Music and History

$\mathcal{M}$USIC

AND

$\mathcal{H}$ISTORY

---⊶∞∞⊷---

Bridging the Disciplines

Edited by Jeffrey H. Jackson and Stanley C. Pelkey

UNIVERSITY PRESS OF MISSISSIPPI • JACKSON

www.upress.state.ms.us

The University Press of Mississippi is a member of the Association of
American University Presses.

First edition 2005

Library of Congress Cataloging-in-Publication Data

Music and history : bridging the disciplines / edited by Jeffrey H. Jackson
and Stanley C. Pelkey.— 1st ed.
    p. cm.
 Includes bibliographical references (p.) and index.
 ISBN 1-57806-762-6 (cloth : alk. paper)
 1. Music—Social aspects. 2. Music—History and criticism. I. Jackson,
Jeffrey H., 1971– II. Pelkey, Stanley C.

ML3916.M86   2005
780'.0306—dc22   2004021647

British Library Cataloging-in-Publication Data available

$\mathcal{C}$ontents

v

Introduction

JEFFREY H. JACKSON AND STANLEY C. PELKEY

This book begins with a simple question: Why haven't historians and musicologists been talking to one another? Such a query will hopefully provoke some thought among both sets of scholars, especially when each group begins to realize that there are many important similarities between their two disciplines. Historians, for example, frequently look to all aspects of human activity, including music, in order to better understand the past. Musicologists inquire into the social, cultural, and historical contexts of musical works and musical practices to develop theories about the meanings of compositions and the significance of musical behavior. In other words, both disciplines examine the many changes in how people represent their experiences. So why has it been so hard for us to converse?

The simplest answer is that the study of music in its historical context has been plagued by significant obstacles. From the historian's point of view, the serious examination of music has traditionally required a particular body of knowledge—the ability to read and to perform music—that many historians simply do not have (or do not have the time to acquire). Worrying that they lack sufficient musical knowledge or training, historians frequently leave music alone and choose to examine other subjects. This emphasis on the "musicality" of music has also been difficult for musicologists to overcome. Generations of musicologists were most interested in formalistic descriptions of how music evolved from one style to the next. Remaining fixed within a discussion of music for music's sake, musicologists (although allowing historical events to shape some of their interpretations of music) have not always actively engaged in larger historical debates by using the music or the musical cultures that they study as evidence for trends in the world of which that music is a part. In other words, they have been content to talk about music at the expense of letting their knowledge inform the broader understanding of human experiences. This may be due, in part, to the fact that musicologists are not only historians of music. They are also often editors, theorists, and performers who engage with musical works as living aesthetic objects, not simply as historical documents. Furthermore, elevating the works of the Western classical traditions to canonical status—by definition, aesthetic objects that have transcended, or are believed to be independent of, their socio-cultural contexts—means that musicologists have often been less interested in music history-as-history than in music history-as-canon formation.

Differences in approach are, of course, also the result of particular educational traditions, methodological requirements, and specialized knowledge. But perhaps more than anything else, historians and musicologists have simply been asking different questions about the human experience. In the case of historians, for instance, many generations of scholars devoted themselves to the study of politics, diplomacy, and war—topics far removed from the concerns of students of music. Few academic historians in the first half of the twentieth century would have chosen to write a book about music because it was simply not accepted within the field. Only in the 1950s and 1960s did the insights of sociologists begin to re-orient historical inquiry away from elites. Social historians worked to include the stories of many forgotten historical actors: workers, peasants, women, slaves, and others traditionally left out of standard narratives of the past. In order to recover as much as possible of the lives of these underrepresented groups, some innovative scholars began to discuss music. Two of the best examples involve reconstructions of the lives of American slaves. Eugene Genovese's classic *Roll Jordon Roll: The World the Slaves Made* weaves many discussions of African-American musical practice (courtship, funeral, and work songs, for instance) into his larger analysis to provide a more textured and nuanced understanding of life under slavery in the United States. Lawrence Levine's *Black Culture and Black Consciousness: Afro-American Folk Thought from Slavery to Freedom* makes music an integral part of African-American history in the United States by showing how music helped to create and sustain a distinctive culture for black Americans.[1]

Levine's work has been particularly important both because it has served as an inspiration to later scholars and because Levine himself has trained a number of historians who study music. We have included an essay by one of Levine's influential students, Burton Peretti, in this collection.

Despite these important examples, most social historians still did not consider music because it remained outside their particular sphere of interest even when music might help to recover the lives of those lost to more traditional forms of history. In the end, social historians have usually been much more concerned with explaining larger social structures, such as changes in class status or the emergence of class consciousness. Influenced by Marxist economic and social theory and by the Annales School of French historians who examined the long-term geographic, economic, and social structures that they believed directed the course of human life, music was simply not brought fully in view.

Important changes began to take place in the 1970s with the advent of a new methodological approach: cultural history. Often controversial, cultural history has borrowed heavily from the fields of anthropology and literary theory to again change the focus of historical inquiry. For cultural historians, nearly all aspects of the human experience are proper subjects for investigation as they seek to reconstruct the mental universes and value systems of people at different moments in time.

Cultural historians interpret the changes in meanings behind events, practices, behaviors, and documents. They seek to discover how those meanings influenced the choices of historical actors. To do so, these historians "read" a wide variety of sources as symbols or "texts" that make sense within a larger cultural framework. They try to uncover the larger patterns of perception and comprehension from the past not only by investigating what people said and did but also what they believed and how those beliefs shaped actions. This emphasis on "reading" is important, the historian Lynn Hunt argues in her introduction to the book *The New Cultural History* (1989), because it connects the traditional historical practice of a close scrutiny of primary source documents with the newer influences of anthropological and literary theory to give the historian an interpretive method. And, she also points out, "Although there are many differences within and between anthropological and literary models, one central tendency in both seems currently to fascinate historians of culture: the use of language as metaphor."[2] In other words, language does not simply consist of words on a page: "Symbolic actions such as riots or cat massacres are framed as texts to be read or languages to be decoded."[3] One might also add a number of other subjects that historians have lately examined: fashion and hairstyles, sexual practices, the human body, or political ceremonies, to name but a few. Therefore, it is no great stretch to include a wide variety of musical performances and practices in such a list. In other words, as historians have stretched the boundaries of their discipline, those who employ the cultural approach are looking for any sign, symbol, or practice that they believe can provide some insight into a particular historical moment—including music.

We should point out that our understanding of history comes from the perspective of those trained in the current mainstream of the discipline. But we must also acknowledge that many other scholars with substantial training in history may approach the subject from a slightly different point of view. In particular, some who perform historical inquiry have come from American Studies or other interdisciplinary programs where historical views are linked with the methods and approaches of other fields of study, including literary scholarship, art history, and cultural studies. They have often built bridges between disciplines when others have not been able do so and have often been more successful than scholars from history programs in incorporating music into their work.

But what about musicology? In his insightful book, *Contemplating Music: Challenges to Musicology* (1985), Joseph Kerman traced the development of musicology as a discipline, especially in America. Kerman wrote at a time when musicology in the U.S. was undergoing a serious transformation in focus and methodology. Although in some respects his essay is now dated, Kerman's insights about the limitations of traditional musicology are helpful in understanding some of the past (and possibly present and future) impediments to a collaborative spirit among historians and musicologists.[4] He suggested that musicologists have traditionally been musical conservatives driven to their field not only by their love of music but also by their dislike of modernism.[5] This attitude fueled the disciplinary-wide retreat into the preparation of texts (scores) of older musics, especially of the Renaissance. At least until the 1960s, it also contributed to the focus on style analysis in order to construct an accurate style history. And even in their capacity as historians, Kerman argued that previous generations of musicologists failed to discuss, as he put it, "the interaction of music history with political, social, and intellectual history."[6]

According to Kerman, an important transformation within musicology began because of a variety of new influences at mid-century. The development of the long-play record made possible a browsable library of music. Listeners and scholars now had access to a wide range of music, including old and forgotten classical music, new modernist works, popular music, and music from around the world.[7] Never before had so much music been available to so many people. This vast collection of musical material inspired a proliferation in musical scholarship and musical criticism. New sonic experiences led to new forms of music scholarship. Furthermore, musicologists such as Susan McClary and others have argued that the modernist classical music of the post-war era alienated a listening public that now had access to and control over many kinds of music, including the popular. For McClary and other young scholars and composers in the 1970s and 1980s, the apparent marginalization of both traditional and modernist classical music in American culture required a radical shift in compositional technique, aesthetic theory, and ultimately of scholarly approaches to the study of music.[8] Musicologists were called upon to move away from description, cataloging, and structural analysis toward new forms of musical criticism.

These changes took time to achieve. The shifting attention of musicologists from the 1960s through the 1980s was not necessarily moving in the same directions as historians with their development of social and cultural history. At the same time that social historians were beginning to reshape the historical profession, traditional musicology in American universities remained focused almost exclusively on the music of the Western classical tradition, not on the musics of the lost voices of the Western world. Even ethnomusicology, which has a history of engaging primarily with non-Western music, has only more recently begun to deal with both Western and non-Western popular music. Indeed, both ethnomusicology and historical musicology are still in flux. Nevertheless, since the mid-1980s, a "New Musicology" has emerged to apply the insights of cultural studies, anthropology, and cultural and literary criticism to the study of music. Ethnomusicology, long influenced by anthropology and musicology, has also begun to produce a greater influence on historical musicology, as some in that field have begun to adopt an ethnomusicologically informed approach to essentially historical musics. In the process, the number of ways in which one can legitimately talk about music within the academy has expanded rapidly. Among the most important trends for "bridging the disciplines" has been the shift away from focus on the sound object within ethnomusicology and away from a focus on the musical work in historical musicology toward a greater interest in "music in culture."[9]

Only within the last few years, therefore, have historians and musicologists begun to use similar approaches in order to ask critical questions about a particular aspect of the human experience: the creation, performance, and consumption of music. Born out of a similar set of questions that have challenged positivist claims about the nature of "history" and "music" as absolute things-in-themselves, historians and musicologists now approach a common ground. As historians wonder about what is "history"—in other words, what are the subjects of the historian's investigation that best help us to uncover the past—musicologists likewise wonder about what "music" is in ways that open up new lines of inquiry.

Still, both sets of scholars ask these questions from different perspectives and for different reasons, and we want to make clear from the outset of this book that our goal is by no means to collapse the two disciplines into one. Historians and musicologists will never be identical. Although they have begun to use similar tools and ask similar questions, they have different ends. This is especially true given the breath of approaches and goals in the study of music that are contained within musicology itself. The musicologist who moves more in the direction of cultural critique, no matter how historically informed that critique is, may be less interested in engaging in a dialogue with the historian than is the musicologist who is more historically oriented in his or her choice of methods and research topics. Similarly, the historical musicologist who has been influenced by ethnomusicological thought may be wary of historical narrative as a potentially alien ideological intrusion into past Western or contemporary non-Western cultures. Nevertheless, both historians and musicologists have something to contribute to the larger understanding of the ways in which people create and represent their lives through music.

What, then, can each side learn from the other? Historians can learn something about music as a particular kind of text with its own special concerns. If cultural historians "read" a wide variety of historical facts as texts to be interpreted, each of those texts comes with its own set of problems and issues. Musicologists can help to guide historians through the particular concerns about music as a text because of their intimate knowledge of it. They can tell historians about how musical styles have changed and why those changes in style are historically important.

Musicologists can learn from historians about a deep engagement with historical context and the ways in which particular musical texts and practices can help to illustrate broader historical issues.[10] Furthermore, in a recent essay, the musicologist Leon Botstein notes that the methods of musical analysis have not been drawn into the other humanities and social sciences, even though musical scholarship has, since the 1980s, drawn heavily from those other fields. Botstein suggests that this appropriation by musicology may not be healthy for the field. Instead, he offers an alternative goal: find ways to make musicology lead the way out of the current fad for methodological skepticism for the humanities and social sciences generally by drawing music out of the margins and positioning it as a central component to life. Botstein argues that music must come to be "treated as a species of fundamental social action."[11] If that were to happen, then musicologists might find ways to use music and music history as a means to recast other points of view, such as social change or culture more generally. Music could become a "primary source" that can "test and perhaps even profoundly revise our sense of the past."[12] But first, musicologists must enter the wider academic community, asserting that theirs is not marginal material but rather that music is central to the human condition.

The chapters that follow this introduction are original contributions to the project of bridging the disciplines of music and history. Some essays are by scholars who have been exploring the middle ground between the two areas for some time. But most are by younger scholars working through the questions that continue to face such interdisciplinary efforts. We begin with a set of personal reflections by noted historian Lawrence Levine that began as an address to the American Musicological Society. Considering how music has shaped his development as a scholar, Levine writes about the "gaps" in historical studies: gaps between the historian and his or her subject, between cultures, between the historian and the performing arts. The last of those gaps is, of course, the central concern of this book. Furthermore, as he did in

Black Culture and Black Consciousness, Levine addresses the use of music as a means of recovering lost voices and personal experiences within the flow of history. This is certainly a challenge for the historian to develop strategies for the use of music as part of his or her professional toolbox. And Levine's comments about the lateral influences among the musics of different cultures is an important point that should spur musicologists to continue to explore the ways in which different kinds of folk, classical, and popular music influence each other. In other words, musicologists may need to develop a richer sense of "culture" and its mechanisms.

Following Levine's essay are six chapters that address widely different aspects of musical culture and history. They are arranged in roughly chronological order, and while each of the essays reflects elements of the methods of the home disciplines of the individual historians and musicologists who wrote them, each also offers ways of bridging the disciplines of history and musicology.

In her essay, Helen Marsh Jeffries considers ways in which the role of the musician in society was changing in the early modern period, but she also critiques the all-too-common emphasis that is placed on change at the expense of continuity within both historical and musicological studies. At the same time, she demonstrates the continuing value that careful archival research can play in the exploration of musico-social phenomena at a time when interpretive strategies are far more central to the New Musicology than is archival research.

In a similar way, in her study of women and popular music in the French Revolution, Laura Mason discusses how the canons of western classical music have negatively influenced the study and aesthetic perception of Revolutionary era music. She also considers ways that the study of representations of music-making, especially among women in the French Revolution, offers another means through which Revolutionary politics and gender relationships can be understood. Finally, she raises important points about popular song as a tool of historical inquiry. On one hand, she implicitly responds to concerns about the supposed lack of musical training among historian. On the other, she also raises some of the concerns about the standards of evidence in musical scholarship that we discuss in the closing essay of the collection.

Dorothy Potter's essay on Mozart's music in America demonstrates the close relationship that often exists between classical repertories and the popular musical market. Thus her essay, like Levine's, brings into relief the potential problem with the entire popular-classical model on which so much musical scholarship and musical education exists.

Finally, some of the essays seek to place music pieces or styles into a larger socio-political context by reflecting on ways in which musical pieces or musical practices mirror aspects of the broader culture. Stanley Pelkey considers ways in which pieces, styles, or repertories that are made national, often through their celebration in literary contexts, are sometimes not only artificially nationalized but are also manifestations of a musical cosmopolitanism that undermines simple identification with the nation. His argument unfolds in part by exploring practices found in both literary and musical periodicals from Britain in the early nineteenth century. Similarly, Charles Freeman discusses several early twentieth-century American operas with plots about immigration. Through close study of their librettos, Freeman reads these operas as cultural documents that mirror ideas that were prevalent in the Progressive Era. In his essay, Burton W. Peretti traces relationships among jazz funding, jazz styles, and political neoconservativism during the late twentieth century. Peretti's essay is particularly rich in that the biographies of individual jazz musicians—especially in terms of their known political sympathies—jazz aesthetics, and jazz styles all become forms of evidence for historical inquiry.

In the section that follows these six chapters, two essays by scholars outside of musicology and history represent a different kind of disciplinary "bridging" between history and music. Michael Antonucci and Sandra Lyne write from within traditions of literary criticism and cultural studies. Antonucci's essay on blues music and American history seeks both to "historicize the blues" (in part by placing blues texts into their historical contexts) and to create "blues history" (by bringing a minority musical tradition into contact with mainstream American history as a witness to another side of the story of American racism). In her essay on nineteenth-century operas with exotic(ized) characters, Lyne addresses how such operas enact nineteenth-century European ideas about race, sexuality, and gender. She discusses these works as both scholar and performer and evaluates the positive and negative attempts at diffusing the racial subtexts of these operas in contemporary performance. We have placed these two essays together not to emphasize that they come from outside musicology and history but rather to highlight an issue to which we will return in the conclusion: the potential evidentiary barriers created by the different methods and epistemologies of historians and musicologists may preclude the bridging which we advocate. In that case, alternative methods may be called for, and these may already be readily available within the tradition of cultural studies. At the very least, that field may provide another kind of common ground from which further attempts at bridging may be accomplished.

Finally, in the last section of the book three essays offer models for bridging the disciplines: through collaborative, multidisciplinary research (Burrows and Weber); through the use of musical materials within humanities courses (Davis); and through the careful plotting of a multidisciplinary approach to the study of popular music that values the exploration of both sonic and contextual aspects of popular music-making (Kramer). The book closes, as indicated earlier, with an epilogue in which we offer some further reflections on the problems of evidence that may create barriers to the successful bridging of history and music.

Does a historian have to learn music to discuss it? Does a musicologist have to learn the entire history of a period in order to analyze the music of that era? We don't believe so. But the issues and problems raised by this book suggest some of the reasons why we should collaborate, read each other's work, or at least talk more openly to one another about the scholarly interests that we have in common.

Notes

1. Eugene D. Genovese, *Roll Jordan Roll: The World the Slaves Made* (New York: Vintage, 1976); Lawrence W. Levine, *Black Culture and Black Consciousness: Afro-American Folk Thought from Slavery to Freedom* (New York: Oxford University Press, 1977).

2. Lynn Hunt ed., *The New Cultural History* (Berkeley: University of California Press, 1989), 16.

3. Hunt, *The New Cultural History*, 16. Here, Hunt is making references to the work of two important scholars, Natalie Zemon Davis, *Society and Culture in Early Modern France* (Stanford: Stanford University Press, 1975) and Robert Darnton, *The Great Cat Massacre and Other Episodes in French Cultural History* (New York: Basic Books, 1984).

4. For an anthology of essays that responds to many of the issues that Kerman raises, see Nicholas Cook and Mark Everist, eds., *Rethinking Music* (Oxford: Oxford University Press, 1999).

5. Joseph Kerman, *Contemplating Music: Challenges to Musicology* (Cambridge, MA: Harvard University Press, 1985), 37–39.

6. Kerman, *Contemplating Music*, 43.

7. Kerman, *Contemplating Music*, 25.

8. Susan McClary, "Terminal Prestige: The Case of Avant-Garde Music Composition," *Cultural Critique* 12 (1989).

9. See "Ethnomusicology and 'Cultural Musicology,'" in *Contemplating Music* for an excellent discussion of the relationship between historical musicology and ethnomusicology. For discussion of historical changes within ethnomusicology, see Gregory F. Barz and Timothy J. Cooley, eds., *Shadows in the Field: New Perspectives for Fieldwork in Ethnomusicology* (Oxford: Oxford, 1997).

10. See, for example, Robert Morgan, "Rethinking Musical Culture: Canonic Reformulations in a Post-Tonal Age," in *Disciplining Music*, ed. Katherine Bergeron and Philip V. Bohlman (Chicago: University of Chicago Press, 1992), 44–63. Morgan traces the history of the musical canon, its relationship to the development of style in the nineteenth and twentieth centuries, and the breakdown of a style consensus in the later twentieth century. Morgan further argues that the diversity and eclecticism of later twentieth-century classical music could be understood as a manifestation of "our fragmented and dissociated manner of life." (58) Thus the essay presents a history of a musical phenomenon—canon formation—but places it within a larger historical context.

11. Leon Botstein, "Cinderella; or Music and the Human Sciences: Unfootnoted Musings from the Margins," *Current Musicology* 53 (1993): 128.

12. Botstein, "Cinderella; or Music and the Human Sciences," 131.

PART I

PERSONAL REFLECTIONS

The Musical Odyssey of an American Historian

Lawrence W. Levine

Over three decades ago I wrote an article entitled: "The Historian and the Culture Gap." It was concerned with the charge, which began to surface with particular force in the 1960s, that certain historians from particular cultures could not really understand and do historical justice to people from certain other cultures. In his Presidential address to the American Historical Association in December, 1962, Carl Bridenbaugh told those young American historians who were "products of lower middle-class or foreign origins" that they were "outsiders on our past and . . . have no experience to assist them," which "will make it impossible for them to communicate to and reconstruct the past for future generations." In the 1968 volume, William Styron's *Nat Turner: Ten Black Writers Respond*, several of the authors maintained that it was "almost impossible, even for the most understanding white writers in the racist, separatist United States" to be "true to history" when writing about Blacks.[1]

As someone brought up in an Eastern European Jewish immigrant family in New York City, who was writing his first book on William Jennings Bryan—the very embodiment of Midwestern American Protestant culture—when Bridenbaugh spoke in 1962, and writing his second book on African American folk culture when the Ten Black Writers made their pronouncements in 1968, I found it impossible to accept casually these caveats about who could and could not write certain types of history, and I responded by arguing that "there are no impassable culture gaps in the realm of historical scholarship." Using my own career as an example, I tried to show that the historian's primary function is always "to perform the central act of empathy—figuratively, to crawl into the skins" of the people being studied. Historians, whoever they were and whatever

past lives they tried to recreate, were inescapably faced by a culture gap—
a discontinuity between their own cultural conditioning and expectations
and those of their subjects. Serious and talented historians were able to
bridge that gap, never completely perhaps, but sufficiently to listen to the
voices of their subjects with imagination and empathy and to recreate
their lives with accuracy and sensitivity.[2]

When I came to think of a title for this reflective piece on my experiences as a historian using musical sources, I realized I could (but obviously chose not to) use the title of that ancient article all over again.
Historians—at least those who cluster in history departments rather
than departments of music, art, drama, literature, language, et al.—
seem to have a culture gap of a sort that has little to do with ethnicity.
This gap has to do with the arts, especially the performing arts. And the
"gap" consists of the fact that, until recently at least, historians of the
United States have widely and largely ignored the arts in their research
and teaching. When I was working with the sources of folk and popular
culture, I assumed that historical neglect of these subjects centered
around the theology of social and cultural hierarchy. Folk songs, spirituals, blues, jazz, band music, musical comedy, the songs of Tin Pan Alley
were, I reasoned, relegated by many of my colleagues to the realm of
mere "entertainment" or, even more damning, mere "escapism," and
were thus beneath the high purposes of serious history. Why else would
they neglect such a wonderfully interesting, ubiquitous, and accessible
body of sources? The answer, I was certain, was the elitism and cultural
snobbery that were omnipresent in great swaths of historical study, and
indeed, of the Academy in general.

But as I came to study cultural hierarchy in the United States in
researching my book *Highbrow/Lowbrow*, I realized that the problem
was more wide-ranging. I learned that American historians were non-
discriminating in their neglect of music and other entire bodies of
cultural expression. They ignored not just African American music or
popular music but all music, not just the popular strains of expressive
culture but almost all expressive culture. They were as blind to opera as
to jazz, to symphonic music as to band music. They ignored not only the
vaudeville stage but the Shakespearean theaters that dotted the landscape of the nineteenth century; not only Dashiell Hammett but Henry
James, not only the tap dancing of the Nicholas Brothers but the ballet

and modern dance of George Balanchine and Agnes DeMille; not only the popular ballads of Cole Porter and Irving Berlin but the symphonies and songs of Charles Ives; not only the blues sung by Bessie Smith but the arias sung by Leontyne Price; not only cartoons and comics in the daily papers but the paintings of Georgia O'Keeffe and Jacob Lawrence; not only the bawdy ballads and limericks of the folk but the poetry of Emily Dickinson and Wallace Stevens. It was not merely elitism—though there was an abundance of that—it was the assumption that expressive culture and the performing arts had little to contribute to our knowledge of ourselves as a people and a nation and need not concern the scholarly historian. The result was a widespread neglect of—and too often a deep ignorance about—these essential currents of our past and the voices they revealed to us.

At the outset of my own career I certainly reflected the same comfortable assumptions. At least I didn't challenge them. Though, as it has turned out, much of my own work on the nineteenth- and twentieth-century American past has revolved around musical expression, I certainly was not trained to examine such sources in my graduate years at Columbia, nor was I hired to teach such subjects at the University of California at Berkeley. When I arrived in Berkeley in 1962 as a young Assistant Professor, it was to teach 20th century U. S. history, and if I had had to label myself it would have been as a political historian. How, then, did I come to the study of culture in general and music in particular? There were, undoubtedly, complex social and political forces at work, for my migration to the study of culture was not sui generis; many other historians have been doing the same thing in recent decades. In fact, I would argue that the field of cultural history as we understand it today was born in the 1960s and 1970s. In this essay, however, I'm going to concentrate on personal and intellectual factors that contributed to my odyssey in the world of musical sources.

I'm tempted to say it all began with the saxophone. Like William Jefferson Clinton I studied the sax as a young person and like the President I decided I had best get a day job. If the saxophone didn't provide a vocation it did provide an entry into some of the technical aspects of the world of music that have been helpful to me as a scholar. In retrospect, I realize that the saxophone was more a symptom than a cause; my choice of the sax rather than more traditional instruments like the violin, which my family would have probably preferred or at least understood better, reflected a process within me that was already well underway. I grew up, as I mentioned earlier, in an immigrant family in New York City and along with the public schools and such venues as the movies and radio, one of my chief forays into the larger American culture came through frequenting jazz clubs in the late 1940s when I was still in my early and mid teens. Thus one of my earliest exposures to American culture outside of the familiar confines of my small Jewish American universe, was the world of young Black musicians like Charlie Parker, Dizzy Gillespie, Thelonious Monk, Ella Fitzgerald, Sarah Vaughan, Billie Holiday, and Lester Young whose innovative music became a central part of my own cultural world. One of the most important acculturative phases of my young life, then, was connected to African American culture, and judging from the diverse mix of people I met at such clubs as the Royal Roost, Birdland, and Bop City, I was not alone.

Indeed, my experience was not particularly new. In the 1920s a group of White youngsters in and around Chicago—Benny Goodman, Eddie Condon, Milton "Mezz" Mezzrow, Gene Krupa, Muggsy Spanier, Frank Teschemacher, Joe Sullivan—encountered the music of such Black jazz musicians as Joe Oliver, Baby Dodds, and Louis Armstrong who were then playing in the clubs on Chicago's South Side. Condon recalled that he and his friends spoke about jazz "as if it were a new religion just come from Jerusalem." The initial excitement of hearing Oliver's band was still vibrant when Condon recalled the experience decades later: "It was hypnosis at first hearing. Everyone was playing what he wanted to play and it was all mixed together as if someone had planned it with a set of micrometer calipers; notes I had never heard were peeling off the edges and dropping through the middle; there was a tone from the trumpets like warm rain on a cold day. The music poured into us like daylight running down a dark hole." When two young White musicians, Hoagy Carmichael from Indiana and Bix Beiderbecke from Iowa, went to a Chicago club where Oliver's band was playing and for the first time encountered the sounds of the young Louis Armstrong, they had a similar reaction: "I dropped my cigarette and gulped my drink," Carmichael has recorded. "Bix was on his feet, his eyes popping. . . . 'Why,' I moaned, 'why isn't everybody in the world here to hear that?"[3]

Here was a cultural medium that allowed these youngsters, many of whom came from immigrant and ethnic families outside the mainstream, to approach the larger society with a degree of musical and personal individuality—the ability to be and express themselves—that appealed mightily to them. At the end of another world war, several of my friends and I, Jewish boys from immigrant families, felt exactly the same way. Through these jazz musicians, we found not only an art that touched us, we also saw the possibility of functioning in the outside society while retaining our individual and ethnic personas; they were doing it and we could find a means of doing it as well. In an ethnically diverse society, cultural models abounded and one had choices and influences far more numerous than many of the theorizers of assimilation and acculturation had recognized.

In short, I was the product of a process that I certainly was not fully conscious of and that I had to rediscover as an academic. That rediscovery began while I was struggling with a book on Black protest thought in twentieth-century America. In my first book, *Defender of the Faith*, a study of William Jennings Bryan's last years, I made certain assertions about how Bryan spoke for the people of the rural and small-town West and South and concluded that understanding Bryan was an important step towards understanding those who identified with him. Unfortunately, I really didn't know how to demonstrate and prove that representativeness. As I began to study African American protest leaders, I realized I was duplicating the pattern of my earlier book. Again, I was assuming that there was a direct link between the "leaders" and their "followers." It was the mid 1960s, a period of protest and ferment during which many of us worried consciously about the relationship of articulate leaders to their followers whose voices were drowned out and lost to posterity and who thus were transformed into what the novelist Ralph Ellison called "the void of faceless faces, of soundless voices lying outside history." "We who write no novels, histories or other books," Ellison's protagonist in *Invisible Man* muses, "What about us?" It was a question that began to engross me.[4]

My attempt to help answer that question initially led me to examine the migrations of Blacks from the South to the North and their role in and reactions to race riots to ascertain if there was any correlation between the actions of the supposed followers and the attitudes of their putative leaders. It gradually occurred to me that the subject of folklore— which I knew scarcely anything about largely because it had been almost totally absent from the curricula of the schools I attended—might prove useful in this quest to understand those who did not leave behind them the kinds of sources historians of the American past were most attracted to. Thus I began to dip tentatively into songs, tales, anecdotes, proverbs, sermons, folk beliefs. I became so overwhelmed by the amount of this rich material and so fascinated by its content that I ultimately abandoned the book on organized protest thought and began an intensive exploration of the world of what I came to think of as African American folk thought. Here, I hoped, would be a way to restore historical voices that had become lost to us. Finding it impossible to fully comprehend the twentieth-century materials without more background, I was led back to antebellum slavery. Thus my original intention to study the thought of African American protest leaders in the twentieth century had turned into something quite different and plunged me into source materials that opened new worlds to me.

In the songs of slaves and freedmen I found the voices of people who, living in oral cultures, had been unusually articulate and who were rendered inarticulate by scholars who had ignored them. The notion that American slavery transformed Africans into passive, atomized beings— a notion that still had considerable credibility in the 1960s—could not be sustained once we began to actually listen to the voices of the slaves themselves. In the large body of slave spirituals there is no trace of the message White ministers incessantly preached from the Epistles of Paul: Slaves obey your masters. Although they were kept largely illiterate, slaves found ways to choose the texts of their songs from those two books of the Bible most meaningful for them: Exodus and Revelation. They based many of their religious songs on the Book of Exodus and its story of the enslavement and liberation of the Children of Israel in Egypt. "And the God dat lived in Moses' time is jus' de same today," they assured themselves. Thus they could sing of oppression and of freedom not only amongst themselves but in the presence of their masters. The heroes they sang of won their deliverance in this world, not the next, and were delivered in ways that engaged the imagination of the slaves who sang over and over of little David subduing the great Goliath with a stone, of the blind and humiliated Samson bringing down the mansions of his conquerors, of the ridiculed Noah patiently building the ark that would deliver him from the doom of a mocking world, of the timid Jonah attaining freedom from his confinement in the belly of the whale through faith, and especially of Moses leading his people out of bondage and to a Promised Land not in the hereafter but right here on Earth.

Similarly, the slaves chose texts from the Book of Revelation that left them free to sing openly of retribution, judgment, and justice. "You'll see de world on fire," slaves sang in one of their characteristically vivid songs. ". . . See the stars a fallin' . . . see the moon a bleedin' . . . see the forked lightning. . . . Hear the rumblin' thunder . . . see the righteous marching . . . see my Jesus coming. . . ." They drew implications and inspiration from any episode in the Scriptures that applied to them. "O my Lord delivered Daniel," they sang, "O why not deliver me, too?"[5] Listening seriously to the songs of the slaves makes it indisputable that theirs was a religion of this world. The freed slaves who fought with the Union Army found it no more incongruous to accompany their fight for freedom with the sacred songs of their bondage than they had found it inappropriate as slaves to sing their spirituals while picking cotton or shucking corn. In all of this, one can see unmistakable continuities between the sacred concepts they embraced in the New World and those that had informed the cosmology of their ancestors in the Old.

The slaves took their owners' religion and made it their own not only in terms of content but also in terms of style. The ways in which slaves sang, moved, and danced in and out of church left no doubt at all about the extent to which they were able to amalgamate African cultures with the cultures they encountered in the United States. In 1818 a group of White Quaker students observed a Black camp meeting and watched in fascination and bewilderment as the worshipers moved slowly around and around in a circle chanting: "We're traveling to Immanuel's land/ Glory! Halle-lu-jah." Occasionally the dancers paused to blow a tin horn. The meaning of the ceremony gradually dawned upon one of the White youths: he was witnessing, as he put it, "Joshua's chosen men marching around the walls of Jericho, blowing the rams' horns and shouting until the walls fell." The students had beheld the slaves' ring shout—that counter-clockwise, shuffling dance, so prominent in antebellum African American culture. The shout—so derivative of African dance, spirituality, and sacred sense of time—often became a medium through which the ecstatic dancers were transformed into actual participants in history: Joshua's army marching around the walls of Jericho, the children of Israel following Moses through the parted waters of the Red Sea. "Those who have witnessed these shouts can never forget them," Abigail Christensen has written. "The fascination of the music and the swaying motion of the dance is so great that one can hardly refrain from joining the magic circle in response to the invitation of the enthusiastic clappers."[6]

Slave music refutes the argument—still influential as late as the 1960s—that Africans were the one group in the United States who were stripped of their indigenous cultures and left as a kind of vast *tabula rasa* upon which the dominant groups in their new homeland could imprint what they chose. African slaves, no less than European immigrants, retained large parts of the cultures they had brought with them, and they and their progeny syncretized these into a new cultural amalgam in the New World. Similarly, the debate about whether slaves retained a sense of community is put to rest not only by the words but by the antiphonal structure of their music. There was almost no solo music in slavery; slaves sang in call-and-response fashion as they or their ancestors had done in Africa and, as in Africa, their musical spontaneity and inventiveness depended upon a communal repertory of phrases and images they could use and embroider upon. Because they refashioned significant elements of their traditional culture into an African American culture, slaves did not merely mimic European-Americans but constituted a cultural influence of their own that had an impact upon wide areas of American religious and secular expressive culture.

The study of slave music constituted a crucial element in the demise of the simple and comfortable evolutionary notion that cultural diffusion operated in one direction: from top down, from "higher" to "lower;" a notion that blinded generations of scholars to the complexities of cultural influences and interactions. Thus in 1918 the White folklorist Louise Pound refuted the claim that "Weeping Mary" was an African American song solely on the grounds that her grandmother had learned the spiritual from a White woman who heard it at a White Methodist camp meeting in the late 1820s. If Whites knew and sang the song, Pound's sense of the way things worked left her no alternative but to conclude that Whites had originated and disseminated it; the alternative—that White people had learned an original African American song from Black people—was inconceivable to her. Similarly, Frederick W. Root, in his welcoming address to the International Folk-Lore Congress of the World's Columbian Exposition in Chicago in 1893, envisioned the panorama of music as a development "from the formless and untutored sounds of savage people to the refined utterances of our highest civilization." This justified omitting from the Congress' Concert of Folk Songs and National Music "the utterances of the savage peoples . . . these being hardly developed to the point at which they might be called music." Even the African American scholar John Wesley Work, who believed that many spirituals were derived from Africa, adopted this hierarchical model in describing the "evolution" of an African song in the United States: "In proportion as the life of the New World was above that of Africa, in proportion as the light of this New World was brighter than the dim haziness of the dark continent, in that same proportion is this new song brighter and more spiritual."[7]

The fact is, of course, that insofar as White evangelical music departed from traditional Protestant hymnody and embodied the complex rhythmic structure, the percussive qualities, the polymeter, the syncopation, the emphasis on overlapping call-and-response patterns that characterized Black music both in West Africa and the New World, the influence of the slaves who attended and joined in the singing at religious meetings is hard to deny. Even at those camp meetings where the races were separated, the plank partition was commonly removed on the final day of the meeting and Blacks and Whites joined together in a song festival or "singing ecstasy." In any case, music was impervious to the barriers of wooden fences and segregated seating and praying. The Reverend Samuel Davies, who preached to Whites and Blacks in Virginia between 1747 and 1774, wrote a friend in London that "The Negroes, above all the human species that ever I knew, have an ear for music and a kind of extatic delight in psalmody," and described to another correspondent the pleasure he took during Sabbath services listening to the slaves in their segregated gallery "breaking out in a torrent of sacred harmony, enough to bear away the whole congregation to heaven." The Reverend Lucius Bellinger described a Methodist quarterly meeting during the 1820s in South Carolina: "The crowds continue to increase and song after song climbs the hills of heaven. . . . The negroes are out in great crowds, and sing with voices that make the woods ring." "Our white folks," an ex-slave recalled, "when they have camp meeting would have all the colored come up and sing over the mourners. You know they still say that colored can beat the white folks singing." The careful study of musical creation, re-creation, and diffusion frees us from the verticality of the hierarchical model for a lateral, horizontal model that allows us to perceive and explore movement between cultures and within cultures.[8]

Once we listen to the voices of the slaves themselves, our picture of their history is revised substantially. But not only of their history. Contrary to the claims that paying scholarly attention to the distinct groups in the United States has a fragmenting effect, the study of a single group has much to teach us about the entire society. The African American relationship to the larger culture suggests that the old notions of acculturation as a relentless progressive movement in one direction is in need of revision. Blacks shared with a number of other ethnic minorities a deep ambivalence about losing themselves in mainstream American culture. In my study of postbellum Black culture I searched for musical developments sufficiently distinct from those in slavery to indicate deep acculturation to modern Western sensibilities. The development of the blues in the late nineteenth and early twentieth centuries seemed to be a perfect example of such acculturation. Blues represented the first true African American solo music in the United States. Certainly, individual voices were prominent in slave music; in both church music and secular work songs, song leaders were crucial but in both cases their contributions blended into an antiphonal communal whole. In church, the song leader was invariably answered by the group, and this was generally the case in the workplace as well. In both instances, the songs were sung in communal settings. The two primary forms of solo music in slavery were lullabies and field hollers, both of which arose out of situations of physical or social distance: Lullabies were addressed to children who were often too young to respond while field hollers arose out of spatial isolation.

Thus it's fair to say that blues was the first African American music to be dominated by the individual persona of the singer. From the beginning the blues was marked by what Abbe Niles referred to as "the element of pure self."[9] The song centered upon the singer's feelings, experiences, fears, dreams, acquaintances, problems, idiosyncrasies. In all of these respects the blues represented not so much a new form of music as a new form of self-conception and signaled an important degree of acculturation into the larger American society with its focus upon the individual and personal expression. But the musical style of the blues with its emphasis upon improvisation, its retention of the call-and-response pattern (though now it was most often the singer answering herself or himself), its polyrhythmic effects, and its methods of vocal production which included slides, slurs, vocal leaps, and the use of falsetto, tied it to traditional African American musical roots at the very moment when the migration of Blacks throughout the country and the rise of mass culture could have spelled the demise of a distinctive African American musical style. The blues illustrates the way in which a group could adopt central features of the larger society while simultaneously revitalizing aspects of its traditional culture.

Exactly the same intricate phenomenon can be seen in the rise of twentieth-century African American gospel music. If we concentrate on the lyrics and the message, gospel music—which focused on Jesus and the next world far more than the slave spirituals with their emphasis upon the story of the Hebrew children and redemption in this world—contained a cosmology more familiar to modern Western culture than the spirituals that exuded a sacralized spirit closer to their African roots. But before we hold gospel songs up as an unadulterated example of postbellum acculturation into the larger society, we have to examine their musical structure, and here the story is quite different. Gospel music is more an instance of cultural revitalization than of acculturation. Gospel songs helped bring back into black church music the sounds and the structure not only of the slave spirituals but also of works songs and nineteenth-century cries and hollers. But they did more than this; they borrowed freely from the ragtime, blues, and jazz of the secular Black world and helped to keep alive the stylistic continuum that has characterized African American music in the United States. Put simply, the antebellum songs of the praise house and field strongly influenced the work songs, blues, and jazz of the postbellum years that were incorporated into the gospel music that in turn helped to shape the secular rhythm and blues, jazz, and soul music of the post World War II years.

Among Black Americans assimilation was not a simple one-way affair; it was a reciprocal process that resulted in an ongoing dialogue that changed but nevertheless maintained the distinctiveness of all the cultures involved. African American music helps us to come to the realization—which we too often have difficulty accepting—that a culture can move in two directions at the same time: African Americans manifested the tendency to surge outward into the larger society even as they nurtured a strong centripetal urge that continually drew them back to fundamental components of their own traditions. The Black experience alone should prompt us to re-evaluate the entire image and theory of the melting pot and the ways in which various groups have related to American culture. It's an extremely dynamic story and music is a crucially important element in helping us to understand that dynamism.

In these respects Black Americans were far from unique. My own findings were duplicated by Mark Slobin in his study of Jewish music in the United States. We each independently found that such recent developments as the modern recording industry acted not only as a force for cultural amalgamation but also served to preserve important elements of group tradition. Developments that common sense and logic tell us must have reduced a group's cultural autonomy turn out on closer inspection to have been more complex and to have enabled people to make choices. The effects of the phonograph upon Black folk song, for example, are not easy to sum up. There is no question that recordings could stultify originality and corrupt discrete styles. Studying the effect of "the mechanical, nickel phonograph" in the work camps of rural Florida during the Great Depression, Zora Neale Hurston found that the songs of the locality began to give way to recorded songs. "The song on the phonograph record soon becomes the music of the work-crew," Hurston concluded, "but with this interesting change: the original words and music are changed to satisfy the taste of the community's own singers." In this way local styles were certainly diluted and influenced by commercial recordings. However, what took place was not a total erosion of regional styles in favor of some standard product but rather a blending process. The eclectic flexibility so characteristic of African American music was enhanced by the phonograph as well as by radio.[10]

Through the recorded blues local traditions could now become quickly known to Blacks in every section of the country; the developments in the new urban centers could be spread throughout the South even while the traditions of the South could be perpetuated and strengthened among the recent urban migrants. Black people living far apart could now share not only expressive styles but experiences, attitudes, folk wisdom, language in a way that was simply not as possible before the advent of the phonograph. In this sense, records can be seen as bearers and preservers rather than primarily destroyers of folk traditions. Their most important effect was to allow millions to continue to possess and millions more to repossess a body of tradition and expression that otherwise must surely have perished in the conditions of modern industrial life. The blues corresponds to the portrait Professor Slobin paints of Jewish American music and further confirms his rejection of the older progressive models of cultural change and accommodation in favor of the recognition that what we are faced with is "a dynamic state of flux."[11]

After completing my book on African American folk culture in 1977, I returned to my interest in the culture of the Great Depression and was struck once again by the dearth of attention historians had paid to music and most of the other arts. My comprehension of how vast that vacuum was increased when I turned back to the nineteenth century to investigate the place of Shakespeare in American culture. Discovering that the Bard was nineteenth-century America's most popular dramatist, known and appreciated everywhere in the nation, rather than the property of the educated, as he had become in the next century, I decided to test whether Shakespeare's vast popularity in the nineteenth century was aberrant or if it extended to such other putatively high culture forms as opera, ballet, and symphonic music. To do this I once again had to stretch out to embrace new perspectives and neglected materials.

The nineteenth-century America I studied in college and university and taught as a young professor contained no figures like Theodore Thomas, who traveled with his orchestra from one coast to another bringing European composers from Bach to Richard Strauss to large numbers of Americans like the young Charles Edward Russell who heard Thomas in a Mississippi River town in 1877 and exclaimed that for those in the audience "life was never the same afterward . . . There had been shown to them things and potentialities they had never suspected. So then there really existed as a fact, and not as something heard of and unattainable, this world of beauty . . . Anybody could go into it at any time . . . The door was open; this man had opened it." There were no bandmasters like Harvey Dodworth, Patrick Gilmore, or John Philip Sousa whose widely-heard repertories interspersed marches, polkas, and popular songs with music by Mozart, Schubert, Haydn, Handel, Mendelssohn, Beethoven, Wagner, and Liszt. "Every night about sun down," a soldier wrote home to Massachusetts during the Civil War, "[our band] gives us a splendid concert, playing selections from the operas and some very pretty marches, quicksteps, waltzes and the like."[12]

In the nineteenth century I learned about there were no foreign and domestic opera companies traveling back and forth across the land packing in such impressive audiences that the New Orleans Bee could report in 1836 that "Operas appear to amuse our citizens more than any other form of public amusement—except balls." The Bee's observation was documented over and over. After attending a performance of Bellini's La Sonnambula in New York during the summer of 1851, George Templeton Strong noted in his diary: "The people are Sonnambula-mad. Everybody goes, and nob and snob, Fifth Avene and Chatham Street, sit side by side fraternally on the hard benches." When George Makpeace Towle returned from his tour of duty as American Consul in England after the Civil War and set about rediscovering his native land, he recorded the extent to which opera was part of the public domain: "Lucretia Borgia and Faust, The Barber of Seville and Don Giovanni are everywhere popular; you may hear their airs in the drawing rooms and concert halls, as well as whistled by the street boys and ground out on the hand organs." There were no triumphal and enormously lucrative tours throughout America of the Swedish soprano Jenny Lind, the Norwegian violinist Ole Bull, and the Viennese ballerina Fanny Elssler—three of the most popular European visitors to the United States in the first half of the nineteenth century, greeted and lauded by Americans of all regions and types. During Lind's 1850 tour, Nathaniel Parker Willis, editor of the New York Journal, remarked on "the quiet ease with which the luxury of the exclusives—Italian music—has passed into the hands of the people.... Now it is as much theirs as anybody's! ... Opera music has ... become a popular taste." There were no indications that music of a wide variety of genres was enjoyed by audiences as eclectic as the music they heard in an open, often collaborative atmosphere no longer common or, increasingly, even possible in the twentieth century. There was not a hint of the ways in which musics from Europe and Africa were blended and syncretized into an American music.[13]

These people and episodes and developments were missing, and the lessons and insights we could derive from them about the eclectic nature and complexity of American culture, about the surprising flexibility and inclusiveness of nineteenth-century America, and about the profound cultural differences between nineteenth- and twentieth-century American culture were, of consequence, missing as well. It's not that these musical episodes were not well known and deeply influential in the nineteenth century; they were. It's that they disappeared from our collective memories by the neglect of the very people who are supposed to be the guardians of those memories.

Similarly ubiquitous and similarly forgotten by historians of the twentieth century were the musics we lump into the genre Jazz. Indeed, earlier in this century jazz was so influential—so liberating to some and so threatening to many others—that it became the very antithesis of the newly defined sense of Culture (with a capital "C") that emerged at the turn of the century. Jazz was the new product of a new age; Culture was traditional—the creation of centuries. Jazz was raucous and discordant; Culture was harmonious, embodying order and reason. Jazz was accessible and spontaneous; Culture was exclusive and complex, available only through hard study and training. Jazz was interactive and participatory, obscuring the line between audiences and performers; Culture was professional and didactic, relegating the audience to a passive role. Jazz was distinctively American, attractive to so many around the world precisely because of this distinctiveness; Culture was Eurocentric, convinced that the best and noblest were the products of the Old World which the United States had to emulate.[14]

To study these two entities side by side was to comprehend radically different impulses in America. Culture represented that side of ourselves that craved order, stability, and definition in terms of Northern and Western Europe. It was the expression of a colonial side of ourselves that we have not done nearly enough to understand. For much of the twentieth century we remained, in so many of our educational and cultural institutions, a colonized people attempting to define our culture in the shadow of the former imperial power. Jazz expressed that other side of ourselves that recognized the positive aspects of our newness and heterogeneity; that was comfortable with the fact that a significant part of our heritage derived from Africa and other non-Western and Northern

European sources; that saw our syncretized culture not as an embarrassing weakness but as a dynamic source of strength.

Not to understand the dichotomy between these two impulses was not
to comprehend much that we need to know about our past in order to
understand ourselves. To ignore jazz and American popular musics, as
historians have done until recently, was to ignore a vital part of ourselves,
our history, and our culture and constituted a regrettable retreat from the
complex process of understanding who we are as a people and a culture.

Using music as a historical source helped me understand the wisdom
of Robert Louis Stevenson's beautiful essay "The Lantern Bearers" in
which Stevenson described how he and his schoolmates used to place a
bull's-eye lantern under the greatcoats they wore in the cold weather and
took nighttime walks on the links, exulting in the fact that though they
were mere pillars of darkness to strangers, there were hidden lanterns
shining brightly at their belts. Stevenson used these scenes of boyhood
bliss as a paradigm for the human condition. A good part of reality,
Stevenson concluded, "runs underground. The observer (poor soul, with
his documents!) is all abroad. For to look at the man is but to court
deception. . . . To one who had not the secret of the lanterns, the scene
upon the links is meaningless. And hence the haunting and truly spectral
unreality of realistic books."[15]

The "secret of the lanterns" has remained to plague generations of
American historians. Music is one of the central sources that has helped
me to recognize and write about and free myself from the influence of
the "haunting and truly spectral unreality of realistic books" and has
allowed me and a growing number of my colleagues greater access to
"the personal poetry . . . the rainbow work of fancy," the hidden lanterns
that Stevenson insisted lay concealed within the human beings and the
human societies we study.

Notes

1. Carl Bridenbaugh, "The Great Mutation," *American Historical Review*, 68 (January
1963): 322–323; *William Styron's Nat Turner: Ten Black Writers Respond*, ed. John Henrik
Clarke (Boston: Beacon Press, 1968), 29, 32, 36, 43, 50.

2. Lawrence W. Levine, "The Historian and the Culture Gap," in *The Historian's Workshop: Original Essays by Sixteen Historians*, ed. L. P. Curtis, Jr. (New York: Knopf, 1970).

3. Eddie Condon, *We Called It Music* (New York: Holt, 1947), 107; Hoagy Carmichael,
The Stardust Road (New York: Rinehart, 1946), 53.

4. Lawrence W. Levine, *Defender of the Faith: William Jennings Bryan, the Last Decade, 1915–1925* (New York: Oxford University Press, 1965); Ralph Ellison, *Invisible Man* (New York: Random House, 1952), 331–332.

5. For these and other sacred songs of slavery, see Lawrence W. Levine, *Black Culture and Black Consciousness: Afro-American Folk Thought from Slavery to Freedom* (New York: Oxford University Press, 1977), chapter 1.

6. Don Yoder, *Pennsylvania Spirituals* (Lancaster, PA: Pennsylvania Folklore Society, 1961), 54–55; Abigail M. Holmes Christensen, "Spirituals and 'Shouts' of Southern Negroes," *Journal of American Folklore 7* (1894): 154–155.

7. Louise Pound, "The Ancestry of a 'Negro Spiritual,'" *Modern Language Notes* 33 (1918): 442–444; Frederick W. Root, "Folk-Music," International Folk-Lore Congress of the World's Columbian Exposition, Chicago, 1893, I: 424–425; John Wesley Work, *Folk Song of the American Negro* (Nashville: Press of Fisk University, 1915), 18.

8. Charles C. Jones, *The Religious Instruction of the Negroes in the United States* (1842; reprint ed., New York, 1969), 36–38; Joseph B. Earnest, Jr., *The Religious Development of the Negro in Virginia* (Charlottesville, 1914), 41–42; Lucius Bellinger, *Stray Leaves from the Port-Folio of a Methodist Local Preacher* (Macon, Ga., 1870), 17; Fisk University, Unwritten History of Slavery: Autobiographical Accounts of Negro Ex-Slaves, Ophelia Settle Egypt, J. Masuoka, and Charles S. Johnson, eds. (Nashville, 1945, unpublished typescript), 320.

9. Abbe Niles, "Blue Notes," *New Republic* 45 (1926): 292.

10. Hurston's report is in the WPA manuscripts, Florida File, Archive of Folk Culture, Library of Congress.

11. Levine, *Black Culture and Black Consciousness*, chapters 3 and 4; Marc Slobin, *Tenement Songs: The Popular Music of the Jewish Immigrants* (Urbana, IL: University of Illinois Press, 1982).

12. Charles Edward Russell, *The American Orchestra and Theodore Thomas* (Garden City, NY: Doubleday, 1927), 1–6; The soldier is quoted in Margaret Hindle Hazen and Robert M. Hazen, *The Music Men: An Illustrated History of Brass Bands in America, 1800–1922* (Washington, DC: Smithsonian Institution Press, 1987), 155–156.

13. Katherine K. Preston, *Opera on the Road: Traveling Opera Troupes in the United States, 1825–1860* (Urbana: University of Illinois Press, 1993); Henry A. Kmen, *Music in New Orleans: The Formative Years, 1791–1841* (Baton Rouge: Louisiana State University Press, 1966), 56–200; Ronald L. Davis, *A History of Opera in the American West* (Englewood Cliffs, NJ: Prentice Hall, 1965), chapters 1–2; George Makepeace Towle, *American Society* (London, 1870), II: 4; *The Diary of George Templeton Strong,* ed. Allan Nevins and Milton Halsey Thomas (New York: University of Washington Press, 1952), II: 59; Nathaniel Parker Willis, *Memoranda of the Life of Jenny Lind* (Philadelphia, 1851), 144–145; Lawrence W. Levine, *Highbrow/Lowbrow: The Emergence of Cultural Hierarchy in America* (Cambridge, MA: Harvard University Press 1988), chapter 2.

14. Lawrence W. Levine, "Jazz and American Culture," in Levine, *The Unpredictable Past: Explorations in American Cultural History* (New York: Oxford University Press, 1993).

15. Robert Louis Stevenson, *Across the Plains* (London, 1892), 206–228.

PART II

Attempts to Bridge the Disciplines

"But a Musician"—The Importance of the Underdog in Musico-Historical Research
Music Professionalism in a Small Sixteenth-Century Oxford College[1]

HELEN MARSH JEFFRIES

The study of early Tudor music is dominated by the great institutions—the royal household chapel, the noble chapels, cathedrals, and great collegiate institutions. Historians and musicologists alike have tended to ignore not only each other's work but also the smaller, less obviously interesting institutions. The tendency to focus on large, progressive centers of activity has led to a false picture of the development of music professionalism in fifteenth- and sixteenth-century England.

For many, the story of the fifteenth century in English music is one of movement from the use of amateur to professional musicians to sing the liturgy:

> In the early part of the [fifteenth] century, funds had been found at many churches to enable the acquisition and employment of singers competent to perform polyphonic music. . . . In order to secure a place in the choir which these expert musicians could occupy, the post of clerk of the second form had to be drastically transformed . . . so as to accommodate the career lay-clerk.[2]

The existence of these expert musicians and career lay-clerks in some cathedrals, colleges, and households has led to the greatest emphasis being placed by writers on those institutions that employed them. The relatively well-documented rise of the employment of "professional musicians" in the fifteenth century easily produces a tacit presumption that by the sixteenth century all church singers must have looked on such singing as their career.[3] This cannot have been the case at that time, or any other. In the case of Oxford College Chapels, most research has been carried out on those colleges with the largest musical complements.[4] The smaller, less prestigious institutions that employed nonspecialist singers have been overlooked.

Recent research has increasingly questioned the scholarly model that focuses exclusively on great "centers" while ignoring the "periphery."[5] The disciplines of history and musicology are no longer content to address the great and canonical works and institutions while ignoring their lesser counterparts. Accordingly, the following discussion examines the role of music and musicians in a hitherto little studied institution, Corpus Christi College, Oxford and attempts to show that as a case study and an example of micro-history, there is much that it can contribute to our historical and musicological knowledge of sixteenth-century Oxford.

Corpus from the outset was a small college and founded for the improvement of the clergy. Being so close in location and date to Thomas Wolsey's great foundation, Cardinal College, historians and musicians interested in the period have largely overlooked Corpus as a much less obviously impressive college. Consequently, the few studies of Corpus' history that do exist are those by former members of the college, motivated by college loyalty.[6] The available archival sources consist of the statutes, admissions records, and lists of payments by the college. Despite the absence of a single study of the college and its music, the relatively rich and unexplored archive enables us to begin to recreate the musical life of the institution, and therefore to observe life in one of Oxford's smaller colleges.

The role of the chapel in defining the college's identity is of particular importance, in relation to the chapel personnel's interaction with the academic members of the college, and as a more general phenomenon. The ethos intended for the college by its founder and depicted in the statutes will form an important part of this study, as will the way in which those statutes were interpreted and enacted by the men in charge of the college. A few case studies of members of the chapel at Corpus particularly illuminate their roles as part of the college, and shed new light on the place of the musician in secular colleges of this period. There will finally be a comparison of the exceptional Cardinal College with the more typical Corpus Christi College in order to demonstrate the important but differing roles played by musicians in these two temporally and geographically close but widely dissimilar colleges.

This study draws heavily on the *Liber Magnus* of Corpus Christi College, a book containing the records of payments made to and by the college.[7] The accounts contain lists of all those members of college receiving stipends: the majority are identified by name, but a few, such as the president, vice-president, and servants or *famuli*, are identified by their office. The amount paid to each individual is recorded as well as any special circumstances surrounding that payment. There are also accounts of the amounts paid for college members' clothing, as all those receiving stipends were also entitled to clothes at the college's expense.

The lists of names are usually arranged in the same order for each year and may cast light on the esteem in which the various offices within college were held. For example, work on the Wardrobe Books of the royal household for the late fifteenth century supports the view that ordering within lists denoted status for this period.[8] Typically, the lists of stipends and clothing allowances at Corpus in the *Liber Magnus* employ the following order of sub-headings: President, Deans, Bursars, Lecturers in Greek and Logic, Fellows, Sacristan and Clerks [Clerics], Probationary Fellows and Undergraduates, and finally Servants. The general consistency as regards the ordering of the stipend and clothing lists suggests that they represent a rough hierarchy within the college with the President at the top and the servants at the bottom. The position of the chapel personnel in this sequence is of significance.

The information found in the *Liber Magnus* is complemented by further details concerning individuals found in the *Liber Admissorum*, which contains the name, age, county of origin, and position within college of each member.[9] The book records the date of a person's formal admission to Corpus, and thus provides confirmation of dates deduced from *Liber Magnus*. If a person appears in *Liber Magnus* but not in *Liber Admissorum*, we may deduce that he filled a position with a stipend or clothing allowance but were not an academic member of Corpus. Thus comparison of the two books allows us to establish which of those present in college were not full members. Chapel singers regarded as professional musicians rather than members of the academic community would fall into this category.

The records of payments give a reliable guide to the activity taking place in the college: more reliable than either the statutes, which constitute what the founder wanted to happen rather than what actually did, or contemporary prose accounts, which are inevitably filtered through the opinions of the writer.

The statutes are also a valuable witness to the early life of the college, provided they are used in the knowledge of the circumstances of their creation. They represent the only lasting testament the founder could leave as to his intentions for the college. As prose rather than financial accounts, they are a literary source, and offer a more stylised impression of the character of the founder and college. While they convey a sense of the intended ethos of the foundation, the statutes also dictate the number of people to be in the college and what activity they were to perform. The Corpus statutes were constructed by addition to preceding versions, producing a layered document compiled gradually. They were originally created in 1517 by the college's founder, Richard Fox, Bishop of Winchester, and revised in 1528.[10] Fox was a secretary to Henry VII and, from 1487, keeper of the privy seal.[11] He died in 1528 and was buried in Winchester Cathedral, where he had a chantry chapel.[12]

Fox's original intention had been to found a monastic College in Oxford for the monks of St Swithin's at Winchester; a royal licence was granted for this in 1513.[13] According to the story given in Holinshed's *Chronicles* of 1587, Hugh Oldham, Bishop of Exeter and a close friend of Fox, persuaded him to revise his plans on the grounds that the time of monks was probably past.[14] Another royal licence was granted in 1516, the charter of foundation was created on 1 March 1517, and the initial statutes the following June.[15] Corpus was not to take students on academic merit alone, as all students had to possess the potential to take holy orders. No student, however intelligent, was admitted if there was a reason why he could not become a priest.[16]

The statutes of Corpus reveal that the undergraduate community was to form an integral part of the institution.[17] A picture of Corpus as a small, intimate and largely closed foundation emerges repeatedly from the literature.[18] There is some evidence in the statutes to support the view that Corpus was a relatively inward-looking college and this would have had a substantial impact on the music of the chapel, as the chapel cannot, in a closed institution, be used for large-scale ceremonial effect.

In a smaller, devotional college it is likely that that the music will be equally private and pious.

The internal structure and statutory regulations at Corpus display the founder's desire to promote the people of areas with which he was familiar, rather than the College's Oxford surroundings, and in that sense it appears to the modern eye as somewhat backward-looking. Fox's succession of dioceses—Durham, Bath, Exeter and Winchester—is immortalised in the statutes of Corpus, in which he provides for two College members from each. It is for this reason that the *Liber Admissorum* records the county of origin of new College members. Provision was also made to recruit from Fox's birth county of Lincolnshire, which was allocated one member, as could the kin of William Frost, his steward and a College benefactor.[19]

Corpus's main benefactor, Hugh Oldham, was also compensated with the allocation of one place to his birth county of Lancashire.[20] Besides those members already mentioned, there were also to be two each from Surrey, Kent, and from Gloucestershire and Worcestershire together, and one each from Bedfordshire, Oxfordshire, and Wiltshire.[21] Corpus appears to have been a college dedicated to equality across the named countries and would probably not have taken the most able candidates unless they came from the required areas. There is notably no provision for students from London, which was already a major city.

The chapel played a central role in the college's day, each member being required to attend mass on pain of an increasing scale of penalties.[22] Having such an important place in college life, the chapel must also have been a major part of the members' image of their college. It was one of the important communal meeting places. The twice-weekly disputations at which all graduates and ministers of the chapel were obliged to be present provided another portion of college life that was held in common for academics and chapel ministers.[23] There is also the possibility, as we shall see, that some members may have become involved with the chapel on a more active basis. There was, therefore, a significant amount of integration of college and chapel, which would have contributed to the sense of college identity.

Corpus was never a large college, and all its members could have known one another. The original statutory provision for the college was for a president, 20 fellows, 20 undergraduates, and chapel personnel and servants.[24] There were only four chapel men—a precentor, sacristan, sub-sacristan and organist—but the significance of a place such as the chapel, where all the college members would see each other every day, must have been large. The corresponding importance of the chapel personnel is indicated by the detail in which they are described in the statutes. Further, in 1528, the year of Fox's death, the original 1517 statutes were changed, and the number of chapel personnel was increased by two choristers.[25] This addition has not been fully appreciated by previous writers on the subject, although it is clear that in the *Liber Magnus* the two choristers appear for the first time following the change of statutes in 1528.[26]

The addition of choristers in 1528, presumably as Fox was dying, could indicate that they were to sing in intercession for him. Alternatively, they could have been to increase the possibilities for singing polyphony in chapel, although with only two boys this could not have been very complex music. In either case, it indicates an increase in the consequence of chapel music, corresponding to the larger number of people involved. It also suggests that Corpus was keeping pace with the more general intro-duction of boy singers into sacred musical life that had taken place throughout the fifteenth century. Although a small body of singers, the Corpus chapel musicians were thus able to perform the same types, if not the same standard of repertory, as their neighbors at the much grander Cardinal College, which had been founded shortly afterwards by Cardinal Wolsey.

It has been suggested that those poor boys who came up to Corpus to begin their education with a view to eventually becoming undergraduates may have paid their way by being choristers.[27] We have already seen that services and disputations involved the whole collegiate body—academics and clerics—meeting together. The existence of a procedure whereby choristers could proceed to academic membership of the college demon-strates that boys might, instead of leaving immediately when their voices broke, want and be able to remain. In turn, this suggests that they did not have a purely musically dependent position within the college, and that it could provide their future academic or priestly career. It was common practice in the royal household for boys whose voices had changed to be sent to a related institution, such as King's College, Cambridge, to be edu-cated. It is less frequently recorded that boys who had been choristers were absorbed into the same body in which they had served as singers, and this is what makes Corpus so interesting. The progression of a boy from chorister to scholar cannot but reflect on the way in which the chapel community was integrated into the college as a whole.

The first appearance of a chorister's name in the college accounts is in 1528/9. The name "Garrett" appears in the *Impense pro vestibus* (first names are almost never listed in these accounts), together with a payment of ten shillings—that allowed to undergraduates. Garrett does not, however, appear in any of the lists of *Stipendia*, which indicates that he could not have been an undergraduate in Corpus at that time. The only statutory provision for persons in College receiving clothes but no stipend was for the choristers.[28] Garrett provides a valuable case study because he did not end his connection with the college when his voice broke.

The entry in the *Liber Admissorum* for 1532 gives details of his official entry into the College as an undergraduate; we know that his first name was John, he was 16 at that time and came originally from Lincolnshire.[29] The accounts make clear that in 1531/2 John Garrett was receiving clothing allowance as a chorister, and in 1532/33 had started receiving an undergraduate stipend.[30] He remained at Corpus and was admitted as a probationary fellow in 1536 and a full fellow in 1538.[31] It is thus possible, in this case, to follow a chorister's career out of the chapel and into academic life. The likelihood of this being a widespread phenomenon, and the consequent implications for the status of musicians in Corpus, are discussed below.

It is worth first considering the view of former choristers presented in the statutes. Fox states (in Ward):

> We allow [choristers] to remain in College until the first breaking of their voice. . . . However, if they behave well, [and] all the qualifications also requisite for a Student shall be found in them, we will that they shall be preferred to their compeers.[32]

These "requisite qualifications" were exacting: new undergraduates were required not only to be literate, but also to have the ability to write Latin verse.[33] Milne has argued that it would be difficult for a boy to acquire these abilities in the rural areas of the counties from which members of college were drawn. He suggests that service as a chorister was a route taken by promising potential students to allow them to pay their way in Oxford until such time as they fulfilled the requirements of entry to College.[34]

Some sense of choristers' academic potential is given by the requirements made of them in the statutes—that they must be, before entry:

> Instructed in all kinds of singing, at least in the plain and the involved ("prikked" they call it,) before they are engaged.[35]

Candidates had already to be partially literate in Latin (in order to sing the Latin liturgy) and to have substantial musical experience. This presents an apparent problem. How would a Corpus chorister have acquired this knowledge before entry to the college? It seems as prohibitive as the requirements made of an undergraduate.

A boy able to afford private tutoring at home would be unlikely to become a chorister, given that it would be unlikely to accord with the career path laid out for him by his rich father. It would not even make sense for a boy to have come up to Corpus as a chorister to fill time before he was able to become an undergraduate if he were already qualified but too young, since undergraduates were admitted from the age of 12. Thus, the choristers at Corpus must have made a definite decision not to begin their life in Oxford as *discipuli*, since they came into the college already possessing much (possibly all) of the ability required of a new student and at a comparable age. As the academic requirements were unlikely to have been acquired from a tutor, it is probable that such boys learned either at such schools as there were, or from educated relatives.

The statutes offer some interesting evidence about the education of choristers while in Oxford: they appear to imply that the chorister's knowledge of singing prior to entry would enable his immediate progression to grammar and literature:

> They [choristers] must be instructed in all kinds of singing . . . so that they may directly learn grammar and good authors; either in the College at the expense of their friends, or at Magdalen School.[36]

If the boys were educated at their own expense in college, then they were probably being taught with the undergraduates. This was presumably the best possible preparation for entry into college, although it entailed some expense to the boy's family. At Corpus, choristers continued to be educated, thus preserving the possibility of their pursuing a career in academia or the church.

The statutes require that during their time as *discipuli*, the students would be instructed in plainsong and examined in it before admission to a fellowship.[37] This means that the choristers would already have learned, before they took up their posts, something that undergraduates would probably only be beginning to be taught. It was necessary, of course, for all students at Corpus to be accomplished in singing plainsong if they were to go on to become priests, as was Fox's intention. The choristers' experience of serving in chapel would have given them early "work experience" for the priesthood and thus made them particularly suitable for admission to college if, as was presumably Fox's pious hope, they wished to become priests and not musicians. Far from being peripheral to the institution's life, choristers, it would seem, had the necessary skills to become ideal undergraduates in Fox's college.

As we have seen from the statutes, the place of origin of an undergraduate was important to Fox, although he made no specifications for choristers. As an undergraduate, Garrett is recorded in *Liber Admissorum* as originating in Lincolnshire, and thus would have traveled a long way to Oxford to become a chorister. This factor may further illuminate his story in relation to Corpus. There must have been some substantial advantage or impetus that led him to leave home at such a young age and with no guaranteed academic or clerical career ahead of him.[38] The college, looking around for suitable choristers, as larger colleges did, may well have consulted former members of college or those of other institutions nearby. That the college's first chorister should have come from Lincolnshire and not somewhere closer seems strange—unless, perhaps, there was a link between John Garrett and Oxford that is not immediately apparent.

That link may be a man called Thomas Garrett,[39] who described himself as "of Cardinallis College" in a letter to Cardinal Wolsey in 1528.[40] Previously, however, he had been a member of Corpus, and had been admitted in 1517 aged 19, from the county of Lincolnshire.[41] This man, then, came from the same county as John Garrett, had the same family name, was on hand at Cardinal College, and had a previous association with Corpus, a college whose founder also hailed from Lincolnshire.[42]

If John and Thomas Garrett were relatives, this could account for the presence of John in Oxford: Thomas, having connections in Oxford already, could have introduced the young boy to the city. It may also be through Thomas Garrett that John became known to his employers at Corpus: Thomas's associations with the college may have enabled him to promote a young relative.[43] This hypothesis is all the more persuasive given some additional evidence showing Thomas's link with the director of a famous group of musicians in Oxford: he was the man whose supply of heretical books in 1528 led to the famous composer John Taverner being accused of heresy while at Cardinal College.[44] The 1528 incident in Oxford, of which Thomas Garrett was the lynchpin, has become (in)famous among musicians because Cardinal Wolsey acquitted Taverner on the grounds that he was "but a musician."[45]

Thomas Garrett's other associates, Udall and Diott, both left Corpus the year before John Garrett arrived, but, as fellows, they might have been privy to discussions concerning future choristers in 1527–8.[46] The serious charge of heresy does not seem to have caused disaster and ruin for them: even Thomas Garrett escaped serious reprisals, although he had to flee from Oxford. It is not likely, therefore, that this scandal would automatically disqualify any child, by association with Thomas Garrett, from a career in Oxford. Udall and Diott could have remembered the family of Thomas Garrett and helped them by assisting a family member to become a chorister.

The Garretts' Lincolnshire origins provide one more possible piece of evidence of their associations with institutions supporting music. It is known that in 1525–6 Thomas Garrett was a chaplain at the Guild of the Blessed Virgin Mary, and master of the grammar school in Boston, Lincolnshire.[47] It is unfortunately not known from which town in that county John Garrett was brought to Oxford, but it could have been either Boston or Tattershall, where John Taverner had worked.[48] If John Garrett had lived in Boston, there is a chance he could have received the education that enabled him to come to Corpus from the grammar school and from service as a chorister in one of the town's guilds.[49]

The above discussion concerning Thomas Garrett is speculative as it has so far proved impossible to discover any definite records of the family of either Thomas or John Garrett. Having established that John Garrett was a chorister, undergraduate and fellow of Corpus Christi

College, however, it is clear that there was a route for members of the Chapel into the academic college, and that it was more than possible for a boy chorister to rise through the academic ranks.

It is apparent that there was considerable interaction between the chapel singers and the academic scholars. The statutes regarding choristers' entry into college as undergraduates indicate that Bishop Fox envisaged this happening. He did not expect all Corpus choristers to be future professional singers: John Garrett's story illustrates a possible *cursus honorem* for ex-choristers. This may, in turn, contribute to our understanding of the gradual rise of professionalism within church music. It provides a relatively late example of a patron not wanting to hire professional singers but to integrate those who provided music into the body of the college. This is in direct contrast to Cardinal College, where musicians were regarded as "but musicians" by Wolsey, as is clear from his dismissive remark about Taverner. It seems unlikely that any chapel singer at Corpus, being a full or future member of the college, could have escaped punishment for lack of religious understanding on the same grounds.

The place of chapel music within Corpus is thus illuminated not only by the role of the choristers within the college, but also by that of the men of the chapel. It will become clear that there was interaction between chapel and college at all levels, some provided by statute and some only inferable from the accounts. Of the four men of the Chapel provided by statute, two were to be priests: "one Precentor of the Choir, and the other *Edituus* or Sacristan," and two "not Priests, but Clerks and Acolytes, or at least initiated by the primary tonsure." Of the latter, "one of them is to be the Organist, and the other the Sub-sacrist."[50] It is unfortunately unknown when the college acquired a chapel organ: the first mention of one is of its destruction towards the end of the sixteenth century. Consequently, it is impossible to determine whether there could actually have been an organist from the college's foundation and the discussion of the organist and the sub-sacrist must focus on their duties as singers. The two men were required to be "so laudably proficient in chanting that they may do service in the choir."[51] This indicates that perhaps polyphony may have been sung, given the proficiency requirement.

While the college's statutes provide for four men of the chapel, the college accounts only show payments to three men at least until 1532. These are clearly arranged in order of precedence, because the third man receives less money than the first two when they are all being paid for the same amount of time. The first occasion on which this happens is in 1528/9:

Stipends of Sacristan and Clerks
Paid to Travys for four terms – 40s
Paid to Eston for four terms – 40s
Paid to John Hychyns for four terms – 26s 8d[52]

It is worth noting that, besides John Hychyns in this instance, only college servants are recorded in the accounts by their first names. Thus the use of Hychyns' first name here is, with his lower pay, indicative of a status lower than that of his two colleagues. This distinction also manifests itself in the lists of names in the *Impense pro vestibus* of the *Liber Magnus* for the same year: Travys and Eston appear after the last of the Fellows and before the first of the undergraduates, but Hychyns is placed at the very end. Hychyns is thus made, from the layout of the accounts at least, to seem of less importance than all the undergraduates, while his colleagues were placed before them.

In 1521/2 the chapel men received no recorded clothing allowance, but in the subsequent years' lists a pattern emerges with two appearing after the fellows and one amongst the undergraduates, the amount of the allowances corresponding with these positions. It seems likely, then, that the regular composition of the chapel personnel was two men of status approximately equal to probationary fellows, and one on a par at most with the undergraduates. Only once do the three chapel men appear together: in the *Impense vestium* for 1530/1, where the third, Hychyns again, is distinguished by the word *clerico* after his name, which the other two, Travys and Eston, do not have. The positioning of their names is such that the chapel group as a whole, rather than just the senior two, falls between fellows and undergraduates. The distinction, however, is still present graphically, as Hychyns appears in the layout almost as the first of the undergraduate group rather than the last of the chapel men, and receiving the same allowance as the undergraduates rather than his colleagues. The figures recording stipends or allowances at the right hand side of the accounts in *Liber Magnus* make a considerable visual impression of groups of differing importance.

The clear distinction between two chapel ministers and the third, in both financial terms and through inference from the ordering of names within the accounts lists, indicates that the college was employing the two priests specified in the statutes, but only one man of lower status who might have been either organist or sub-sacristan.[53] It is possible to interpret this as evidence that the college had not yet acquired an organ and was thus not employing an organist, the third name therefore belonging to the sub-sacristan. The presence of a sub-sacristan is supported by the fact that it is apparent that the college had bells at this time—one of his duties was "to ring the bells for the divine offices."[54] It is clear that there were bells because there are payments related to their maintenance in the *Impense Sacelli* of the *Liber Magnus*: for example, 16d was paid in 1530/1 for repairs to the bells.[55] Whatever the specific duties besides singing of the chapel men, there were still only three of them when the statutes required four.

The question arises whether and how the place of a fourth singing man was filled. The matter is more complicated than it seems, because in 1521/2, 1528/9, 1529/30 and 1530/1, one or more of the Fellows is named in the *Stipendia sociorum* of *Liber Magnus* as having performed the functions of a priest in chapel. For example, the 1528/9 account records a payment to Rodys "for four terms, one of them [acting] as priest."[56] The senior fellows would all have been priests, because a member of Corpus was obliged, on completing his MA, either to receive holy orders or to leave the college. No member, however, was permitted to be ordained before he had completed his MA.[57] Thus there was no difficulty in finding men to perform the duties of priests from within college if the need arose. Taken with the fact of there being only three chapel men employed instead of four, this presents the possibility of the fourth position being filled from within college. It is unlikely, however, that a Fellow would have officially taken up the fourth post, as it has been made clear that the vacancy was of the lower of two levels of status and unsuitable for an ordained priest.

In the years 1529/30 and 1530/31, six and five of the fellows respectively are noted in the accounts as having acted as priests for all or part of the year.[58] Indeed, in 1529/30 the first of the remaining three fellows after the above list is specified as *non sacerdoti*, the large number of priests having created a presumption that priesthood was the normal status for fellows, and a need to specify those who were not in holy orders. The fact that those who were paid for less than a full year (four terms) do not appear in the next year, that the four paid for a full year in 1529/30 appear again in 1530/31, and that the priests are, in these years, at the top of the list of fellows, suggest that this is merely a convention of naming those senior fellows who were in priest's orders as such in the accounts. This was not the convention in the preceding and succeeding years as there is only ever one fellow indicated as being paid as a priest and often not even one.

If there were a change in the handwriting or style of presentation for the years 1529–31 this would have indicated that a different clerk wrote the accounts for those years and would have supported the idea that the differences in numbers of priests were produced by changing styles of account presentation alone. If anything, however, it appears that different people compiled 1529/30 and 1530/31, as the notational conventions are different. In most entries "a[d]" of 1529/30 is replaced by an abbreviation that appears to be "a[d]ro[n]" in 1530/31, and in the former the number of academic terms is almost always given in Arabic numerals, whereas in the latter the number of terms is often written in Latin words.[59]

It is possible that for some reason it was decided in 1529 that status as priests should be recorded in the *Stipendia* accounts and that that decision was revoked in 1531. It is also possible, however, that these large numbers of fellows actually were performing some extra priestly duties in chapel, perhaps ones that were required for two years but not before or after. It is worth noting that these years, 1529–31, are immediately after choristers were introduced and could be a period of increased choral activity. The fact that Richard Fox died in 1528 makes it possible that extra requiem masses were being sung for him in these years, thus accounting for the augmented chapel personnel.

The individual entries of payments *fuit sacerdos* in other years, however, are more problematic because they are unlikely to have been to single fellows who simply happened to be priests. If they were, they would have resulted, as they do not, in that individual being placed at the top of the list of fellows as would have befitted his implied seniority. Further, it seems unlikely that in 1525–7 there were no fellows who had taken their MA and thus been ordained, but none is denoted as having done so. Equally, Wytallys and Donne, who appear in 1530/1 as priests, are not denoted as such in 1531/2 and thus either a change in situation or in accounting practice must have occurred between the two sets of accounts, neither of which can be demonstrated to have taken place, unless the men were being paid extra for special duties.

Even without this example of fellows acting as priests, there are other instances: it seems most probable that the single entries of 1521/2 and 1528/9 do refer to individuals who did service in the chapel beyond their ordinary duties. This, if the case, would indicate movement from the academic side of the college to the chapel to add to the movement, seen in John Garrett's case, from the chapel to academia. Academics singing in chapel may have been as easily accepted as choristers becoming academics.

There is substantial evidence that any or all senior members might have taken part in some form of musical activity within the college but outside the chapel, which can only strengthen the supposition that they could also sing liturgically. The statutes of New College, for example, allow scholars and fellows to remain by the fire in hall after dinner in winter "for the sake of recreation in singing and other honest solaces." [60] This instruction was copied almost word for word in the statutes of several other colleges, including those of Corpus.[61] If the fellows were accustomed to sing after dinner, there is no reason to suppose that the chapel men would not have been welcome to join them, thus bringing the chapel and academic personnel together in secular and devotional music if not in liturgy. Thus music could serve a communal function in the college rather than just a liturgical and ceremonial one in chapel.

To summarize: the chapel of Corpus Christi College was to a large extent integrated into the college as a whole, and probably more so than in other, larger colleges. As participants in twice-weekly disputations with the senior members of college, and as colleagues in the priesthood of some of those members, the men of the chapel at Corpus must have been held in higher regard than those at other colleges who were only professional singers.[62] At the levels both of chorister and priest, the Corpus chapel personnel worked with the other members of college on terms of considerable parity. There is no evidence of the kind of musical professionalism that had been developing in large institutions and none of the sharp differentiation between the musical and academic sides of the institution's existence. This, as mentioned earlier, is in marked contrast to the much-documented trend towards professionalisation supposedly taking place in the fifteenth century.[63] The point is emphasized by the following quotation from Roger Bowers concerning the two Cardinal Colleges where:

> [Cardinal Wolsey did not] leave the worship of the college chapel to be conducted as a secondary priority by the *academic members*; rather for each [of his two colleges] he supplied a *full-staffed professional chapel choir*.[64] [my Italicizations]

Bowers's clear-cut distinction between "academic members" and "professional chapel choir," while apparently perfectly justified in the case of Cardinal College, Oxford, implies that that distinction needs no further qualification. It also suggests that if worship was performed by the academics, it must necessarily be a less satisfactory version of the Cardinal College system, thus making musical excellence the only criterion of worth in a college chapel, as does not seem to have been the case at Corpus.

It is clear that a modern tendency to look for professionals and study large institutions more than small ones has contributed to an imprecise picture of the chapels of this period. Music can easily be viewed as segregated, leading to a presumption that musicians were a breed apart. During the sixteenth century, this applied to John Taverner ("but a musician") but clearly not to singers at Corpus.

Corpus Christi College was founded only nine years before Cardinal College was opened on the feast of St Frideswide in October 1526.[65] In order to assess the information provided by Corpus regarding its music and general structure, it will clearly be productive to compare it to this other establishment so close in date and location but so dissimilar in size and status. Cardinal Wolsey's elaborate building programs and huge household were all designed to convey his greatness to the world. Chapels were clearly part of this display:

> The objective informing the maintenance of an elaborate chapel of the household was far more than merely the ordering by competent staff of the daily devotions of a great man. . . . [Among other things] it was . . . a channel for a conspicuous display of his wealth and magnificence, so establishing his status in the eyes of those with whom he dealt in business both diplomatic and political. . . . The chapel was a vehicle for pageantry and spectacle.[66]

Cardinal College appeared as a rival in size and magnificence to King's College, Cambridge, founded by Henry VI, and contained a great monastic church as its chapel to compare with the chapel of King's.[67]

The number of people employed in the chapel of Cardinal College was nearly seven times greater than that of Corpus. There were 13 chaplains, 12 clerks and 16 boy choristers, and Wolsey demanded only the best musicians.[68] Selecting a master of the choristers, Wolsey lighted on John Taverner, a man already proven to be excellent at his job, although not Wolsey's first choice. It was not an impediment that Taverner was already employed at the church of the Holy Trinity in Tattershall, Lincolnshire,[69] and he was tempted to Oxford with wages of £15 a year (50% more than the stipend of the President of Corpus!).[70] By mid 1526 Taverner was in Wolsey's employ and recruiting singers for Cardinal College.

During this period, in order that standards might be maintained in important choirs, some were allowed to demand good singers of their choice from lesser establishments. The Chapel Royal, of course, could take singers from anywhere else, after which there was a group of choirs that could select, with the king's permission, from the rest. This permission was obtained by purchasing the equivalent of a licence at the crown's discretion. The opposite was also sold, a document allowing choirs protection from having their singers removed.[71] In the case of Cardinal College, Wolsey lost no time in acquiring the necessary commission from the King that would enable him to take singing men and boys from around the country.[72] There is no evidence that Bishop Fox performed a similar manoeuvre on behalf of Corpus Christi College, and it seems alien to his vision of the college as depicted in the statutes. If Wolsey had not been anxious to create an image for himself to use in matters of state, it seems unlikely that he would have exerted himself to form such a choir as that of Cardinal College.

The place that a choir could have in establishing the status of a college in the early sixteenth century is demonstrated by a comment quoted by Bowers and made in relation to Wolsey's Ipswich college choir:

> The opinion of William Capon, dean of Cardinal College, Ipswich, [addressed to Wolsey, was] that "in our quere standeth the honnor of your grace's collage."[73]

If the choir could thus be the honour of a college, it must have been strongly identified with the college as a whole and a visible sign of that college's status. In the case of Corpus, status does not seem to have been too important as the college was "planned to stay small." [74]

While the singers at Cardinal College remained isolated from the academic college in a way that the ones at Corpus did not, there remains the anomaly that John Taverner was clearly connected with academics at his own and surrounding colleges. He became involved in the heretical dealings of Thomas Garrett in Oxford, as indeed did John Radley, one of the singers that Taverner had brought from Lincolnshire.[75] The accounts of the affair make clear that the people concerned were a mutually sympathetic group with whom Taverner is likely to have had contact. If this was the case, then there is the possibility that some of the kind of interaction between academics and chapel taking place at Corpus also occurred in an informal, unofficial way in other, larger colleges. With the provision for singing after meals in hall at Corpus there appears the possibility of internal music making for pleasure: the self-contained chapel services conducted by those within the body of the college would also have been private. Not for the greater glory of founder or college, this music would be part of the life of the college in a way that more impressive, professional music never could be.

There has been consistent neglect of un-professional behavior in sixteenth-century church musicians: modern writers tend to look for evidence of change rather than continuity, and movement towards the present. Such results in an unbalanced and unhistoricized picture of musical life. Corpus Christi College, Oxford, provides an example of how amateur music making by people who pursued careers in the church rather than music continued to be of great importance well into the sixteenth century. They should not be overlooked.

Notes

1. This paper draws on research I carried out while working for my first degree at St. Hugh's College, Oxford.

2. Roger Bowers, "Obligation, Agency, and *laissez-faire*: the Promotion of Polyphonic Composition for the Church in Fifteenth-Century England," in *Music in Medieval and Early Modern Europe: Patronage, Sources and Texts*, ed. Ian Fenlon (Cambridge: Cambridge University Press, 1981), 4.

3. See Bowers "Obligation, Agency and *laissez-faire*," and Manfred F. Bukofzer, *Studies in Medieval and Renaissance Music* (London: Dent, 1951); Frank Ll. Harrison, *Music in*

Medieval Britain (London: Routledge and Paul, 1963); Christopher A. Reynolds, "Sacred Polyphony" in *Performance Practice: Music before 1600*, ed. Howard Mayer Brown and Stanley Sadie (London, 1987).

4. In his chapter "The Institutions and the Cultivation of Polyphony from 1400 to the Reformation," in *Music in Medieval Britain*, 156–219, Harrison refers to Cardinal, Lincoln, Magdalen, Merton and New Colleges when discussing Oxford. Examples of works that address single colleges are Roger Bowers, "The Cultivation and Promotion of Music in the Household and Orbit of Thomas Wolsey," in *Cardinal Wolsey: Church, State and Art*, ed. S. J. Gunn and P. G. Lindley (Cambridge: Cambridge University Press, 1991), 178–218 [Cardinal College], and Paul R. Hale, "Music and Musicians," in *New College Oxford 1379–1979*, ed. John Buxton and Penry Williams (New College, Oxford, 1979), 267–292.

5. See, for example, Reinhard Strohm, "Centre and Periphery: Mainstream and Provincial Music," in *Companion to Medieval and Renaissance Music*, ed. Tessa Knighton and David Fallows (London: Dent, 1992), 55–59.

6. See, for example, Thomas Fowler (President of Corpus 1881–1904), *Corpus Christi*, "Oxford University College Histories" (London, 1893), and J. G. Milne (undergraduate at Corpus 1886–90 and Librarian 1933–46), *The Early History of Corpus Christi College Oxford* (Oxford: Basil Blackwell, 1946).

7. The chronological order of the *Liber Magnus* is unfortunately unreliable, so all citations from it are made by the year of the accounts as given in pencil by J. G. Milne, former archivist of Corpus. Milne's notes provide clarification: Corpus Christi College Archive: K/2/2.

8. See Helen Jeffries, "Job Descriptions, Nepotism and Part-Time Work: the Minstrels and Trumpeters of the Court of Edward IV of England (1461–83)," *Plainsong and Medieval Music* 12:2 (2003): 165–77.

9. The *Liber Admissorum* has reliable pencil foliation as well as accurate dating, so citations are made using both of these methods of reference.

10. G. R. M. Ward, *The Foundation Statutes of Bishop Fox for Corpus Christi College in the University of Oxford* (London, 1843).

11. James McConica, ed., *The Collegiate University*, vol. 3, The History of the University of Oxford, ed. T. H. Aston, III (Oxford: Clarendon Press, 1986), 17.

12. Thomas Fowler, "Foxe or Fox, Richard 1448?–1528," *Dictionary of National Biography*, CD-ROM Version (Oxford, 1995), 6.

13. McConica, *The Collegiate University*, 17.

14. Raphael Holinshed, *Chronicles comprising . . . the Description and Historie of England . . . Ireland . . . and Scotland, by R. Holinshed, W. Harrison, and Others* (London, 1587), in Fowler, "Foxe or Fox, Richard," 6

15. McConica, *The Collegiate University*, 18.

16. W. O. Hassall, "Corpus Christi College," in *The University of Oxford*, ed. H. E. Salter and M. D. Lobel, 3 vols., The Victoria History of the Counties of England (Oxford, 1954), vol. III, 220–221.

17. McConica, *The Collegiate University*, 21.

18. Fowler, *Corpus Christi*, 37–59; Milne, *Early History*, 1–10; and McConica, *The Collegiate University*, 18.

19. Hassall, "Corpus Christi College," 220.

20. McConica, *The Collegiate University*, 18.

21. Hassall, "Corpus Christi College," 220.

22. Fowler, *Corpus Christi*, 52, 54.

23. McConica, *The Collegiate University*, 24.

24. Ward, *Statutes*, 2–3; and McConica, *The Collegiate University*, 18.

25. *Liber Magnus*; and McConica, *The Collegiate University*, 18.

26. There is an entry regarding the clothing for *Duobus choristio* in 1521/2, but the handwriting and ink are clearly different from the surrounding accounts and are consistent with the entry being a later addition.

27. Milne, *Early History*, 7.

28. Ward, *Statutes*, 79.

29. *Liber Admissorum*, f.13r 1532: Apr 27.

30. 1531/32 *Impense pro vestibus . . . choristorum*: Solutum garret—x s; 1532/33 *Stipendia scolarum in probatione et discipuli*: Solutum garret—xxvi s viii d, *Impensae pro vestibus*: [Solutum] garret—x s.

31. *Liber Admissorum*; and A. B. Emden, *A Biographical Register of the University of Oxford A. D. 1501 to 1540* (Oxford, 1974), 228.

32. Ward, *Statutes*, 79.

33. Hassall, "Corpus Christi College," 220.

34. Milne, *Early History*, 7.

35. Ward, *Statutes*, 79.

36. Ward, *Statutes*, 79.

37. McConica, *The Collegiate University*, 20.

38. Being 16 years old in 1532, he would have been about 12 in 1528/9 when he arrived in Corpus.

39. I am grateful to David Skinner for bringing this man to my attention as a possible connection of John Garrett.

40. Emden, *Biographical Register*, 228.

41. *Liber Admissorum*, f.2v 1517: aug 9.

42. Fowler, "Foxe or Fox, Richard," 1.

43. This kind of nepotism has been found in royal chapel singers and royal minstrels; see Marsh Jeffries "Job Descriptions, Nepotism and Part-time Work."

44. David S. Josephson, *John Taverner Tudor Composer*, vol. 5, Studies in Musicology (Michigan: UMI Research Press, 1979), 69.

45. Josephson, *John Taverner*, 69.

46. *Liber Magnus*, 1527/8.

47. Josephson, *John Taverner*, 90.

48. Josephson, *John Taverner*, 85.

49. Josephson, *John Taverner*, 88.

50. Ward, *Statutes*, 76, 3, 78.

51. Ward, *Statutes*, 78.

52. *Stipendia edituum et clericor[um]*

Solut[um] a[d] travys p[ro] 4 t[er]minis:——xl s
S[olu]t[um] a[d] eston p[ro] 4 termini[s]:——xl s
S[olu]t[um] Joa[n]ni hychyns p[ro] 4 t[er]mi[nis]:——xxvi s viii d
Liber Magnus, 1528/9.

53. It should be noted that this conflicts with the accounts heading *edituus et clerici*, which gives the higher status in the singular and the lower in the plural.

54. Ward, *Statutes*, 78.

55. *Liber Magnus*, 1530/1.

56. S[olu]t[um] a[d] Rodys p[ro] 4 t[er]minis uno ex illis sacer[doti]——xliii s iiii d
Liber Magnus, 1528/9.

57. Hassall, "Corpus Christi College," 219.

58. 1529/30—Clerkson: Priest for three terms: 40s; Current: Priest for one term: 13s 4d; Wytallys: Priest for four terms: 53s 4d; Mertyn: Priest for four terms: 53s 4d; Bolday: Priest for four terms: 53s 4d; Rodys: Priest for four terms: 53s [*sic*]. In 1530/1—Wytallys: Priest for four terms: 53s 4d; Martyn: Priest for four terms: 53s 4d; Bolday: Priest for "all the terms": 53s 4d; Rodys: Priest for one term: 13s 4d; Done: Priest for four terms: 40s.

59. *Liber Magnus*, 1529/30 and 1530/31, *Stipendia* section.

60. "quando of Die reverentiam, ac suae matris, vel alterius Sancti cujuscunque, tempore hyemali ignis in aula Sociis ministratur; tunc scholaribus et Sociis, post tempus prandii aut coenae, liceat gratia recreationis in aula in cantilemus et aliis solatiis honestiis moram focere condecentem, et poemata, regnorum chronicas, et mundi hujus mirabilia, ac caetera quae statum clericalem condecorant, seriosus pertractare." Quoted in Janet Coleman, *Public Reading and Reading Public*, vol. 26, Cambridge Studies in Medieval Literature (Cambridge, 1996), 136–137.

61. Coleman, *Public Reading*, 137.

62. McConica, *The Collegiate University*, 24.

63. See, for example, Bowers, "Obligation, agency, and *laissez-faire*"; Bukofzer, *Studies in Medieval and Renaissance Music*; Harrison, *Music In Medieval Britain*; and Reynolds, "Sacred Polyphony."

64. Bowers, "The Cultivation and Promotion of Music," 196.

65. Bowers, "The Cultivation and Promotion of Music," 197.

66. Bowers, "The Cultivation and Promotion of Music," 178.

67. Josephson, *John Taverner*, 52.

68. Josephson, *John Taverner*, 54.

69. Bowers, "The Cultivation and Promotion of Music," 197; and Josephson, *John Taverner*, 45, 58.

70. Josephson, *John Taverner*, 59.

71. Bowers, "The Cultivation and Promotion of Music," 178–196.

72. Bowers, "The Cultivation and Promotion of Music," 196.

73. Bowers, "The Cultivation and Promotion of Music," 196.

74. McConica, *The Collegiate University*, 18.

75. Josephson, *John Taverner*, 63, 64–67.

Angels and Furies
Women and Popular Song during the French Revolution

Laura Mason

The traditional view of the relationship between music and the French Revolution was that it was hardly worth acknowledging. Generations of music scholars dismissed the revolutionary decade as a creative wasteland that failed to produce operas, symphonies, or chamber music of lasting significance. Complaining that revolutionary France did not produce a Beethoven or a Mozart or, more positively, that the musical world did not generate talent equal to that of revolutionary painter Jacques-Louis David, and dismayed by the visible impact of politics on the arts, historians of music elided the revolutionary years as they skipped from the operas and musical quarrels of the 1770s to the compositions of Berlioz in the 1830s.[1]

Those opinions changed late in the twentieth century when the bicentennial of the French Revolution coincided with the emergence of new academic approaches to music. Now emphasizing rather than occulting interaction between politics and music, scholars re-evaluated the revolutionary decade by focusing on distinctive compositions of the period—festival and theatrical music, topical operas, and songs—and the institutions that nourished them. Although they did not uncover a neglected genius to rival David, they did foster new appreciation of the breadth and variety of musical creativity in those years. Equally important, scholars are beginning to fill the void that once yawned between the eighteenth and nineteenth centuries, illustrating how particular musical traditions survived the Revolution and what innovations revolutionaries bequeathed to their musical heirs at home and abroad.

For all of these achievements, however, such scholarship still defines music and revolution alike in unnecessarily narrow terms. Music is defined in terms of compositions and the institutions in which or for which they were produced. This emphasis reveals the social, cultural, and political contexts of musical invention by highlighting how revolutionary values were expressed in opera and popular and theatrical songs, and it assesses the relative impact of tradition and innovation on compositional technique, music theory, and pedagogy.[2] This approach serves the purposes of music history and has the added advantage of meshing well with traditional histories of revolutionary song, which celebrate song lyrics as vehicles of public opinion and consider the relationship of those lyrics to the events they represented, and the individuals and institutions that produced them.[3]

What both bodies of scholarship leave untouched, however, are the dimensions of musical experience that became apparent in performance. How did men and women perform these compositions? What kinds of responses did they elicit from listeners? Such questions are vital to a fuller understanding of revolutionary music because performance takes us beyond the world of composers and pedagogues to illuminate how music insinuated itself into the daily lives and intimate political expressions of ordinary people.

The French Revolution offers unusually rich and varied examples of musical practices because the Revolution mobilized citizens to a degree hitherto unknown, and because singing served as a unique means to express that sense of mobilization. Familiar and highly malleable, singing would prove particularly important to the many citizens who lacked the literacy, political influence, or cultural contacts to produce pamphlets and newspapers, motions to the National Assembly, or speeches at the local Jacobin club. So songs became nearly ubiquitous during the Revolution, serving to express opinions across the political spectrum. And these opinions were not confined to lyrics; singers who were attuned to the rich possibilities of their largely oral culture manipulated tunes, inflected particular words, and used a rich repertoire of gesture to convey revolutionary commitment or opposition.[4]

This brings us to our second term: revolution. Studies of music and song lyrics alike too often define revolution as a relatively coherent package of pre-existing political ideals that composers and lyricists accepted or rejected outright. But the French Revolution encompassed far more than regime change or the sorting of republicans from royalists.

Revolutionaries concerned themselves with all dimensions of public and private life as they debated the nature and aims of the state, the meaning of politics, race and religion, hierarchies within families and between the sexes, and even the social and political implications of sexual practices. The list is breath-taking and the conclusions revolutionaries reached had consequences that lasted for generations; in many instances, they continue to shape how we understand the world today. All of these issues were susceptible to musical treatment for, as scholars like Jane Fulcher and Susan McClary have shown for other periods, composition and performance regularly breached the limits of seemingly fixed categories of genre, aesthetics, and subject matter to express deep-seated and often unexamined assumptions about matters as diverse as nationalism and sexuality.[5]

I want to consider the implications of defining music and revolution more broadly. In so doing, I hope to demonstrate how the methods of cultural historians may illuminate new dimensions of revolutionary musical experience by proposing the means to find traces of musical performance—and amateur performance in particular—in the past. I mean to do so by examining a specific case, that of Sophie Lapierre, a political activist tried for conspiracy and famed for singing revolutionary anthems in the courtroom. I want to argue that Lapierre's performances and the reactions they excited violate musicologists' expectations about traditional relationships between gender and singing, and historians' assertions about women and politics during the French Revolution.

French revolutionary attitudes toward women's singing are likely to surprise scholars of music and history alike. On the one hand, ethnographers and musicologists assert that most cultures, before the mid-twentieth century, drew sharp distinctions between men's and women's musical performances, distinctions that evoked public/private dichotomies. Women's musical performances were usually associated with the household or household activities; when women did perform in public, they were likely to find traditional restrictions on performance and repertoire that expressed their subordination to men and their status as exceptional beings.[6] At the same time, historians of the French Revolution assert that revolutionaries' hostility to powerful women of the Old Regime—those who exercised influence at court and were believed, like Marie-Antoinette, to have corrupted the monarchy—shaped representations of women and encouraged legislators to forge a republic that silenced women and excluded them from public politics.[7] In light of both bodies of scholarship, then, we might expect revolutionaries to have been unsettled by the sight of women singing in public, or to have attempted to limit the kinds of songs that women might legitimately perform.

Such was not the case, however, for revolutionaries privileged a singer's political intent over her gender. This did not, of course, preclude the application of gender stereotypes, but such stereotypes were more often determined by *a priori* opinions about the singer's politics than her sex. Thus, Paris police spy Marauz was not disconcerted to hear a woman singing "patriotic songs next to the former church of St. Germain l'Auxerois," nor did the commune of St. Sever consider it inappropriate to organize a choir of young women to perform patriotic songs and revolutionary hymns for the inauguration of the local temple of Truth.[8] In other words, whether performing as independent agents or under the auspices of an official ceremony, women's public singing was praised when it promoted revolutionary goals. This point becomes most clear when we consider two different representations of women singing during the summer of 1793, as the Terror gained momentum.

The first is an account by citizen Perrières, a police spy who described a women's choir performing the "Marseillaise" at nightfall in a public garden. The "Marseillaise" is not simply the song that would become the French national anthem at the end of the nineteenth century; it may legitimately be described as distinctively masculine hymn in both cultural association and composition. Popularized by soldiers shortly after France declared war on Austria, the "Marseillaise" pairs a vigorous and relatively complex tune that moves steadily toward the lower registers of the voice, with lyrics that describe the nation's enemies as "ferocious soldiers/ . . . come into your very midst/To slaughter your sons, your wives!" before roaring, "To arms citizens . . . let impure blood water our fields." And yet, rather than expressing shock upon hearing women sing such a song, Perrières was transported. He described the singers as, "all young . . . and pretty, I would like to believe."

> Ah! sing ladies and your husbands, your beloved will fly into combat;
> that is the true means of enlistment. These gentle, penetrating voices
> reminded me of the choirs of women and charming girls I so often heard

in the non-conformists' assemblies in England. . . . There is not one of those angels I would not have liked to take as my wife. . . .[9]

The second account stands in sharp contrast. Describing a crowd of women who sang counter-revolutionary songs just a couple of months later, Perrières's fellow spy, Beraud, conjured up a monstrous horde that did not sing but "vomit[ed] . . . horrible songs against the Jacobins."[10]

In sum, what made women's singing desirable or repellant was its use to proclaim particular political opinions. Women who sang in public became angels or furies because of the kinds of political opinions they performed and, as we shall see, because of the ways in which they situated themselves with regard to revolutionary authorities. To examine this point in greater detail and consider how singing intersected with the complex political alignments of the Revolution, let us turn to representations of the singer and democratic activist, Sophie Lapierre, who was tried with sixty-three other men and women for fomenting insurrection.

By the winter of 1797, many French citizens believed the Revolution was over. The Terror had ended more than three years before, and reactionary violence seemed to be wearing itself out. As the sitting government of the Directory struggled to reimpose order in the countryside and stabilize a faltering economy, journalists and private citizens debated the Revolution's meaning and France's political future. In this context, the trial of the Equals opened before a high court in the small town of Vendôme.

The Equals, a group of sixty-four men and women who included the radical journalist Gracchus Babeuf, were charged with conspiring to overthrow the Directory in order to abolish private property and restore the popular government of the Terror. Although many of the accused were simply provincial activists, swept up by local police who considered them trouble-makers, there was at their center a knot of Parisian democrats who had been attempting to organize the working people of the capital at the time of their arrest. This cohort had used songs to circulate its message, and once the accused were gathered in the prisons of Vendôme, all of the detainees sang together. They did not, however, sing the radical Babouvist songs of Paris; they chose more common favorites with which to keep up their spirits and entertain themselves. While awaiting trial, for example, they marked the anniversary of the king's execution by singing a few verses of the *Carmagnole* and a new song on the subject rhymed to the tune of a popular drinking song.[11]

But the defendants' most remarkable performances did not surface until the high court was in session: then, they began to sing republican hymns at the close of each hearing. The first such performance was of the "Marseillaise," an energetic and iconic expression of republican enthusiasm that had also been the source of lengthy and violent contests between soldiers and reactionaries during the Thermidoran Reaction. Later, the defendants took up "Veillons au salut de l'empire," which warned, "Tyrants tremble/Sooner death than slavery," and "Goujon's Lament," which commemorated those "martyred" in the wake of Prairial, the last popular insurrection of the Revolution. The Equals continued to sing for almost a month, until the high court judges ordered them to be silent, after which "the accused withdrew quietly."[12]

The political implications of the Equal's singing were entirely clear to members of the court and to the trial's observers, for their performances echoed what the defendants said about themselves in unrhymed prose.[13] The Equals declared themselves innocent of conspiracy and claimed they were being persecuted for defending the Revolution's achievements. The prosecution's evidence, they continued, was fabricated by the Paris police force at the behest of a hostile government intent on burying the Revolution's democratic legacy. Carrying this offensive strategy into the courtroom, the defendants and their lawyers committed themselves to turning the tables on their prosecutors and putting the government on trial by questioning the court's legitimacy and condemning public policy as antidemocratic. In sum, the Equals asserted that they were the Revolution's true defenders; indeed, they claimed to defend the Revolution against the government itself. Their performances reinforced their arguments for, in choice of song and act of singing alike, they evoked popular radicalism and the high-water mark of revolutionary democracy.

Democratic newspapers sympathetic to the Equals represented their singing in the same terms: "The accused sing the first verse of the hymn of the Prairial martyrs. Their voices deepen at the words: *we are those who depraved men dare to menace with death.*"[14] According to such accounts, when the Equals sang, they did so as a group: "... the accused sang hymns to liberty until the last moment, when they were given the cruel order to separate."[15] These accounts evoked the memory of sans-culottes who sang together in parks and cafés at the height of the Revolution; sympathetic readers might well have told themselves that, like the sans-culottes, so now the Equals sang in spite of being encircled by threatening enemies.

The Equals' opponents—police spies, prosecutors, moderate and royalist newspaper editors—did not see matters in these terms. They believed the defendants were anarchists and terrorists: the Equals had conspired to overturn the stable civil order for which the public longed, in order to revive the partisan violence and chaos of the Terror. And just as the Equals' opponents defined the latter's politics in their own terms, so they represented the defendants' courtroom singing in a fundamentally different way. Rather than describing them as peers who sang collectively and spontaneously, hostile newspapers portrayed them as members of a choir led or, more properly, provoked by a woman.

> The 14th of [Ventôse], Sophie Lapierre struck up a lament. . . . The last verse was sung in chorus, and followed by shouts of long *live the republic! long live liberty!*

> At the closing of the session, Sophie Lapierre struck up the usual hymns, and the choir replied.[16]

If we are to believe the official transcript of the trial, Sophie Lapierre, a seamstress and former teacher, led the Equals on four of the fifteen occasions that they sang in court.[17] Although democratic papers made no special mention of these performances—some said nothing about them at all—royalists and liberals dwelt on them almost exclusively, using the act of singing to define Sophie Lapierre.[18] Such newspapers were joined in this by the Equals' legal opponents. The police spy Bourdon, sent to watch the proceedings on behalf of the Paris Minister of Police, noted that when the judges silenced the defendants, "Sophie Lapierre, who won't speak in this case except to sing, withdrew without saying anything."[19] At the end of the trial, the prosecutor who acknowledged he could not prove Lapierre's participation in the conspiracy, nonetheless reminded jurors that she was the one "known for her taste for singing, which she practiced in the café of the Chinese baths, and the same who for a long time ended all court sessions with patriotic hymns, the choruses of which were repeated by a sizable choir."[20] So much did the label stick that late nine-teenth-century histories of revolutionary women and histories of song still evoked "Sophie [who] mocked her judges, and at the end of each court session [. . .] struck up choruses, which the conspirators repeated at the tops of their lungs while looking at their prison."[21]

Certainly, Sophie Lapierre sang in the courtroom at Vendôme. Whether she simply added her voice to those of the other defendants or led them in song is impossible to determine, given the partisan interests of all accounts. What concerns me is who highlighted her singing and why. Why did the opponents of the Equals focus on Sophie Lapierre when describing the defendants' singing? What associations did she evoke in them, and what associations did such opponents hope to evoke among the readers, politicians, and jury members to whom they spoke? Finally, what may this tell us about singing and revolutionary politics? To begin to answer these questions, we must go back still further, to 1789.

It is now something of a historical truism that revolutionary represen-tations of women, and republican representations in particular, express growing hostility to women's political activity during the first half of the Revolution. Most scholars highlight attacks on aristocratic women, and the Queen in particular, to explain republican misogyny: radicals believed women had corrupted men and politics under the Old Regime by feminizing them, and they were determined to prevent a recurrence of such activity in a revolutionary nation.[22] Dominque Godineau, however, has offered a more nuanced and historically-specific explanation of rev-olutionary ideas about women. The Revolution was not simply anti-feminist, she argues. Militant women played an important part in the Revolution; when their aims coincided with those of the Revolution's leaders, they were celebrated in speeches and festivals and welcomed into the movement. But when they pursued independent goals, as during the critical summer of 1793 and again in the Germinal and Prairial insurrec-tions of 1795, the same political leaders rhapsodized about women's "proper" social role to gain political support for demobilizing them.[23]

By taking into consideration the role that militant women played in shaping the anti-feminist legislation of the Revolution, Godineau's account may also help to explain why republicans had no monopoly on the image of the unruly woman. For what historians have less commonly remarked upon is the degree to which all sides to the revolutionary contest associated their enemies with debauched, unyielding women. From across the Channel, the father of conservatism, Edmund Burke, famously described the procession that returned from Versailles in 1789 with the King and Queen in their midst as filled with, "horrid yells, and shrilling screams . . . and all the unutterable abominations of the furies of hell, in the abused shape of the vilest of women."[24] In France, the activist Theroigne de Méricourt became the object of a virulently misogynist campaign by royalist newspapers that painted her as a hermaphrodite or "the patriot's 'whore'."[25] Similarly, male leaders of the Revolution were portrayed by their opponents as having fallen under the sway of unnatural women.

> This widow Helvétius, who leads a witches' Sabbath at Auteuil, licks her lips whenever she hears that more victims have been sacrificed. Cabanis, Brissot, Condorcet, Manuel and the abbé Sieyes, one by one, eagerly bring her disastrous news from . . . all parts of France that it pleased the Jacobins to inundate with blood. The Shrew smiles, her accomplices applaud and sing in chorus the tune of the cannibals, *ça ira*.[26]

When royalists were swept from public view by Terror in 1793, their caricatures of monstrous women went with them, but only temporarily. These images resurfaced in the wake of Thermidor, during the violent political reaction that followed the fall of Robespierre and the Committee of Public Safety. Wielded by reactionaries who hoped to demobilize republican radicalism by hounding Jacobins and sans-culottes into retirement, such images did not just express a timeless fear of political women. Rather, they reflected on the last phase of revolutionary female militancy as women moved to the forefront of activism during the Thermidoran reaction, capitalizing on looser organizational strategies and compensating for the declining activism of sans-culottes men who had been arrested or were simply worn out.[27] Thus, when "gilded youth"— draft dodgers who served as the shock troops of urban reaction— attacked the Paris Jacobin Club to initiate days of street fighting, they took particular care to humiliate the "furies" of the galleries. They beat, stripped, and spanked women they chased from the Club, to the visible delight of a reactionary press that did its utmost to fuel such violence. The journalist Fréron, for example, targeted a legislator's wife among gallery attendees, claiming that this Mme. Crassous acted as a "drum major for all the female battalions that pack [the galleries]." After Crassous had been beaten (and sexually abused?), Fréron continued by crowing that "the bruises on [her] behind [are] reflected in the painful lines on her dear husband's visage."[28] Months later, when gilded youth turned against sans-culottes in the galleries of the National Convention, reactionary newspapers again focused on women in the audience, whose "hideous faces bespeak dissoluteness, debauchery and debasement," asserting that "If it is another thrashing that these tricoteuses need to be brought to their senses, then that is what they will get."[29]

Reactionary diatribes against Jacobin women intensified following the popular insurrections of Germinal and Prairial the following spring. These were the last popular insurrections of the Revolution, and women played a more visible role here than in any revolutionary event since the march to Versailles in October 1789. Following the Germinal insurrection (1–2 April 1795), police reported having heard some women say "the men are cowards" as they accused their husbands of not acting quickly or energetically enough, while the *Journal de Paris* argued that female insurgents' unique fury arose from their ignorance and impressionability.[30] Once the Prairial insurrection (20–23 May 1795) had been suppressed by bloody street-to-street battles between gilded youth and sans-culottes, the National Convention resumed its strategy of using anti-feminine rhetoric for broader political ends as it passed several laws targeting the women of Paris, the most famous of which forbade them to gather publicly in groups of more than five until order was restored to the city.[31]

These were the predominant images of radical and activist women when, a year later, police agents under the new republican government of the Directory began to infiltrate what they believed were Babouvist gatherings in working-class cafés. Dominique Godineau has argued that women retreated from politics after the suppression of the Prairial insurrection, but police spies feared otherwise: although they followed the men in 1796, they took careful note of the women. Of the femme Baptiste, in whose café reputed conspirators met, a spy remarked, "[she] said . . . if [her husband] showed himself cowardly enough to retreat, she would go in his place;" he added that Sophie Lapierre was a woman "who could be called Harpie, [she] excited the entire group and provoked them to murder."[32]

It was consistent with opponents' expectations that such women would include songs among their means to excite political frenzy. Like their Enlightenment forbears, revolutionaries considered music and song uniquely effective means to stir emotions and impart ideas.[33] More important still were the connotations that accrued to particular kinds of singing by the time of the Equals trial in late winter 1797, when accounts of Sophie Lapierre and her "choir" began to circulate. Police, cultural elites, and even private citizens had by this time come to treat public performances of political songs as open incitement to disorder. During the Terror (1793–94), songs helped to mobilize a revolutionary populace that many now hoped to see calmed; during the Thermidoran Reaction (1794–95), singing regularly degenerated into open violence during wearying battles between republican proponents of the "Marseillaise" and reactionary singers of the "Réveil du peuple." By 1797, even many loyal republicans considered political singers to be troublemakers.

There was, as well, the activity of Sophie Lapierre herself. Although she sang, she would not speak, for she was among a minority of accused who refused to defend themselves or tell the court anything beyond name, age, and profession. These defendants charged that the court was illegitimate; to participate in their prosecution would be to share in violating the constitution. Lapierre would only say that, ". . . love of the fatherland takes precedence in my heart over all other emotion; . . . I challenge the high court and will challenge it forever."[34] Although the prosecution failed to produce evidence of Lapierre's activism before her arrest, her resolute courtroom silence identified her as a self-conscious militant.

All of these associations came together for those who represented Sophie Lapierre as a siren leading her choir of Equals through a verse of the "Marseillaise" or "Goujon's Lament." The Equals were democratic radicals whose ranks were filled, or so believed their opponents, with dissolute and frenzied women. Such women were intent on stirring the men around them to ever-greater acts of chaotic violence, and they found an excellent means to do so in singing, for this act was already proven in its ability to incite auditors. So tightly bound had become the associations between radicals and female militants, between troublemakers and political songs, that journalists did not need to spell them out. It was enough merely to say, "Sophie Lapierre . . . sang today, at the end of the court session, *Veillons au salut de l'Empire,* and the choir repeated the last words of each verse"; the readers consuming such images could fill in the rest.

Sophie Lapierre's case has several implications for our understanding of revolutionary music and revolutionary politics. In the first place, it highlights the value of reaching beyond texts and institutions to consider the changing nature of performances and their reception. Let us consider only one of the songs that Lapierre sang: the "Marseillaise." Analyses of the music and lyrics of that song tell us about the composer's musical forbears and illuminate key images with which revolutionaries chose to represent themselves at the height of the Revolution. But the study of music or lyrics alone does not and can not exhaust the multiple and contradictory meanings imputed to this iconic hymn during the volatile years between its appearance in 1792 and Napoleon's coup in 1799. Police spy Perrières's choir of angels, for example, inspired romantic admiration when they performed the song during the Terror, encouraging Perrières to conflate religious and patriotic fervor as he imagined taking one of the singers as a wife. And yet, when Sophie Lapierre sang the same song in Vendôme in 1797, she divided her audience. In the eyes of opponents, many of whom identified themselves as republicans, singer and song had ceased to be generators of republican unity and had become, instead, sowers of discord. This was so because of the different kinds of performances of the "Marseillaise" that had emerged in the intervening years; because of the ways in which the republic was being redefined; and because of the immediate circumstances under which Lapierre herself performed the song. In sum, while the music and the lyrics of the "Marseillaise" remained the same between 1793 and 1797, we can scarcely say that this was the same song.

The power of performance and context to shape the meaning of a song serve as a reminder of the very particular and intimate ways in which music insinuated itself into individual lives and broad political movements in the past. That music was so readily appropriated is not news; indeed, varieties of appropriation are at the heart of ethnomusicology. The challenge lies in finding ways to undercover that appropriation in the past. This is the terrain of cultural historians and those trained in their methods, for cultural historians have, for almost two generations, been producing studies based on the application of anthropological questions to ephemeral literature and institutional documents alike. This kind of work suggests the possibilities for uncovering such apparently elusive features of daily life as gesture and gaining progressively greater insight into the lives and aspirations of ordinary people.

Sophie Lapierre's case does not only highlight new historical approaches to music and song; it also suggests how songs may help us better to understand the past. Although song lyrics may, at first glance, appear to trace a simple divide between revolutionary and counter-revolutionary, their performance reveals the complexity of political opinions and alliances during the French Revolution. Let us take up the matter of gender.

The song performances I describe here reinforce Dominique Godineau's arguments about republican attitudes toward women. The now classic scholarship on republican misogyny that is based on representations of women is being eroded by more recent studies that illuminate the much more contradictory impact on women of republican legislation concerning citizenship, divorce, and inheritance.[35] We can only reconcile this growing tension between representation and legislation if we take seriously Godineau's injunction that we heed the political specificity of rhetoric and legislation that targeted women. Activist women drew the ire of revolutionary leaders when they pursued goals independent of those leaders' aims. When the aims of both groups were congruent, women's revolutionary activism was cause for celebration. Once again, song performances by Perrières's "angels" and Sophie Lapierre underscore this: the women's choral performance of the "Marseillaise" drew admiration because it encouraged men to "fly" to the front; Sophie Lapierre's singing was castigated by opponents who defined her as another militant woman preventing sans-culottes men from retreating to the quiescence deemed necessary to resolve the Revolution. In neither case, did witnesses draw on a priori notions of what or whether these women should sing; they were more concerned with what the women hoped to accomplish with their songs.

All of this is not to say that representations of these women were free of preconceptions about gender and sexual hierarchy; we ought to consider, however, whether such preconceptions were restricted to women. As I suggested above, republicans were not alone in targeting women of the opposition as unruly and dissolute; such images were popularized across the political spectrum. If a horrified fascination with monstrous women was not restricted to republicans, then we must consider what political purposes it served and whether those images were not directed as much at male as female opponents. Did not republicans who described aristocratic women as duplicitous and domineering implicitly charge aristocratic men of having been emasculated? Did not royalist and reactionary critics who decried ferocious market women accuse sans-culottes men of failing to sustain proper sexual authority in their households and, by implication, the nation? In other words, we need to look beyond the explicit content of revolutionary and counter-revolutionary attacks on women to consider how pointedly they took aim at men as well.[36]

Finally, popular songs allow historians to extend their reach to varieties of political activism that might otherwise remain hidden. For example, having so generously described women's activism across the first two-thirds of the Revolution, Dominique Godineau consigns them to silence in the final years: "The archives on the Conspiracy of Equals do not show figures of militant women as we find in previous years."[37] Such an assertion seems reasonable until we untangle the implications of Sophie Lapierre's singing, for militants and conservative opponents alike. Although republicans did not represent Lapierre as leading the Equals in song, they could understand what her silence and singing telegraphed: that she defined herself as an activist as firmly committed to the Equals' principles as men like Babeuf and Buonarroti, and that she was committed to performing her militancy in the courtroom in the most effective ways possible. Meanwhile, reactionaries defined her according to the same terms they applied to the "furies" at the Jacobin club and the women who invaded the Convention during the Germinal and Prairial insurrections in 1795: she was yet another unruly woman preventing sans-culottes men from keeping the peace they ought to respect. In sum, whether they approved or not, observers of the Equals' trial understood that women's revolutionary activism was not yet extinguished. Without the evidence of singing practices, that dimension of the past would be lost to us.

Notes

1. Adelaide de la Place, introduction to *La vie musicale en France au temps de la Révolution* (Paris, 1989); David Charlton, "Introduction," in *Music and the French Revolution*, ed. Malcolm Boyd (Cambridge, 1992).

2. M. Elizabeth C. Bartlet, "The New Repertory at the Opéra During the Reign of Terror: Revolutionary Rhetoric and Operatic Consequences," and Cynthia M Gessele,

"The Conservatoire de Musique and National Music Education in France, 1795–1801," in *Music and the French Revolution*, ed. Malcolm Boyd; Simone Wallon, "La chanson des rues contre-révolutionnaires en France de 1790–1795," in *Orphée Phrygien: Les musiques de la Révolution*, eds. Jean-Rémy Julien and Jean-Claude Klein (Paris: Editions du May, 1989).

3. Constant Pierre, "Aperçu général," *Les hymnes et chansons de la Révolution* (Paris: Imprimerie nationale, 1904); Cornwall B. Rogers, *The Spirit of Revolution in 1789: A Study of Public Opinion as Revealed in Political Songs and Other Popular Literature at the Beginning of the French Revolution* (New York: Greenwood Press, 1949); James Leith, "Music as an Ideological Weapon during the French Revolution," *Canadian Historial Association Report* (1966): 126–39; Robert Brécy, "La chanson révolutionnaire de 1789–1799," *Annales historiques de la Révolution française* 53/244 (1981): 279–303; "La chanson babouviste," *Annales historiques de la Révolution française* 54/249 (1982): 453–475; and Michel Vovelle, "La Marseillaise : la guerre ou la paix," in *Les lieux de mémoire*, vol. 1, *La République*, ed. Pierre Nora (Paris: Gallimard, 1984).

4. Laura Mason, *Singing the French Revolution: Popular Culture and Politics, 1787–1799* (Ithaca NY: Cornell University Press, 1996).

5. Jane Fulcher, *French Cultural Politics and Music: from the Dreyfus Affair to the First World War* (New York: Oxford University Press, 1999); Susan McClary, *Feminine Endings: Music, Gender, and Sexuality* (Minneapolis: University of Minnesota Press, 1991).

6. Jennifer Post summarizes these arguments and provides an overview of scholarship in "Erasing the Boundaries between Public and Private in Women's Performance Traditions," in *Cecilia Reclaimed: Feminist Perspectives on Gender and Music*, eds. Susan Cook and Judy Tsou (Urbana & Chicago: University of Illinois Press, 1994).

7. Joan Landes put this argument in its most schematic terms, describing the Revolution as the origin of a split between public and private spheres. See *Women and the Public Sphere in the Age of the French Revolution* (Ithaca, NY: Cornell University Press, 1988). Other scholars have moderated Landes's argument while continuing to call attention to revolutionaries' misogynist and exclusionary representations of public and political women. See Elizabeth Colwill, "Just Another Citoyenne? Marie-Antoinette on Trial, 1790–1793," *History Workshop* 28 (Autumn 1989): 63–87; Lynn Hunt, *The Family Romance of the French Revolution* (Berkeley: University of California Press, 1992); Madelyn Gutwirth, *The Twilight of the Goddesses: Women and Representation in the French Revolutionary Era* (New Brunswick: Rutgers University Press, 1992); Geneviève Fraisse, *Reason's Muse: Sexual Difference and the Birth of Democracy*, trans. Jane Marie Todd (Chicago: University of Chicago Press, 1994).

8. Report of Marauz (4 nivôse II), AN: F7 3688/3; procès-verbal from the commune of St. Sever (2 nivôse II), AN: F17 1008/D #1638.

9. Report of Perrières for 8 June 1793, AN: F1c III Seine 27.

10. Report of Beraud for 20 September 1793, AN: F7 36883.

11. *Journal de la haute-cour de justice, ou L'écho des homme libres, vrais, et sensibles* (4 pluviose V/ 23 janvier 1797).

12. *Débats du proces instruit par la haute-cour de justice, séante- Vendôme, contre Drouet, Babeuf, et autres*, part 71 (Paris: chez Baudouin, 1797). Séance of 11 germinal.

13. I develop this argument in *Singing the French Revolution*, 174–177.

14. *Journal de la haute-cour de justice* (22 ventôse V).

15. *L'ami du peuple* (11 frimaire V).

16. *Clef du Cabinet* (21 ventôse V); *Courrier républicain* (5 germinal V).

17. *Débats du proces, op cit.*

18. See also *Clef du Cabinet* (5 germinal V); *Courrier républicain* (7 germinal V); *Le Rédacteur*.

19. Bourdon to Cochon (11 germinal V). AN: F⁷ 7178.

20. *Le Rédacteur* (18 floréal V).

21. *Feuilleton de la Gazette de France* (5 novembre 1878) quoting from Victor Fournel, "La chanson et les chanteurs populaires sous la Révolution," *Rues du vieux Paris, galerie populaire et pittoresque* (Paris, 1878) and E. Lairtullier, *Les femmes pendant la Révolution* (Paris, 1878).

22. See above, note 7.

23. Dominique Godineau, *The Women of Paris and their French Revolution*, trans. Katherine Streip (Berkeley: University of California Press, 1998).

24. Edmund Burke, *Reflections on the Revolution in France*, edited with an introduction by Conor Cruise O'Brien (New York, 1968), 165.

25. *Actes des Apôtres*, #169 [sd]; Elizabeth Roudinesco, *Théroigne de Méricourt: A Melancholic Woman during the French Revolution*, trans. Martin Thom (London, 1991), 30–33.

26. *A deux liards*, première mois, #29 [sd/oct. 1791].

27. Dominique Godineau, *The Women of Paris*, 303–315.

28. Quoted in François Gendron, *The Gilded Youth of Thermidor*, trans. James Cookson (Montreal & Kingston: McGill-Queen's University Press, 1993), 29. See pages 24–29 for a discussion of the battles at the Jacobin Club.

29. *L'orateur du peuple* and *Le messager du soir*, quoted in Gendron, *The Gilded Youth*, 43.

30. Police spy quoted by Olwen Hufton, *Women and the Limits of Citizenship in the French Revolution* (Toronto: University of Toronto Press, 1992), 43. *Journal de Paris* (18 germinal III).

31. Olwen Hufton, *Women and the Limits of Citizenship in the French Revolution*, 48–49. For the text of the law against women's gatherings see translation of *Moniteur universel* (23 mai 1795) in Laura Mason and Tracey Rizzo, *The French Revolution: A Document Collection* (Boston: Houghton-Mifflin, 1999), 270–275. For an account of women's participation in the insurrection, see Dominique Godineau, *The Women of Paris and their French Revolution*, 331–346.

32. Dossier 4954, regarding Jean Baptiste Breton, Jeanne Ansiot and others. AN: W 560.

33. Jean-Louis Jam, "Fonction des hymnes révolutionnaires," Jean Ehrard & Paul Viallaneix, *Les f?tes de la Révolution* (Paris: Société des études Robespierristes, 1977).

34. *L'ami du peuple* (14 frimaire V).

35. Suzanne Desan, "War between Brothers and Sisters: Inheritance Law and Gender Politics in Revolutionary France," *French Historical Studies* 20 (1997): 597–634; and

"Reconstituting the Social after the Terror: Family, Property, and the Law in Popular Politics," *Past and Present* 164 (Aug. 1999: 81–121; Jennifer Heuer, "Foreigners, Families, and Citizens: Contradictions of National Citizenship in France, 1789–1830" (Ph.D. dissertation, University of Chicago, 1998).

36. Lynn Hunt considers the relative positions of masculine and feminine in the revolutionary imaginary in *The Family Romance of the French Revolution* (Berkeley: University of California Press, 1992), but the subject has received little attention elsewhere.

37. Dominique Godineau, *The Women of Paris*, 363.

Music, Memory, and the People in Selected British Periodicals of the Late Eighteenth and Early Nineteenth Centuries

Stanley C. Pelkey

Introduction

My primary professional training has been as a historical musicologist, but while in residence at the University of Rochester, I also completed course work in the Department of History. As I was exposed to the methods of cultural history, the ideas of Clifford Geertz, and the New Historicism of Stephen Greenblatt, I moved away from my initial interest as a musicologist—seeing the musical work as a sonic redaction of a text—toward a commitment to studying music as part of a matrix of mutually-informing sociocultural systems that can include literature, art, theology, or any other type of cultural document that records human thought and experience.

This is one approach to the study of music and history that allows the scholar to place musical pieces, practices, or entire musical cultures within broader sociocultural contexts. Thus, for example, by studying periodical reviews of folk-song publications from the late 1700s and early 1800s, one can come to understand how folk music was discussed and valued in that time, which should shape one's understanding of, for example, a piano sonata that uses folk tunes as melodic source material. But this approach also makes possible the use of musical pieces, musical styles, or musical cultures as part of a framework for understanding other aspects of society and culture, such as politics, national identity, or literature.[1] Furthermore, if a poem, a musical composition, and a periodical review or article from the same moment in history attest to similar sociocultural values or experiences—and thus form a matrix of mutu-ally-informing data—then we can trust them more fully together as evidence for our moment in cultural history than we could any one of them separately.[2]

This second approach, making musical pieces and musical style part of the context of broader historical and cultural moments, requires that the scholar engage with notated musical pieces at a fairly intimate level, and this throws the process of cross-disciplinary communication between the musicologist and the historian into doubt because of the specialized vocabulary of musical analysis. While the historian may help to elucidate the context of musical pieces or music making generally, it is the musicologist who will need to pick apart the musical language of particular pieces if they are going to be studied meaningfully as part of this contextualizing process. It then becomes necessary to find a way to communicate the results of musical analysis to non-specialist audiences.

In most of my past attempts to bridge history and musicology, I have not done this, rather I have been content to use writings about music from the past as the means to understand the musical aspects of broader historical issues or phenomena, such as national identity. If I did address musical style or musical pieces, I did so at the most rudimentary level. But I have grown unhappy with this approach. To shy away from "music itself," or "sonic experience," or "the musical work," or however one wants to define the actual musical moment, whether notated in a score or not, even when trying to make the case for a nonmusical sociocultural phenomena, is to fail to address musical pieces as cultural artifacts on their own terms. New Historicists call into question traditional close readings of literature even as they expand the kinds of texts and images that can be read and interpreted by the scholar; nevertheless, "major works of art remain centrally important."[3] In the same way, I believe that there must be a way to study music as music while also using it as a tool for historical understanding, and I believe this even though I am not convinced that I have found that way myself yet.

This conviction has become even stronger for me since I read a set of essays by a group of ethnomusicologists who address the problem of fieldwork in their discipline. Reflecting on current trends in their discipline, these ethnomusicologists argue that to know a culture is to participate in a culture. Thus they have moved toward a participatory model for fieldwork in which the scholar becomes a practicing musician within a different culture.[4] Although this participatory model within ethnomusicology de-emphasizes the older, supposedly objective focus on sonic objects (such as intervals to be measured or rhythms to be transcribed), the fact that the scholar's participation is active—she is part of the music-making process—rather than merely observational is key to my own most recent thinking about the necessity of staying engaged with musical materials when doing cultural history. At present, I believe that "participation as knowledge" provides a way for me to hold in tension both the musical experience of musical pieces as a performer, which is essentially an aesthetic experience, and the desire for a deeper awareness of the past by way of musical repertories, which I believe as a scholar.[5]

The autonomous musical work elevated out of its historical and social contexts must go, but even if our focus centers primarily on music as the locus around which meaningful social behaviors take place, the sounding materials of music should remain part of the story, just as they do for ethnomusicologists, who tend to have a wider definition of music that includes both sonic phenomena and the sociocultural systems that make those phenomena meaningful. In an ideal world, this would require us historical musicologists to successfully retrain the academic community as amateur musicians who can join with us in meaningful participation in music. In the real world, it will likely mean close collaboration with sympathetic historians in our scholarship and hopefully in our classrooms as well.

In the remainder of this essay, I will discuss how certain types of articles in British periodical literature in the late eighteenth and early nineteenth centuries served as a means of generating a sense of the national community through the rehearsing of collective memories about places and famous people or historical figures. I will then highlight some examples of the use of this literary tradition within periodical literature about music, before moving to a final example from a nineteenth-century source about a body of music that I care about as a musicologist and performer. For that final example, I will turn to musical style history as a means of assessing the supposedly national quality of that particular repertory of music. The chain of events thus runs from a broad historical phenomenon—national identity—embodied in literary culture to the same phenomenon within musical culture to a particular body of music whose reception can, in its turn, further illuminate the nature of national identity itself.

Constructing an Artificial, National Musical Culture

In *Imagined Communities: Reflections on the Origin and Spread of Nationalism*, Benedict Anderson discusses the role of territorial maps, archaeological surveys and reports, and restoration of monuments within the boundaries of postcolonial states as part of the process by which new nations were imagined and constructed out of the ruins of nineteenth-century colonial conquests. These cultural activities were part of even broader processes of national imagining through print culture that Anderson reconstructs throughout his study.[6] I take that discussion as a model for interpreting the sociocultural significance of certain types of articles on places, people, and music in England and Scotland published in British periodicals during the late eighteenth and early nineteenth centuries.

I will assume that most readers are familiar with the literature on national identity, nationalism, and ethnicity that has appeared during the past twenty years and in particular with the work of Anderson, Ernest Gellner, Eric Hosbawm, and Anthony Smith. The theories of these men and two recent studies by Colin Kidd on national identities in eighteenth-century Britain inform the foundations of this essay and the larger research project from which it is derived.[7] There were patterns of discourse about the people, the state, and the nation in England and Scotland during the eighteenth and early nineteenth centuries that we can describe as national and that point to Britons' sense of having a national identity; much of this discourse rested upon particular conceptions of history, memory, and myth—and these could be either real or imagined. Furthermore, it is clear from Kidd's research, from delving into the world of late eighteenth- and early nineteenth- century British periodicals, and from developing familiarity with British musical materials themselves that the content and the object of national identity, whether English, Scottish, or broadly British, was often contested in the eighteenth and nineteenth centuries. Thus, in the case of Scottish periodicals, for example, we find both exclusively Scottish identities and more cosmopolitan British identities, and there were, I would argue, corresponding possibilities for identity in English periodicals as well. Colin Kidd uses the concepts strong Anglo-Britishness and weak Britishness as a means of conveying the existence of both older loyalties and newer ones within eighteenth-century Scotland and England.[8]

A striking example from the periodical literature that demonstrates the workings of this sense of national identity can be found in the article "On the Love of our Country," which appeared in the *Scots Magazine or General Repository* in 1794. The sentiments of the article push past mere identity toward a more robust, modern conception of nationalism. It opens with the following passage:

> The love of our country is one of the noblest passions that can warm and animate the human breast. It includes all the limited and particular affections to our parents, friends, neighbours, fellow citizens, and countrymen. It ought to direct and limit their more confined and partial actions within their proper and natural bounds, and never let them encroach on those sacred and first regards we owe to the great public to which we belong.[9]

Later we read:

> Wherever [love of country] prevails in its genuine vigour and extent, it swallows up all sordid and selfish regards; it conquers the love of ease, power, pleasure, and wealth; nay, when the amiable partialities of friendship, gratitude, private affection, or regards to a family, come in competition with it, it will teach us bravely to sacrifice all, in order to maintain the rights, and promote or defend the honour and happiness, of our country.

The idea that one owes a sacred and primary duty to the national community, which is even higher than one's duty to self, friends, and family, is one of the features that scholars of nationalism have stressed as making nationalism a particularly modern phenomenon. Furthermore, the author of this article has an Andersonian-like vision of the imagined community:

> This love of our country does not import an attachment to any particular soil, climate, or spot of earth, where perhaps we first drew our breath,

though those natural ideas are often associated with the moral ones, and, like external signs or symbols, help to ascertain and bind them; but it imports an affection to that moral system, or community, which is governed by the same laws and magistrates, and whose several parts are variously connected one with the other, and all united upon the bottom of a common interest. Perhaps, indeed, every member of the community cannot comprehend so large an object, especially if it extends through large provinces, and over vast tracts of land; and still less can he form such an idea, if there is no public, i.e. if all are subject to the caprice and unlimited will of one man.

Note the quasi-sacramental language of external sign and symbol in which the trappings of what we might call patriotism and nostalgic memories of hearth, home, and birthplace become the visual and emotional representation of the more abstract attachment to the moral community. The moral community in its turn is governed by a common law—which is discussed during the course of the article as the bond that holds all social orders together—and a duly appointed body of lawmakers. The author's conclusion: this is the constitution of Great Britain.

A society thus constituted by common reason, and formed on the plan of a common interest, becomes immediately an object of public attention, public veneration, public obedience, a public and inviolable attachment, which ought neither to be seduced by bribes, nor awed by terror . . . and to sacrifice his ease, his wealth, his power, nay life itself, and, what is dearer still, his family and friends, to defend or save it, is the duty, the honour, the interest, and the happiness of every citizen.

As a historian of music and musical life in Great Britain during the eighteenth and early nineteenth centuries, I am particularly interested in the manner in which the supposedly natural, expressive utterance of the people in the form of their national music may actually be concocted, marketed, or manipulated into being, sometimes doing violence to the actual facts of musical style history. When studying late eighteenth- and early nineteenth-century British periodicals for what they reveal about national identity generally and national music specifically, one finds examples of cultures being compared as either natural or artificial, with

European cultures often falling into the later category.[10] For example, eighteenth-century discussions of the relative merits of Native American and European cultures sometimes branded the latter as artificial (that is, non-natural, non-organic, and crafted by purposeful human agency) but the former as organic, that is, springing naturally from the spirit of a people, given their particular social and environmental conditions.

Thus, an article entitled "Remarks on the Savages of North-America" by Benjamin Franklin, which appeared in the March 1792 issue of the *Literary Magazine and British Review*, refers to the division of labor among the men and women of the native tribes. Regarding these arrangement, Franklin writes, "These employments of men and women are accounted natural and honourable. Having few artificial wants, they have abundance of leisure for improvement of conversation. Our labourious manner of life compared with theirs, they esteem slavish and base; and the learning on which we value ourselves, they regard as frivolous and useless" (206). This organic view of culture (and ultimately, in the nineteenth century, of the nation) is modern in spirit and points us toward the fact that the later eighteenth century, with the rise of national sentiment in Britain, France, and the early American republic, marks a significant turning point in the relationship between culture, state, and ethnicity in Western civilization.

Music and musical cultures were also received within this intellectual framework. Thus "national song" was, for many Britons in this period, a flexible category that included patriotic pieces, such as "God Save the King," popular songs drawn from English operas or from the pleasure gardens, authentic (and inauthentic) folk songs and dances from Scotland, Wales, and Ireland, and other music associated with British political or religious life. *The Loyal and National Songs of England, for One, Two, and Three Voices* (London, 1823) compiled by William Kitchiner, provided an opportunity for a reviewer in the May 1823 issue of the *Harmonicon* to discuss what he believed could legitimately be considered as national song and to reflect on the importance of national song to national life.

National Song is the most interesting of all musical subjects: it is so intimately connected with the history, morals, habits, and, we may almost venture to add, the politics of a country, that it has not been thought unworthy of serious notice by the greatest philosophers and ablest writers

of ancient and modern times. Its influence over the people is too well
known to be questioned, and is proved by facts both numerous and convincing. A certain moralist, speaking of the various modes of regulating
the manners, and governing the opinion of the multitude, even went so
far as to say, 'It matters not who makes the laws, provided you take care
who writes the songs.'[11]

The reviewer continues by criticizing the collection for including
much music that is not, in his opinion, English. For example, "The first
piece in the work is Handel's Coronation Anthem, 'Zadok the Priest,' and
we must express our doubts whether, being composed by a foreigner, it
comes properly under the term National Music." This assessment of
Handel's "Zadok" as non-national is particularly revealing because it
implies that only music written by native composers can qualify as being
national. Even though Handel became a British citizen in 1727, and even
though this anthem was composed for the coronation of George II as
a setting of a text traditionally used in the British coronation rite, the
reviewer cannot see beyond the origins of the composer to assess the role
that social context or tradition has in conferring national status on a
piece of music.[12]

The reviewer prefers "God Save the King," "Rule, Britannia," and
Purcell's "Come if You Dare" as examples of British national song,
although he is critical of their "bloated" settings in Kitchiner's volume.
He then takes exception, again, to more music by Handel appearing in
the volume. He argues that Kitchiner must have included "See the Conquering Hero Comes" and "Disdainful of Danger" from *Judas Maccabeus*
merely "to swell the size of the book ... for what connexion can be shewn
between these chorusses [sic] and our English loyal or national music? As
to loyalty, they are directly opposed to it, for Judas fought in defense of
republicanism against the Syrian monarchy: and as Britons are not,
either directly or collaterally descended from any of the leaders of Israel,
it will require all Dr. Kitchiner's eloquence to shew our right to music,
composed to a drama founded on the *Jewish* history, by a native of
Germany."

Again, one could take issue with this negative assessment of these
particular pieces by Handel as national songs on a number of points.
Judas Maccabeus was composed to celebrate the victory of the Duke of

Cumberland over the Jacobite forces at the Battle of Culloden in 1746. The reviewer also demonstrates his ignorance of a tradition prevalent in eighteenth-century English sermons and theological writings that equated England with Israel.[13]

A review of *Canadian Airs, collected by Lieutenant Back, R. N., during the late Arctic Expedition under Captain Franklin* provides additional evidence that shared ethnicity was a central feature of the conception of the nation and its for some Britons.[14]

> Genuine national melodies are often delightful, and always interesting. Should even every other charm be wanting in them, they never fail to produce some sort of pleasure by an originality which they are sure to possess. That the airs now under notice are authentic, we have the word of an officer in His Majesty's service to justify us in believing; but whether what is called a Canadian melody comes correctly under the term national, may be a question; for the natives of that portion of North America under the dominion of the French, and now subject to Great Britain,—a people derived from the crossings of the two latter nations, mixed up with the descendants of the first settlers at Hudson's Bay, and the aboriginal inhabitants,—people with the laws of one country, and the customs of another, can hardly be said to have a peculiar, or national, song. Accordingly we trace in these 'Canadian airs' a descent from European ancestors; the *vaudeville* of France in great measure, and the ballads of England, Scotland, and Ireland, in less degree, have we suspect, contributed to form the music of our brother-subjects in the frozen regions of the Western continent.

Our reviewer implies that the nation, any nation, in order to be a true one, must consist of a homogenous ethnic population that shares a common language and culture. This view of the nation and of national cultural implies an organicism for the nation that does not really exist. Indeed, note that the reviewer's nation is ambiguous. Great Britain, England, Scotland, and Ireland are all mentioned in opposition to France as supplying the main non-French components to the Canadian people and their culture.

The natural/organic view of the nation and national song was not the only one to be found in late eighteenth- and early nineteenth-century

Britain. More artificial means to construct the nation and its culture can also be found, as I will show below. Nevertheless, much of the music that was produced in the eighteenth and early nineteenth centuries in England, Scotland, and Ireland, such as "Auld Lang Syne" or "Rule, Britannia," and constructed as national song has survived and is widely recognized today as folk, folk-like, or national song (and being "natural," it is also often thought to be "ageless").

Having shown that British periodicals of the later eighteenth and early nineteenth century often included ideas about the national, national identity, and national music, I want to shift the discussion to two particular types of articles—reports on national sites and national biographies—that appear frequently in the periodical literature and that can be seen as a kind of mapping of the nation.

Scottish periodicals in this period constructed the imagined community in part through the rehearsing of the community's moral, social, and political history. This was done, among other ways, through the inclusion of biographical sketches of Britons, often times from the seventeenth and early eighteenth centuries, and through the inclusion of views of Scotland. For example, in the first issue of the *Scots Magazine or General Repository* of 1795, the editors explained that they were going to introduce into the periodical views and discussions of the topography and natural history of Scotland, which would be both instructive and entertaining. The implication is Andersonian—they wish to create the imagined space in which the imagined community exists, especially for those who do not travel about the country, and to better prepare those who do travel for the points of interest that they will encounter.

In the first decade of the nineteenth century, many issues of the *Scots Magazine, and Edinburgh Literary Miscellany* included similar engravings of views and descriptions, such as maps of the new roads through the Highlands (January 1806); a view of the monument to be erected in Edinburgh to "the Memory of Lord Nelson" (February 1806), which was meant to "excite others to imitate his great example" (83); a map of the canal from Glasgow to the Harbor of Ardrossan (May 1806); a view of the proposed tunnel under the Firth of Forth (August 1806); an account of the laying of the foundation stone for Nelson's monument in Glasgow (August 1806); a view of the proposed canal from Perth to Lock-Earn (February 1807); and a view of the Forth from Hopetoun House to Rosyth

Castle, with a section of the proposed tunnel underneath (November 1807). Pride in material and mechanical progress, the veneration of British military heroes, and Scottish topographies all rested contentedly together as part of a matrix of nation-imagining views.

By including such national views, these two Scottish periodicals were engaging in a cultural pattern found in earlier Scottish periodicals, such as the *Edinburgh Magazine, or Literary Miscellany*. In that periodical, engraved "Views of Scotland" graced the first page of each issue. Among the views in the 1780s and 1790s were Castles Campbell, Down Perthshire, Kilchurn, Strathaven, Claderwood, Wenyss, Slaine, Dunbarton, Crighton, and Elan Stalker; a view of Edinburgh; and views of Perth Bridge, the Abbey of Lincluden, and Cambuskenneth Abbey. From May 1774 to November 1774, there was also an extended discussion of "Antiquities in Stirlingshire."

All such views helped to create the imagined space in which the imagined national community existed. That community itself was then invoked through the second principal means by which the community's history was mapped, the biographical sketches of famous Scottish or British citizens. Such sketches were frequently placed prominently at the beginning of an issue. Subjects of biographical sketches in the *Edinburgh Magazine and Review* included William Carstairs, the Principal of Edinburgh University who, according to his sketch, saved Scottish Presbyterianism by convincing William of Orange not to establish the Episcopal Church in its place in Scotland (January 1774); George Buchanan, the sixteenth-century scholar whose ideas so strongly shaped Scottish Whig ideology (March 1774); Dr. Alexander Monroe, a professor of Anatomy at the University of Edinburgh whose family fought against Cromwell and for William III (April 1774); and John Knox (July 1774), Charles II (May 1775), and William III (June 1775).

Similarly, the *Scots Magazine or General Repository* included biographical essays in sections sometimes referred to as "characteristic sketches of eminent Britons." Queen Elizabeth, James VI and I, and Charles I (February 1794), Archbishop Laud (September 1794), Adam Smith (1796), James MacPherson (April 1796), James Beattie, the son of Dr. Beattie (September 1796), Tobias Smollett (November 1796), and Hume and Lord North (December 1796) appeared as part of this group. In addition to these figures, who tended to appear prominently in articles that opened each issue of the periodical, there were also a variety of other articles not so prominently treated that, nevertheless, also participated in the construction of the literary, artistic, and political nation. One such article, "Character of the Most Eminent Scots Writers of the Day," from the *Scots Magazine, and Edinburgh Literary Miscellany*, placed Hume among the leading historians of the day, Beattie and Reid among the leading metaphysicians, Beattie at the head of Scottish poetry, and Beattie's article "Essay on Music and Poetry" among the most important articles in Scottish critical traditions.[15] Another article, "Character of George II with the State of Literature and the Arts During His Reign," from the *Scots Magazine, or General Repository*, included a discussion of two important English composers, Thomas Arne and William Boyce; their fame rested upon the fact that they so "vigorously emulated" the German-born Handel (note that this group of "British" musicians is devoid of native Scotsmen).[16] Both articles mapped a cultural canon of eminent Scotsmen (in the former article) and of eminent Scotsmen and other Britons (in the latter).

In summary, the biographies and the views were means by which a mapping (and remembering) of national history, culture, and space occurred. When combined with news from Scotland and England, and also from America, especially during the Seven Years and American Revolutionary Wars, and the frequent articles about the Constitution, parliament, commerce, and the arts, we have a constructed, self-conscious national identity that is best described as principally Scottish but with links to a broader British conception of the nation.

Prior to 1818, when the first all-music British periodical began to be published, the appearance of music in British periodicals was usually limited to notices of musical performances, occasional reviews of new publications, and rare, extended articles on music. Thus the relatively frequent articles on music in the *Edinburgh Magazine, or Literary Miscellany* during the 1780s is interesting in and of itself. Even more so, however, is their content. Many of these articles are about Scottish music, such as ballads and dances—the folk music of Scotland, if you will. But an almost equal number are about the great G. F. Handel. This is significant, because in England, Handel was appropriated as a national musical figure from the 1750s forward, as I discussed briefly above. That construction was given a boost by the first of many Handel Commemorations held in Westminster

Abbey in 1784. Soon after, hundreds of keyboard arrangements of Handel's music began to appear, which transformed a public, national event into private, domestic entertainment, thus allowing it to be repeated. Was this appropriation of an English musical figure for Scotland, through the inclusion of so much about Handel in the *Edinburgh Magazine, or Literary Miscellany* in 1785 through 1789, part of a conscious construction of a pan-Britannic musical identity? Perhaps; the same periodical also published a series of "Biographical Sketches of Eminent Composers" over the course of 1785—the year after the Handel Commemoration; these were very much like the Scots historical biographies that I discussed above. Note that the way in which these various composers were treated—in a series of short biographical sketches—replicates a publication process and literary tradition that maps the nation. But while Handel might have some claim to being "British," having served the Hanoverian dynasty during the first forty years of the United Kingdom, and having become a British citizen, the thirteen men of the "Sketches of Eminent Composers" were all English composers of the Tudor and early Stuart periods.

The only other musicians discussed in their own articles in this periodical were John Stanley, the famous eighteenth-century English organist and composer, and Garret Wesley, Earl of Mornington, the Irish patrician, father of the Duke of Wellington, and respected musician. Finally, a long article appearing in two parts in November and December 1800 summarized the history of British music during the past century. Its focus was on Italian opera in London. Thus the nation's music included the ballads and dances of Scotland, but, it seems, the works of the great Church musicians of the Tudor period, the canonical Handel, and the Irish Mornington might be part of the nation's music, too.

The intersections between musical life and national identity in periodicals of the time ran the gamut from the natural (Scottish folk tunes) to the artificial and concocted (Handel, Stanley, and Mornington as national composers). From a style history point of view, the underlying musical materials of all of these repertories were very similar, reflecting as they did a pan-European musical language. Therefore, context and tradition rather than musical style alone probably determined whether or not a particular piece was perceived as national.

The Earl of Mornington makes a similar appearance a half century later in the English all-music periodical the *Harmonicon*. Like the

Scottish periodicals just considered, the *Harmonicon* presents, over the course of its publication history, an image of a national identity, in this case, one that is primarily reflected in a new national and pan-Britannic musical culture (although sometimes this national culture flows between more English and more thoroughly British identities). Evidence for this shared musical culture includes the similar concert programs from London, Edinburgh, and the provinces, the letters from contributors— real or imagined—from all over England, Scotland, and Ireland, and the reports of the "state of music" around the British Isles. Throughout many of the articles, reviews, and letters appear references to Britons as a free, commercial people, so common to British self-perceptions.

The existence of this pan-Britannic musical culture is reinforced by study of the musical compositions themselves from throughout the British Isles in the years between the 1750s and the 1830s. This reveals an ever-increasing commonality in terms of genres, styles, and compositional practices throughout the isles from London to Edinburgh to Dublin. And that commonality included musical elements drawn from across the British Isles, such as Irish and Scottish dance topics. It was not simply a "classical" musical culture imposed from London. Indeed, the popularity of Scottish, Welsh, and Irish songs, dances, and folk idioms in music throughout Georgian Great Britain would suggest the opposite, as I discuss elsewhere.[17]

Consider, for example, the "Highland Quick March," from H. Liebe's *Battle of Waterloo, Or La Belle Alliance. A Grand Descriptive Musical Piece* (London: Preston, ca. 1815), which is reproduced in musical example 1. Such keyboard pieces attempted to convey battle scenes through musical-narrative gestures. They were a musical way of invoking the nation through pride in its martial strength, just as Handel arrangements could conjure up the national celebration of that great musical hero. In this case, furthermore, the loyal Highlander within the Imperial army is also invoked by way of the common musical gestures that signaled the Scottish in music in British keyboard music from the eighteenth and early nineteenth centuries.

Although the exclusive treatment of music in the *Harmonicon* was a recent development, the inclusion of biographical sketches in periodicals was not, as we can see from the discussion above. The sketches in the *Harmonicon* included non-Britons as subjects, although many of them,

"Highland Quick March," <u>The Battle of Waterloo</u>   H. Liebe

Musical Example 1

such as Haydn, had close connections to Britain through their travels and performances there. But many British composers and musicians were also included, somewhat surprisingly, given that throughout most of the Georgian period, foreign music and musicians dominated serious musical life in London, to the detriment of the careers of native musicians. Thus the composers Croft, Storace, Arnold, Kent, Jackson, Purcell, and Boyce—who inhabit a range of compositional abilities—join Bach, Handel, Mozart, and Haydn. Musical cosmopolitanism is present, made possible by British economic success, which attracted so many foreign musicians to London, Edinburgh, and the other major cities of the isles, but so, too, is a self-conscious Britishness. This comes out rather consistently and most forcefully in articles that imply that a national musical crisis existed and was manifested in the preference for foreign music and the lack of British musical genius. Various explanations were offered for this situation, but in such discussions we find strongly nationalistic utterances about British music and its relationship to the nation.

This is where Mornington reenters this story: his biographical sketch appeared in the *Harmonicon* in January 1830. The author of the sketch states that few nobles compose music good enough to be noticed, but that among those "of our own patrician order," Lord Mornington, who was born in Ireland in 1720 and became "one of the most accomplished states-men of the period," was "preeminent." His early training in harmony consisted of study of the music of Archangelo Corelli (1653–1713), the famous Italian composer whose string music formed the core of the English musical canon, and composition of English glees, a genre of indigenous vocal music frequently discussed in British musical periodi-cals and one of the few types of music discussed at all in nonmusical peri-odicals. The article even expresses the hope that his son, the Duke of Wellington, and then prime minister (1828–1830), would correct the abuses of earlier ministries.

We have, then, a moment of national sentiment, no doubt sincere, but made up artificially through reflections on an Irish-born musician whose training consisted in the mastery of Italian and English styles that were by 1830 a century or more old and whose son was a famous military hero and British imperial leader. Yet the whole exists within a literary tra-dition found in both Scottish and English periodicals that had regularly constructed a sense of the national. This article on Mornington is, then, a good demonstration of the possibility for a multiplicity of British iden-tities and national practices to intersect through musical means. It also suggests that the study of musical style may demonstrate both the artifi-cial character of music that is perceived to be national and once again that musical style itself is not sufficient to elevate a piece of music to national status.

The Earl of Mornington appears once more, indirectly, in this essay. My last example of the intersection between music, memory, identity, and periodicals relates to an article on the composer Samuel Wesley (1766–1837). It appeared as the first item in a section of the *Freemason Magazine and Masonic Mirror* of July 28, 1858 entitled "Biographical Sketches of Eminent (Deceased) Freemasons." Samuel Wesley, the son of Charles Wesley (1707–1788) and nephew of John Wesley (1703–1791), was among the most important British composers and organists of the Georgian period. His compositions included Latin choral works, Anglican anthems and service music, orchestral pieces, organ voluntaries, and a substantial body of harpsichord and pianoforte music. Although widely respected during his lifetime for his choral and organ compositions and organ playing, Wesley was considered a social and moral maverick, which created professional difficulties for him. Nevertheless, after his death, a group of friends and pupils, including the publisher Vincent Novello (1781–1861), worked to perpetuate his memory as an exceptional musician and as a great national figure. They succeeded, at least in part, because Wesley continued to be the subject of books and articles for the next 150 years, and many of his organ works remained in print throughout that time.

The Freemason article was modeled on Wesley's obituary from the October and November 1837 issues of the *Musical World*, but it made some interesting changes. In the 1837 obituary, Wesley's physical appearance is compared to that of his uncle John, the founder of Methodism. In the Masonic version, Samuel is again compared to his uncle, but he is also compared to the Duke of Wellington, whose family was believed to be distantly related to the Wesleys. Samuel's features are found to be "almost a counterpart to those of the late Duke of Wellington."

This article, which once more stands within the national biography tradition, and, furthermore, yokes the memories of Wesley and Wellington—as the Earl of Mornington and Wellington were also yoked—takes on additional national coloring as it asserts, "Wesley's style of composition was essentially English; square, broad, and rhythmical. His manner of playing is traditionally imitated by every organist today."[18] This national temperament continues through to the conclusion of the article, where we read:

> Hoping we have made good our title in selecting one of our eminent deceased Brethren as the subjects of our first biographical series, we take leave of the most wonderful English child, and man, of musical genius that this country can show, and rejoice to add that our late Bro. Samuel Wesley shined resplendent in our annals, as the first [organist] to the Grand Lodge of England.[19]

The irony is that from a strictly stylistic point of view, Wesley's organ music was only partly English. Like his British contemporaries, he composed for the pianoforte many variation sets and rondos based upon Irish and Scottish tunes. But he also transformed the native English organ voluntary tradition, in part through his appropriation of serious counterpoint modeled on the organ music of the great German master,

J. S. Bach (1685–1750), and through an increasingly complex rhythmic and harmonic vocabulary—most likely also inspired by Bach's music—that was virtually foreign to traditional English voluntaries, as they were then still being composed by Wesley's contemporaries, such as his older brother, Charles Jr. (1757–1834), and William Russell (1777–1813).

It has been Wesley's role as an early advocate for the music of Bach in the British Isles and not the national character of his music (nor the quality of his organ voluntaries) that has kept Wesley earning at least brief mention in standard music history textbooks during the past century. And even when his friends, such as Vincent Novello, spoke in glowing terms of the national character of his music, their assessment of his style reads like a catalog of the principle English and Continental musicians of the sixteenth, seventeenth, and eighteenth centuries. Musical example 2 reproduces "Lord Wellington's March," a section from Wesley's battle sonata *The Siege of Badajoz* (ca. 1812), which is one of his more overtly national compositions. The excerpt is doubly applicable for this essay both as part of a nationalist composition that, like other battle sonatas of the time, aurally invokes the nation, and also as part of a web of interrelated cultural artifacts that attempts to relate the families of Wesley and of Wellington.

Wesley's "Lord Wellington's March" is of a much higher quality than are extracts from many other battle sonatas. Even so, Vincent Novello did not celebrate such overtly national music by Wesley. Rather it was Wesley's self-conscious musical cosmopolitanism—which Wesley reflects upon in his letters, in his lectures, and in his autobiographical *Reminiscences*—that makes him important and worthy of emulation and veneration as a British musical genius.[20] To make self-conscious musical cosmopolitanism the basis on which one endorses a composer as "national" is paradoxical. Granted, one may argue that because a musician achieves a certain level of compositional sophistication, and thereby brings honor to the national community, he achieves national status. But this argument runs contrary to the many voices raised in British periodicals that articulated a vision of a national musical utterance, born out of a nation's supposed unique temperament, character, and ethnicity, as the basis for music that is truly national.

Nevertheless, the "nationalness" of Wesley's organ music is an important contextual component for me to recognize as a musician. I have no

"Lord Wellington's March," <u>Siege of Badajoz</u>   S. Wesley

Musical Example 2

doubt that one reason that Wesley's organ music was published throughout the nineteenth century was that his music and reputation were linked
to the national musical identity. The "nationalness" or "Englishness" of
his music, at least as a matter of reception history, may actually have
some value to the music as participatory experience today. At the same
time, the fact that Wesley's musical style in his organ works—which I do
not have time to fully discuss in this essay—contests a "natural" relationship

with national music is further, specifically musical evidence for the artificiality of national identity generally. That artificiality is a fact that many scholars of national identity and nationalism already acknowledge; I do not claim to be making any major advance in that theory here. What I am trying to do is to place musical style into that mix and to suggest that the study of musical style and its relationship to national identity might yield further, unique insights into that important cultural practice of nation formation.

To conclude, I wish to pose a few questions. Samuel Wesley, by virtue of the fact that he possessed a well-recognized name and was clearly of English extract, could easily be seen as "one of us" by later English organists. By the 1850s, they could look back on the man's music and see it as "ours," even though it was only partly the product of native musical traditions. The German influences from Bach that were in Wesley's music may have become domesticated simply by time and familiarity. But to view Wesley's essentially cosmopolitan style as national (and natural) negates the facts of style history, even if the designation makes sense from the standpoint of tradition formation. According to the workings of national identity and tradition formation, the familiar becomes the natural, the natural the inevitable, and the inevitable the ageless.

Why was it that Wesley's Anglo-German organ music could take on national trappings in subsequent English music history, but John Stanley, the Earl of Mornington, and Handel were not accepted as "Scottish" in subsequent Scottish history? Each of them was "British" in some sense, and some Scottish periodical writers had placed their music into a stream of literary reflections on national identity and culture in Scotland. Furthermore, their compositions participated in the same pan-European musical style, which was strongly shaped by Italian influences. Were those writers who included English musical culture in their invocations of the nation genuinely seeking to reconcile distinct English and Scottish musical histories? Were those writers ahead of their time in viewing Great Britain as a potentially natural and organic Union? Was this the literary parallel to the pan-Britannic sharing of folk tunes and dances that was going on in Wales, Scotland, Ireland, and England at the same time? Were these all attempts at reshaping Britannia? And why did such musical reconciliation ultimately fail? I can only pose the questions here, but the music awaits further study.

Notes

1. Leon Botstein argues that music can be a means to study the nonmusical in "Cinderella; or Music and the Human Sciences. Unfootnoted Musings from the Margins," *Current Musicology* 53 (1993): 124–134.

2. In his book, *Cunning Passages: New Historicism, Cultural Materialism, and Marxism in the Contemporary Literary Debate* (London: Arnold, 1996), Jeremy Hawthorn refers to the process of "triangulation" by which the historian uses "different forms of evidence to ensure that error and falsity can be detected." (209) Likewise, in *Chivalry and Violence in Medieval Europe* (Oxford: Oxford University Press, 1999), Richard Kaeuper writes about the "powerful cumulative traces of experience in literature." (22) He builds his arguments around the careful scrutiny of many different kinds of records, including the imaginative literature of the medieval period, and he finds them trustworthy as a whole because the evidence from the different sources is congruent. Kaeuper was one of my professors at the University of Rochester. His approach to the use of literature for studying history has had a profound influence on my thinking as a musicologist generally and on my understanding of the relationship between musicology and history specifically.

3. See Catherine Gallagher and Stephen Greenblatt, *Practicing New Historicism* (Chicago: University of Chicago Press, 2000), 9.

4. See the collected essays in Gregory F. Barz and Timothy J. Cooley, eds., *Shadows in the Field: New Perspectives for Fieldwork in Ethnomusicology* (Oxford: Oxford University Press, 1997). In his essay, "Casting Shadows in the Field: An Introduction," Cooley discusses how ethnomusicologists are moving away from text-based representations of cultures to experience-based participation in which fieldworkers become "social actors within the cultures they study." (4) The goal is to develop "bimusicality" and to de-emphasize the musical object as the center of scholarly attention. Likewise, Michelle Kisliuk suggests that "a focus on the ethnography of musical performance—overdue in the ethnographic arena—can suggest incisive ways of researching, writing about, and understanding cultural processes." See "(Un)Doing Fieldwork: Sharing Songs, Sharing Lives," in *Shadows*, 23. See also Jeff Todd Titon's "Knowing Fieldwork," with its phenomenological conception of fieldwork and concurrent critique of text-oriented cultural studies generally. Titon writes, "The world is not like a text to be read but like a musical performance to be experienced." See "Knowing Fieldwork," in *Shadows*, 91.

5. The notion of participation as a grounding for knowledge also appeals to me as a performer. Although I cannot quantify it, I feel that when I perform eighteenth- and nineteenth-century keyboard music I have a living connection to that past culture that is different in kind to the experience of that culture that I have when reading its periodicals, novels, or writings about music. Furthermore, it is often in the context of a performance where I feel that I can communicate with an audience immediately about music and its contexts and significance. Botstein argues that by recasting how we talk about music and by more fully exploring the "extramusical dimension" of our favored repertories, we may be able to reengage concert audiences with older musical works and past musical cultures. He cautions, however, against being satisfied with "mere parallelism and surface comparisons." See Botstein, "Cinderella," 129.

6. Benedict Anderson, *Imagined Communities: Reflections on the Origin and Spread of Nationalism*, rev. ed. (London: Verso, 1991).

7. Eric Hobsbawm, *Nations and Nationalism Since 1780: Programme, Myth, Reality* (New York: Cambridge University Press, 1990); Anthony Smith, *National Identity* (Nevada: University of Nevada Press, 1991); Ernest Gellner, *Nations and Nationalism* (Ithaca: Cornell University, 1983); Ernest Gellner, *Encounters with Nationalism* (Oxford: Blackwell, 1994); John A. Hall, ed., *The State of the Nation: Ernest Gellner and the Theory of Nationalism* (London: Cambridge University Press, 1998); Colin Kidd, *Subverting Scotland's Past: Scottish Whig Historians and the Creation of Anglo-British Identity, 1689–ca. 1830* (Cambridge: Cambridge University Press, 1993); Colin Kidd, *British Identities Before Nationalism: Ethnicity and Nationhood in the Atlantic World, 1600–1800* (Cambridge: Cambridge University Press, 1999).

8. Kidd describes "Britishness" as essentially Anglo-Britishness. Rather than being a richly comprehensive Anglo-Scottish British identity, Britishness was "dependent on a historical allegiance to England's evolving constitution of crown and parliament." It has become in the past three hundred years "almost as pervasive in Scotland as in the English heartland of the United Kingdom." See Kidd, *Subverting Scotland*, 1.

9. "On the Love of Our Country," *Scots Magazine or General Repository* (July 1794): 379.

10. I have studied a wide variety of British periodicals from the Georgian period. Some were short lived, others existed for many decades in one form or another. Some had sizeable circulations, while others did not. Nevertheless, consistent patterns of ideas can be seen regarding national identity, national cultural, and national musical life across the full spectrum of periodicals, which causes me to be confident that the sentiments expressed in the articles I discuss in this essay were widely shared within British society. Furthermore, in the Georgian period, the number of copies of a periodical in circulation did not necessarily mark the extent of the reach of the ideas in the periodical. Periodicals liberally reprinted materials from each other, and circulating libraries, the practice of reading out loud, and the availability of copies of periodicals in public places, such as coffee houses, extended the reach of a periodical.

11. Similarly, the reviewer of *A Selection of Popular National Airs, with Symphonies and Accompaniments, by H. R. Bishop the Words by Thomas Moore* writes, "The songs of a nation have been said to picture its character. . . . Neither music nor poetry are likely to become national, (indeed, they are neither worth a thought nor do they attract one) unless they speak to the sensibility, connect themselves inseparably with the affections of the time, raise consentaneous emotions and passions, sink into memory, and become the subjects of tradition. These are the properties which cause ballads to be national, and they are said to portray the character, because they reflect the images and opinions most agreeable to national feelings." See the *Quarterly Musical Magazine and Review* vol. 2 (1820): 233.

12. From the contextual point of view, Handel's "Zadok the Priest" is quintessentially British. "Timotheus," who wrote an extended letter to the editor in the first issue of the *Quarterly Musical Magazine and Review* (1818), also considered whether or not Handel was a British composer. He was somewhat less confident than the reviewer in the

Harmonicon, for he acknowledged that although Handel was not "strictly speaking an English composer," he laid the foundation of contemporary English music: all English composers are his "sons," for they develop their skills through study of his music. Furthermore, Handel "has joined the fulness [sic] and majesty of the German music, the delicacy and elegance of the Italian, to the solidity of the English, constituting in the end a style of magnificence superior to any other nation." (39) Another anonymous letter written in the *Quarterly Musical Magazine and Review* went further and declared that Handel was the successor to the composers Matthew Locke and Henry Purcell, and that "we may certainly claim Handel for our own on the . . . ground [of] naturalization." See *Quarterly Musical Magazine and Review* vol. 6 (1824): 157. Handel was also linked with Purcell and Arne as "the best foundations" on which the great style of English singing could be built in "The Royal Academy of Music," *Quarterly Musical Magazine and Review* vol. 7 (1825): 158. Finally, in a review of Addison's arrangement of *Samson,* a writer for the *Quarterly Musical Magazine and Review* stated that *Messiah* had become almost a part of the religion of England. Furthermore, the fact that it is one of Handel's oratorios that survive in the public concerts "elucidate[s] strongly the national character of the English." That character is warlike, manly, and grave. See *Quarterly Musical Magazine and Review* vol. 11 (1829): 366.

13. For a discussion of Britain as the new Israel and the relationship between this idea and Handel's music, see Ruth Smith, *Handel Oratorios and Eighteenth-Century Thought* (Cambridge: Cambridge University Press, 1995).

14. The collection came with accompaniments by Edward Knight. It was published in London by J. Power and reviewed by the *Harmonicon* in December 1823, on pages 193–194.

15. See "Character of the Most Eminent Scots Writers of the Way," *Scots Magazine, and Edinburgh Literary Miscellany* (October 1806 and November 1806): 743, 817–819.

16. "Character of George II with the State of Literature and the Arts During His Reign," *Scots Magazine or General Repository* (June 1794).

17. See Stanley C. Pelkey, "Song, Dance, and National Identities in Keyboard Arrangements," in "British National Identity and Keyboard Music in the Later Georgian Period" (Ph.D. dissertation, University of Rochester, 2004.)

18. "Biographical Sketches of Eminent (Deceased) Freemasons," *Freemason Magazine and Masonic Mirror* (28 July 1858): 159.

19. "Biographical Sketches," 161.

20. "Self-conscious musical cosmopolitanism" is my term, not Novello's, although it is rooted in my study of Novello's conception of Wesley's music and in my reading of Wesley's writings on his own compositional process. Novello's assessments of Wesley can be found in many annotations by Novello of Wesley manuscripts, such as the following on Lcm 5237, "This Collection is a very fine one, and contains several beautiful compositions (unpublished manuscripts) by one of the greatest musical geniuses and the finest extempore Fugueist that England has produced—Samuel Wesley." Sources for Wesley's views on musical style include his *Reminiscences* (See Lbl. Add. 27593) and his lectures (see Lbl. Add. 35015).

Music by the "Celebrated Mozart"
A Philadelphia Publishing Tradition, 1794–1861

Dorothy Potter

Around 1795 George Willig, a German immigrant music publisher who the year before had begun work in Philadelphia, issued "The Fowler," a piece with piano or guitar accompaniment, subtitled "A Favorite Song by the celebrated Mr. Mozart." Based on Papageno's Act One aria in *Die Zauberflöte*, in which the bird-catcher explains himself to Prince Tamino, this lively three verse song with both English and German words could appeal to many potential customers. Adapted for the average parlor pianist or guitarist, accessible to Philadelphia's large German community as well as English speakers, the work bore the name *Mozart*. That one word informed Willig's customers that he printed and sold superior music.[1]

For Willig and other publishers profit was, of necessity, the primary motivation, but choices made by early entrepreneurs had significant consequences for the future. Printed matter sold in the new nation's major cities—Philadelphia, New York, Boston—largely determined what was read, performed, and later reissued by their counterparts in smaller communities.

Mozart's music was introduced to American audiences in 1786, with the performance of an unspecified sonata in a Philadelphia concert.[2] Within three or four years of his death in 1791, a few Philadelphia and New York publishers began issuing music that bore his name. While titles including "much admired" and "favorite" were typically used to attract customers, describing a composer as celebrated was less common. We cannot be sure why Willig chose this term, or indeed how he acquired his original version of "The Fowler," but the accuracy of the German text and his own origins suggest that he was more familiar with Mozart's works than most of his English and American counterparts. It is unlikely his source was British, since the opera was not staged in London until 1811.

By its very nature music is the most elusive and intangible of the arts, and for this reason is often all too briefly treated in history texts, compared to art, literature, and architecture. Yet in many ways it is the most omnipresent and inclusive, offering a vast range of choices, from the excitement of live performances to more muted background sounds tailored for workplaces, and individual choices for the home. It is vital to many forms of worship, and essential to films, radio, and television programming.

Amid an array of seemingly endless choices, cultivated music remains a recognized and, for many, a preferred form. How we almost intuitively define it relies on definitions that grew out of the late eighteenth and early nineteenth centuries, before audiences and performers began to separate themselves into the tidy categories of "popular" and "classical." The concept of a musical cannon began in eighteenth-century England. Reverence for "Antient [*sic*] music" by Thomas Tallis, Henry Purcell, Arcangelo Corelli and others soon led to George Frederick Handel's admission to the pantheon. Influential British music historians like Charles Burney and Thomas Busby revered Handel but included contemporary composers like Joseph Haydn and Mozart in their multi-volume histories.[3]

A number of non-British composers such as Handel and J. C. Bach had lived in England, or like Haydn had popular concert tours there in adulthood. Mozart's English experience was limited to a brief fifteen months; arriving in London at age eight, he performed with his older sister Nannerl and composed a few modest works. His desire to return to Britain never materialized. However a number of his mature works were performed in London as early as 1784, and appeared in print not long thereafter.[4] Immigrant publishers with British origins, like the Carr family and George Blake, imported and pirated these and many other works to enrich their inventories.

Part of an historian's craft is the pleasure of detective work—the pursuit of elusive facts to hopefully "round up the *unusual* suspects." After the bicentennial of Mozart's death in 1991, I began studying the genesis of his music and reputation in antebellum America. It seemed curious that amid a flood of Amadeus-related concerts, books, films, and kitsch, relatively little attention was paid to the early events and individuals that had made his name a household word.

One challenge in tracing Mozart links to antebellum cultural life in the United States is limited information. A great deal of time is spent perusing music collections, diaries, letters, memoirs and contemporary biographies, newspapers, literary magazines, and even visiting old book shops. Since my research links the "finished product"—concerts, plays, operas, performance sites like City Tavern, the New [later Chesnut] Theatre, and Musical Fund Hall—to the more private worlds of printer-publishers and the domestic market that supported them, it was essential to examine the small number of publishers' catalogues, Philadelphia newspapers, and a few compilations by later scholars, such as Oscar George Sonneck, William Treat Upton, and Richard J. Wolfe.

A different sort of challenge is a natural tendency to equate influence with public performances. Since Mozart's name usually appeared less frequently on concert and opera programs than do the names of Handel, Haydn, Rossini, Beethoven, and others, some authorities have concluded he had little cultural influence beyond Europe until the twentieth century. However this view ignores publishers, the social music that was their "bread and butter," and adaptations of cultivated music in theatre productions of the period.

Purists may despise the 1817 extravaganza *Don Giovanni: or A Spectre on Horseback*, as well as scoff at Henry Rowley Bishop's opera-romance *The Marriage of Figaro*, which opened in London on 6 March 1819, and was staged in Philadelphia on 29 December 1824. However these English adaptations introduced cultivated music to diverse audiences that would not have sat through an opera in Italian. Such productions launched songs whose lyrics might be banal, but whose music captured popular interest. As Lawrence Levine notes:

> Popular songs in English based on operatic arias could be encountered everywhere in nineteenth-century America. As early as the 1790s the popular song "Away with Melancholy" was derived from an aria in Mozart's *Magic Flute*. In 1820 "La ci darem la mano" from *Don Giovanni* took the country by storm as "Now place your hand in mine, dear." And so it continued for decades.[5]

Inclusion on concert programs was an essential component in the creation of fame, but publications informed and directed taste. These ranged, in Mozart's case, from one-page songs to articles in English encyclopedias and literary magazines as early as 1803. The public found his music beautiful, and when adapted to a piano or guitar, not too difficult to play. Victorians also learned that Mozart's life represented qualities of which they approved: love of family, diligence in one's work, plus the added fascination of an early mysterious death.

Throughout the nineteenth century middle-class Americans became increasingly preoccupied with gentility. Middle and upper class women, barred by law and custom from much of the public sphere, were exhorted from the pulpit and encouraged by their mothers and their literary magazines to become guardians of proper behavior. The home became a haven and the parlor a shrine filled with books, music, and journals chosen to display refinement and virtue. Women gathered families around the piano to play, sing, or even dance to music derived from the concerts, plays, and in cities like Philadelphia, operas they had recently attended.

A few Americans, from John Adams to William Henry Fry, tried to ignore or minimize European taste, maintaining that the New World's literature, music, and art needed no foreign influences. However the almost universal choice by publishers to put composers' names in large type within the titles of the ballads, duets, waltzes, and "favorite airs," they turned out in such profusion showed that the public wanted to know who created these works.

During the first two decades of the nineteenth century Philadelphia and Boston were America's two largest publishing centers. While all sorts of music was being produced, by 1825 presses in New York, Baltimore, Philadelphia, Boston, Charleston, and a few smaller cities had issued some 170 Mozart works, compared to about 80 by Haydn, over 50 by Handel, and approximately 30 works by Beethoven.[6] Between 1794 and 1861 more than twenty-one Philadelphia publishers had included Mozart's music (or works ascribed to him) in their inventories. A brief overview of the most influential of these men underscores their influence in Philadelphia and the nation at large.[7]

Philadelphia was the nation's second largest city until around 1830, and its wealth and historic associations also gave it a unique place in antebellum American life. From the eighteenth century onward it had been a major publishing center, and its artisans, printers, and publishers would continue to lead the industry for more than one hundred years. At first largely religious in content, music publishing expanded as the desire grew for secular songs. Typefaces were at first imported from the Netherlands and Great Britain, but by 1800 Americans had begun to produce their own. The development of lithography in the 1820s and chromolithography in the 1840s evolved even as Mozart's music became part of the fabric of American life. These processes made books and music cheaper and more visually attractive to an increasingly literate public.

Pennsylvania's first paper mill began operating in 1690, and within fifty years demand was such that many gristmills were converted to papermaking. In 1810 Isaiah Thomas noted in *The History of Printing in America* that of at least 185 paper mills in the United States, Pennsylvania had "about sixty."[8] Local mills supplied rag paper for Philadelphia's publishing industry and its Mint, which exerted an influence far beyond the State's borders.

Philadelphia's historic publishing district was in the center of the city, where Chesnut and Market Streets intersected second through Fifth Streets. Most pre-Civil War printers, publishers, and music sellers spent some part of their careers here. In mixed neighborhoods of homes, taverns, churches, grocers, bookbinders, and tailors' shops, music dealers worked close together and near the various theatres and Musical Fund Hall. Patrons could easily purchase music they had heard on-stage. Only by mid-century did newer publishers prefer to locate in the more fashionable uptown districts.[9]

Like other nineteenth-century merchants, publishers often occupied two or three ground floor rooms with living quarters above them. The main room, which served as a retail center, might not be very large; the South Fifth Street shop of George Blake, one of Philadelphia's oldest and most successful publishers, was only about twenty by thirty feet. Engraving and printing were done in a back room, unless one's plates were sent out to professional printers.[10]

Throughout America during this period music was sold in separate sheets for purchasers to bind as they chose, with usually twenty to forty sheets in a volume. Many nineteenth-century works survive only because of these personalized collections. From about 1815 through the 1850s, music paper was sometimes colored lavender, pale green, blue, pink, or yellow for the feminine market. Both George Willig and Philadelphia's popular *Godey's Lady's Book* used colored music paper until the 1850s, when it was no longer considered attractive.[11]

Since full calfskin was costly, many private collections had marbleized covers with calf on the corners and spine. A label with the owner's name and a title such as "Sonatas" completed a front cover. Initially the music itself was something of a luxury; in 1816 one sheet cost twelve and a half cents, the same price as a quart of milk or five Havana cigars.[12] Hand-copied music was thus a major component of many collections. For example, Thomas Jefferson's granddaughters Ellen and Virginia supplemented their elders' choices with hand-copied waltzes and opera excerpts. Like many young ladies of their social standing, they were proficient in singing, harpsichord, piano, and guitar.[13]

For a variety of reasons, determining the number of any city's pre-Civil War publishers is challenging. Performers and music teachers issued music for themselves or for their pupils. Imprints sometimes lacked business addresses, and until the 1840s dates were often omitted, since a major selling point was that the music was "New." As in Europe, literary piracy was almost universal. The first American copyright act of 1790 did not include foreign works. The more popular a European book or composition, the sooner it would appear in a pirated American edition. Publishers in the same city often issued competing versions of the same work, with only minor changes in the title or the music itself. Music was not even deemed a copyright category until 1831.

Benjamin Carr would become one of America's most influential early publishers. Carr was born in London in 1768, and an important influence in his early life was the English organist-composer Samuel Arnold. In 1789 Arnold was conductor of the prestigious Academy of Ancient Music. Carr may have decided to come to the United States after it was disbanded in 1792.[14]

Reaching Philadelphia at the outset of a virulent yellow fever epidemic in 1793, Carr was soon joined by his parents Joseph and Mary, and his brother Thomas who settled in Baltimore. With the 1794 opening of a third shop in New York, the Carr family created the nation's first multi-city publishing business. Though not as active a publisher as his brother, Thomas Carr was a composer and arranger. His greatest achievement is that in 1814 he set the words of Francis Scott Key's poem "The Star Spangled Banner" to a British drinking song, "To Anacreon in Heaven." Their ties to London's publishing world and their technical skills helped the Carr family dominate the Philadelphia-Baltimore markets for nearly two decades. During his thirty-eight years in Philadelphia Benjamin Carr pursued many musical careers; along with publishing he was also a singer-actor, composer, church organist, and in 1820, a founding member of the Musical Fund Society.[15]

One of Carr's and colleague Ralph Shaw's earliest collections was *The Gentleman's Amusement*, arrangements for up to three flutes or violins, in seven issues between April 1794 and May 1796. Both the title and the series' six-dollar cost were indicators for whom it was intended. Flutes, recorders, and violins were thought to disturb facial expressions and thus were played by men. The price limited these arrangements to the upper middle class.

"Grand March from the Opera of The Prisoner," a duet for flutes or violins in issue 2, 1794, and an unspecified "Duetto" for either flutes or violins in issue 9 (ca. 1796) are two of the earliest Mozart adaptations published in the United States. They are also rare in that their dates can be determined with some accuracy. Thomas Attwood, Mozart's English piano pupil from 1785 to 1787, composed *The Prisoner* in 1792. "Grand March" was based on the popular aria "Non più andrai" from *Le nozze di Figaro* (1786).[16] *The Gentleman's Amusement*'s success led Carr to offer *Military Amusements* (1796) for the same set of instruments; it included another "Mozart March."

Musical Journal for the Piano Forte (1800–1804), five volumes of vocal and keyboard music, much of it pirated from British ballad operas, was both more ambitious and also intended for both women and men. Number 20—a "Turkish Air"—in instrumental Volume One was a simpler version of Mozart's popular 1783 "Alla Turca" Rondo in A Major (K. 331). The duet with piano accompaniment in the vocal section of Volume Four, no. 95: "Ah perdona al primo affetto," from Act I, Scene II of *La Clemenza di Tito* (K. 621) was also probably chosen because that opera was currently in vogue; though next to the last operatic work that Mozart composed (1791), it was the first to be given in its entirety in Britain (1806).[17] There would be at least ten American reprints in Italian or English of "Ah perdona" between 1802 and the mid-1840s.[18]

After *Musical Journal* the Carrs published less frequently during the three decades before Benjamin Carr's death on 24 May 1831. In 1822, after the death of their father Joseph, Thomas Carr had sold his interest in the Baltimore business to George Willig and come to Philadelphia. In his last Mozart adaptation in 1823, Benjamin Carr returned to *La Clemenza di Tito* for "The Landing of Columbus," a celebratory ode whose music was based on a march and chorus in the opera's first act. Even as the Romans in the opera proclaimed the virtues of Emperor Titus, so the orchestra and chorus of Philadelphia's newly incorporated Musical Fund Society celebrated Christopher Columbus and Queen Isabella.

Spain's queen was a romantic figure to many Americans, so "The Landing of Columbus" may have been given in the Society's third concert on 24 April 1823 in honor of her birthday, April 22.[19] Reprised to celebrate the Society's newly completed Hall on 9 December 1824, it was also part of an 1838 concert at the black Second Presbyterian Church, with works by Handel and Haydn.[20]

Their choice of an obviously European piece may seem curious in the twenty-first century, which celebrates the unique richness of African-American music. However free black communities in northern cities like Philadelphia and New York saw cultivated music as a means to show whites that they shared many Victorian middle class aspirations. "Tunes and hymns of your own composing"—i.e., spirituals—were discouraged by some black Methodists. Formal concerts by African-Americans in New York and Philadelphia in the 1830s and 1840s included Handel, Haydn, Mozart, and Rossini.[21]

Eighteenth- and nineteenth-century Quakers and Baptists habitually condemned theatre and dancing. Theatres were illegal in a number of cities including Philadelphia, prior to the Revolution, and travelling actors were blamed by the godly for everything from encouraging sin to the 1793 yellow fever epidemic. By the early nineteenth century however, most Americans accepted theatre, and it helped familiarize Mozart's music to urban audiences. By 1812 Philadelphia had two (and during some seasons three) theatres vying for audiences. Subjects included farces, romantic melodramas, Shakespeare, and operatic plays in English, including by 1824 *The Marriage of Figaro* and two versions of *Don Giovanni*.

However the most popular domestic music was waltzes for one or two pianists, and it was in this category that Mozart's name most often appeared. In researching waltz tunes in America to 1824, Michael Broyles found fifty-seven attributed to Mozart, compared to seventeen waltzes by pianist-composer Muzio Clementi, and sixteen attributed to New York musician-publisher James Hewitt.[22]

Mozart composed numerous minuets, but technically never a waltz, which was a nineteenth-century dance form. The many "Mozart Waltzes" attributed to him were variations on two or three of his works, probably the most authentic adapted from his Six German Dances (K. 606). However, as Broyles notes, "in this case [the] actual composer is a secondary issue. Who wrote the piece matters less than who people thought wrote the piece." [23] Various "Admired," "Favorite," and "Celebrated" Mozart waltzes abounded throughout the United States.

George Willig issued many waltzes, and indeed all kinds of music. Born in 1764, he began his Philadelphia career by acquiring plates from other businessmen and reprinting their stock as well as his own choices, like "The Fowler." He also taught music and sold pianos and concert tickets. [24] In 1845 *Wealth and Biography of the Wealthy Citizens of Philadelphia* described him as a "respectable and much esteemed teacher and seller of music," and estimated his material worth at $75,000 (a sum roughly equivalent to a $1,000,000 in twenty-first century currency). [25]

Between 1812 and 1850 Willig published more than fifty Mozart titles, including fifteen waltzes. While *Die Zauberflöte*, *Figaro*, *Don Giovanni*, and *La Clemenza di Tito* provided the basis for twenty-one of thirty-four songs, other pieces were taken from a variety of Mozart Lieder. [26] However Willig's major contribution to American music was his three catalogues. Before this innovation publishers might list a few titles on the back of a music sheet, or advertised their latest stock in a newspaper.

Catalogue of Songs. Printed & Sold by G. Willig at his Musical Magazine . . . [1807–1808] was the first of its type in the United States. Four pages long plus a supplement, it had about 750 titles, including works from other publishers. At least nine titles were attributed to Mozart. The 1824 *Catalogue of Vocal and Instrumental Music Published by George Willig, Importer of Musical Instruments and Music Publisher . . .* included more than 800 Willig imprints arranged in groups; songs filled four pages, followed by marches, dances, airs, sonatas, and other instrumental categories. This catalogue listed twenty-nine Mozart works or adaptations. [27]

Willig's last catalogue (1835) included more than 2000 items. Of about forty Mozart pieces, nineteen were songs in English or Italian; six waltzes were the next largest category. Willig made clear in his introductory paragraph that he set his sights on potential customers far beyond Philadelphia:

> G.W. is constantly supplied with new European and American musical publications. Orders from any part of the United States, West Indies, or South America [are] attended to with care and dispatch. [28]

A quarter century of publishing had also led to decreasing prices. The average two-page song, which cost twenty-five cents in 1807, was twelve and a half cents by 1835, while single sheets formerly twelve cents were now six cents.[29] More efficient distribution by rail, and advertising in popular national magazines like *Godey's Lady's Book*, contributed to Willig's success for more than half a century. He died on 30 December 1851, aged eighty-seven. About five years later his former clerks, George W. Lee and Julius Walker acquired the Philadelphia shop. Willig's son and grandsons kept the Baltimore branch of the business until 1910.

From 1849 to 1851 Lee & Walker briefly took advantage of a unique locale; their store was on the first floor of P. T. Barnum's Museum at 162 Chesnut Street. When it burned in December 1851 they relocated to a less public site two blocks away and acquired a fireproof vault. Walker died in 1857, but Lee remained in business another eighteen years publishing sacred music, popular songs such as "Dixie," and operatic adaptations from, among others, *Die Entführung aus dem Serail*, *Don Giovanni*, *Die Zauberflöte*, and *Figaro*. Seventy years after Carr and Shaw issued "Non più andrai," Lee & Walker sold their own version.[30]

A. Bacon & Company was another important Philadelphia firm. Allyn Bacon moved from Connecticut around 1813, and soon his store at No. 11 South Fourth Street became a gathering-place for local musicians.[31] While not as long-lived as the Carrs, Willig, Blake, or his successor John G. Klemm (1823–1879), Bacon issued eight "Mozart waltzes," a march, two "airs and variations" for piano, and two books of *Select Airs from the Celebrated Operas Composed by Mozart*—twelve *Don Giovanni* arias arranged for piano and flute.

Prior to lithography, American music was sparsely illustrated. Typical images included simple borders on title pages, flowers, birds, wreaths, military symbols, or musical instruments. Thus the title page of Bacon's two volume *Select Airs from the Celebrated Operas Composed by Mozart. Arranged for the Piano Forte . . .* (ca. 1819) is visually remarkable. Below the intricately lettered title sits a young man before a plinth inscribed "Mozart." The plinth is decorated with a lyre, eternal flame, and crown of stars and is surmounted by a truncated column, symbolic of untimely death. The youth holds an open book inscribed "Oeuvres de Mozart." Behind the monument are willow trees, and below the figure lies a fallen branch, also denoting death.

Bacon would hardly have authorized such elaborate artwork unless he was sure this visual tribute would generate sales. The name "C. Gobrecht" forms part of the title's decoration. Around 1820 Christian Gobrecht was an ambitious young artist. By 1836 he was the Assistant Engraver at the United States Mint. Once becoming Chief Engraver (1840) he redesigned much of America's coinage.[32]

Each of these publishers made unique contributions to his occupation and to America's cultural history. In addition to providing superior quality music for an increasingly sophisticated public, Gustav André was directly linked to Mozart through his father and grandfather. The family publishing house was founded in Offenbach am Main in 1774 by Johann André, an amateur composer and friend of Mozart and Joseph Haydn. Shortly after Johann's death in 1799, his son Johann Anton André purchased a large number of manuscripts from Mozart's widow Constanze.[33]

Friendship played a significant part in Constanze's choice; Mozart had visited the Andrés during a journey to Frankfurt in 1790, and young J. Anton had been present with him at a rehearsal of *Don Giovanni* in Mannheim that same year. André published about fifty-five Mozart compositions between 1800 and 1830, and began organizing his manuscripts in hopes of issuing a complete chronological catalogue. His efforts were used by Edward Holmes in the first English-language biography of Mozart in 1845, and in Ludwig Ritter von Köchel's *Chronologisch-thematisches Verzeichnis sämtlicher Tonwerke Wolfgang Amadé Mozarts* (1862).[34]

J. Anton André had fifteen children, several of whom became publishers, musicians, instrument makers, or music dealers. Carl August, Julius, and Johann August's biographies are in *The New Grove* or the *Norton-Grove Music Printing and Publishing*, but Gustav was one of five other sons, about whom less is known. He published and imported music in London at several addresses in 1838–1839, moved to New York in 1843, and then to Philadelphia, where his firm remained in business from 1850 to 1879.[35] Family connections gave Gustav an obvious advantage over his competitors; for example, an 1850s André edition of Mozart's piano concertos included the note that they were based on original manuscripts.[36]

The era of Philadelphia's early publishers ended with the death of George Blake in 1871. Born in England about 1775, the multi-talented Blake came to Philadelphia around 1793, and began giving flute and clarinet lessons. By the first decade of the nineteenth century he was making pianos. He also created a musical circulating library and became one of eighty-five charter members of the Musical Fund Society.

From around 1810 through the 1830s Blake was America's most prolific music publisher, issuing popular songs, sacred works, British and American theatre music, and excerpts from Italian operas. His imprints were sold in urban shops from New York to New Orleans, and to private collectors in Virginia, including Jefferson and the Cockes of Bremo.[37]

Blake published more than sixty Mozart works, attributions, or adaptations, with at least twelve titles identical or similar to ones issued by the Carrs or Willig.[38] His most extensive series, *A Selection from the Vocal Compositions of Mozart United to English Verses, The Accompaniments for the Piano Forte Arranged from the Original Scores by Muzio Clementi. The Poetry by David Thomson. To the Admirers of Mozart, this Work is Respectfully Dedicated by the Publisher* was issued in three parts (each $1.50) between 1815–1821.

This particular set shows Blake's keen business sense on several levels. Italian-born Muzio Clementi, who spent much of his life in England, was well known on both sides of the Atlantic as a composer, arranger, and businessman. Add to Clementi the magical name of Mozart, and customers had the sort of music that would grace any parlor, works which would show the owner to be a person of taste and wealth.

Of the twenty-three songs with English titles and verses by minor British poet David Thomson, eleven were duets or solos based on arias in *Le nozze di Figaro, Don Giovanni, Die Entführung aus dem Serail, Così fan tutte, Die Zauberflöte,* or *La Clemenza di Tito.* Blake would have known that many potential customers had heard excerpts from *La Clemenza di Tito* and *Figaro* in various concerts, and had seen *The Libertine* either in New York, or at Philadelphia's New Theatre in December 1818. Twelve other songs were derived from several editions of Mozart's works.[39]

Blake was most active through the 1830s; by the 1850s he was issuing no new music. The absence of his name on a list of twenty-seven men, including six Philadelphians, who signed the Board of Music Trade's articles of association at their New York convention on June 6–8, 1855 implies he had lost interest in current events.[40] Still Philadelphia's senior publisher kept his shop open until his death on 20 February 1871.

During more than six decades an increased knowledge of Mozart and his music offered something to nearly everyone, whether professionals, publishers, or consumers. Musicians were nearly unanimous in praising his genius. Editors and publishers knew that Mozart's name on a title page facilitated sales. Romantics saw him as one of the chosen few who interpreted the eternal harmonies of God to humanity. Amateurs who purchased his music—including the waltzes that bore his name—felt that, as with Shakespeare, some knowledge and appreciation of Wolfgang Mozart was a vital form of self-education.

Mozart and his music were, in effect, serving two dissimilar masters: musical idealism and mass entertainment. While other musical geniuses, most notably Beethoven, would later become equally omnipresent in both the concert hall and the marketplace, Mozart was the first composer and performer to be elevated by the English-speaking world to superstardom. This process still continues.

Notes

1. "The Fowler. A Favorite Song by the celebrated Mr. Mozart. Printed and sold at G. Willig's Musical Magazine." [ca. 1795] For added appeal the German verses were set in Gothic type. Both German and English verses accurately reflect the opera's libretto.

2. The first performance in the United States of a Mozart work—a "Sonata Piano Forte" by Alexander Reinagle—took place on 14 December 1786, in a concert at Philadelphia's City Tavern. *The Pennsylvania Journal and Weekly Advertiser*. 13 December 1786.

3. William Weber, *The Rise of Musical Classics in Eighteenth-Century England: A Study in Canon, Ritual, and Ideology* (Oxford: Clarendon Press, 1992), 3–5, 99–100, 124–125, 223–224.

4. John Jenkins, *Mozart and the English Connection* (London: Cygnus Arts, 1998), 142. Cliff Eisen, *New Mozart Documents: A Supplement to O. E. Deutsch's Documentary Biography* (Stanford, CA: Stanford University Press, 1991), 136–142.

5. Lawrence W. Levine, *Highbrow/Lowbrow: The Emergence of Cultural Hierarchy in America* (Cambridge MA: Harvard University Press, 1988), 96.

6. Carlton Sprague Smith, Introduction to *Secular Music in America 1801–1825: A Bibliography*, 3 vols, by Richard J. Wolfe (New York: New York Public Library, 1964), vol. I, x.

7. Publishers include John Aitken, the Carr family, Ralph Shaw, George Willig, George Blake, J. C. Hommann, William McCulloch, George Balls, Henry Lewis, Allyn Bacon, J. G. Klemm, R. H. Hobson, Fiot & Meignen, Kretschmar & Nunns, James Kay, Edmund Ferrett, Lee & Walker, C. F. Hupfeld, Gustav André, Frederick Rullman, J. G. Auner, and J. C. Viereck.

8. Isaiah Thomas, *The History of Printing in America* (Worcester: MA, 1810), quoted in Dard Hunter, *Papermaking In Pioneer America* (Philadelphia: University of Pennsylvania Press, 1952), 19.

9. Harry Dichter and Elliott Shapiro, *Early American Sheet Music: Its Lure and Its Lore 1768–1889* (New York: R. R. Bowker Co., 1941), 166–169, 172, 177–179, 191, 197, 211, 214, 244.

10. Richard J. Wolfe, *Early American Music Engraving and Printing* (Urbana: University of Illinois Press, 1980), 71–74.

11. Julia Eklund Koza, "Music and References to Music in *Godey's Lady's Book*, 1830–1877" (Ph.D. dissertation, Minneapolis: University of Minnesota, 1988), 453–454.

12. Charles H. Haswell, *Reminiscences of an Octogenarian of the City of New York: 1816–1860* (New York: Harper & Brothers, 1896), 57–58.

13. The Monticello Music Collection, the University of Virginia, Charlottesville, VA.

14. Stephen C. Siek, "Musical Taste in post-Revolutionary America as Seen Through Carr's 'Musical Journal for the Piano Forte.'" (Ph.D. dissertation, University of Cincinnati, 1991), 49–53, 55–56, 60–62.

15. Oscar George Theodore Sonneck, *Bibliography of Early Secular American Music: [18th Century]*. Revised and enlarged by William Treat Upton. (Washington, DC: Library of Congress Music Division. 1945), 501–502, 575–578. Siek, ii, 131–132.

16. Roger Fiske, *English Theatre Music in the Eighteenth Century* (Oxford: Oxford University Press, 1986), 518–519.

17. Benjamin Carr, *Musical Journal for the Piano Forte* (Wilmington, DE: Scholarly Research Inc., 1972), 2 vols. Instrumental, vol. I, 37; Vocal, vol. II, 69–71.

18. Carr included an English translation of the libretto. Wolfe, *Secular Music*, II, 603, 606.

19. Assuming the concert date was not random, Isabella seems to best fit the facts. Columbus' birth year is uncertain; the sighting of San Salvador occurred on 12 October 1492. Columbus died on 20 May 1506; Isabella had died on 24 November 1504.

20. "The Landing of Columbus . . . music from Mozart's opera of La Clemenza di Tito and performed . . . at the concerts of the Musical Fund Society of Philadelphia. The adaptation by Benjamin Carr." (New York: I. P. Cole, 1825). *Public Ledger*, 4 January 1838.

21. Eileen Southern, "Musical Practices in Black Churches of Philadelphia and New York, ca. 1800–1844," *Journal of the American Musicological Society*, 30/2: 296–299, 302, 306–307.

22. Michael Broyles, "Mozart: America's First Waltz-King," 6. A paper given 10 February 2001, Mozart Society of America conference, University of Nevada, Las Vegas. I am grateful to Dr. Broyles for a copy of his text.

23. Broyles, "Mozart: America's First Waltz-King," 5.

24. Donald W. Krummel, "Philadelphia Music Engraving and Publishing 1800–1820" (Ph.D. dissertation, University of Michigan, 1958), 109. Wolfe, *Secular Music*, vol. II, 622–624.

25. *Wealth and Biography of the Wealthy Citizens of Philadelphia, Containing an Alphabetical Arrangement of Persons Estimated to be Worth $50,000 and Upwards* (Philadelphia: G. B. Zieber, 1845), 22.

26. Wolfe, *Secular Music*, vol. II, 607.

27. Mozart works/arrangements in the 1824 *Catalogue of Vocal and Instrumental Music* include fifteen songs, two marches, four waltzes, a minuet, a rondo, three variations, a piano duet, a sonata, and a flute arrangement. Wolfe, *Secular Music*, III, 970.

28. *Catalogue of Vocal and Instrumental Music . . . by George Willig* (1835), 1–3, 5–8, 10–12.

29. *Catalogue of Vocal and Instrumental Music Published and for Sale by George Willig* (Philadelphia: Willig, 1835).

30. "Noteworthy Philadelphia: A City's Musical Heritage, 1750–1915," Exhibition catalog. The Library Company of Philadelphia: 1997, 33–34. Oliver Ditson of Boston acquired the firm after Lee's death in 1875.

31. *The Sunday Dispatch,* 13 February 1859.

32. Gobrecht's redesigned coinage ranged from half cents to ten dollar gold pieces; his design for the five dollar gold piece (or half eagle) lasted from 1839 to 1908.

33. Otto Erich Deutsch, *Mozart: A Documentary Biography*, trans. Eric Blom, Peter Branscombe, and Jeremy Noble (Stanford, CA: Stanford University Press, 1965), 490–492. August Hermann André, *Zur Geschichte der Familie André* (Offenbach am Main: Offenbacher Geschichtsverein, 1962), 18–19.

34. Deutsch, *Mozart*, 492. Wolfgang Plath, "André," *The New Grove Dictionary of Music and Musicians*, eds. Stanley Sadie, John Tyrrell, and Laura Macy (London: Macmillan, 2001), vol. I, 618–621.

35. Charles Humphries and William C. Smith, *Music Publishing in the British Isles: From the Beginning until the Middle of the Nineteenth Century: A Dictionary of Engravers, Printers, Publishers and Music Sellers, with a Historical Introduction* (New York: Barnes & Noble, 1970), 52–53. A. H. André, 33, Dichter and Shapiro, 166.

36. "W. A. Mozart's Klavier-Conzerte in Partitur . . ." [1852–1859].

37. Wolfe, *Early American Music Engraving and Publishing*, 45–47. Krummel and Sadie, 177. I am indebted to Dr. Ronald R. Kidd at Purdue University for information on the Cockes; the Bremo music is in Swemm Library, the College of William and Mary.

38. Dorothy Turner Potter, "The Cultural Influences of W. A. Mozart's Music in Philadelphia: 1786–1861," (Ph.D. dissertation, University of Virginia, 2000), 348–352.

39. Wolfe, *Secular Music*, vol. II, 610, 612–613, 629–630.

40. Philadelphia members were G. André, James N. Beck, J. E. Gould, Lee & Walker, Edward L. Walker, and Winner & Schuster. Dena J. Epstein, "Music Publishing in the Age of Piracy: the Board of Music Trade and its Catalogue," *Notes: The Quarterly Journal of the Music Library Association* 31 (September 1974): 10–12.

Republican Jazz?

Symbolism, Arts Policy, and the New Right

BURTON W. PERETTI

American political history seems to be curiously devoid of musical sub-currents. The resolute practicality and legalistic nature of the U. S. political tradition seems to drive out any clear association with the nation's expressive culture. Ulysses S. Grant's alleged comment, "I know only two tunes—one is 'Yankee Doodle' and the other isn't," epitomizes the general situation. Upon closer inspection, of course, one can detect scattered evidence of interaction between the two fields. Among presidents, for example, Thomas Jefferson played the violin, Harry Truman and Richard Nixon the piano; young Warren Harding dabbled in all of the brass instruments in the Marion, Ohio town band; and Bill Clinton blows riffs on his saxophone. The White House, furthermore, has been a notable venue for music for at least a century and a half, and far-flung martial and ceremonial events have inspired a rich tradition of performances.[1] Is it possible, though, for historians to make the leap from these incidental musical trends to an understanding of intellectual and ideological connections between American political and music history?

As a historian of jazz, I have tried to connect the music's history with general trends in American history, including race relations, economics, class divisions, and urbanization. Other historians have begun to connect jazz with general political ideologies. In recent social histories of 1930s swing music, especially, David Stowe and Paul Lopes have pioneered the exploration of jazz history's interaction with partisan politics, with a particular focus on the pro-New Deal and Democratic orientation of many swing musicians in the 1930s and early 1940s.[2] These promising findings suggested that jazz might have evolved a basic political identity in its big-band swing years, and that relationships between partisan ideologies and the ideological content of jazz musicians' and listeners' activities might have been established.

In looking for such relationships, one might think that because jazz is such a notably biracial music, and because beginning in the 1930s it brought unprecedented prominence to important African American musicians, that jazz's political profile would be particularly evident in the evolution of civil rights policy. Certainly many black musicians, such as Duke Ellington and Teddy Wilson, were active crusaders for racial equality, and the white jazz promoter John Hammond consciously wedded his musical activities with his NAACP work.[3] Some black musicians, such as Wilson, even championed a socialist critique of American racial oppression.

However, for the most part, as Paul Lopes has shown in his recent study *The Rise of a Jazz Art World*, jazz's New Deal partisans were much more cautious. Like Franklin Roosevelt's Democratic party itself, big-band Democrats such as Benny Goodman and Artie Shaw largely endorsed the New Deal as a vehicle for the assimilation of working-class Americans of recent immigrant stock into the mainstream of U. S. society and economy. The more radical notion of racial equality was hotly debated by the mostly white critics who publicized swing, but only as it pertained to conditions within the jazz world itself. Thus, the elimination of Jim Crow in society did not become a rallying cry among jazz aficionados, but critics eagerly explored the issue of whether black musicians "naturally" played jazz better than whites.[4]

In the 1940s, again, while far-left jazz writers such as Sidney Finkelstein found radical implications in the music's development, the vast majority of commentators in jazz either endorsed Roosevelt's mildly left-wing New Deal and wartime agendas or remained silent. World War II and the ensuing Cold War, of course, dampened even this moderate liberalism throughout the United States, and the cautious politics of the jazz world in the late 1940s and 1950s fully conformed to this. Critics such as André Hodeir and Marshall Stearns set about to define the safe "mainstream" of jazz history and filed off any of the sharp ideological edges that the history of the music might have exhibited.[5] Young bebop artists such as Dizzy Gillespie did express an aggressive black nationalism, but at midcentury these views—like socialism and communism—were outside the mainstream political spectrum and won jazz no general political cachet. By contrast, though, the civil rights movement of the 1950s and 1960s brought black liberationist traditions and undercurrents of the left-wing political tradition into the mainstream discourse. Jazz artists such as Abbey Lincoln, Jackie McLean, and Charles Mingus put their music to the service of the cause of equality and racial pride. Much of the 1960s jazz avant-garde became associated with a cultural politics that were far more radical than the welfare-state liberalism of Lyndon B. Johnson's Great Society agenda.

This background serves as a preface to this essay, an initial and tentative inquiry into the possible existence of a historical relationship between jazz and the most important post-1960s political trend in the United States: the conservative revival. By "conservative" I mean specifically the "New Right" ideology that has overtaken the Republican Party since the early 1970s. This ideology, opposed to the welfare state and social tolerance and in favor of aggressive military action and so-called "traditional" social and religious values, was prophesied in 1964 by Barry Goldwater in his losing presidential campaign, honed by Richard Nixon's "Southern strategy" designed to win over conservative white Democrats, and reached increasingly definitive forms in the presidencies of Ronald Reagan, George H. W. Bush, and George W. Bush. Their ascendency to the White House, of course, attests to the electoral success of the New Right in the late twentieth century.

One avenue into the history of this relationship would be to explore the political conservatism of certain jazz musicians themselves. For this purpose, an obvious example would be Lionel Hampton, the great swing vibraphonist and bandleader. While he is best remembered for his role in that signal event in the chronicle of jazz liberalism—the creation in 1936 of the first publicly integrated jazz combo, the Benny Goodman Quartet—Hampton was a life-long Republican. Inheriting his parents' Reconstruction-style loyalty to the party of Lincoln, he scorned Democrats for "us[ing] blacks just to get their vote" and for "picking my pocket" every year at income tax time. In the 1940s Hampton campaigned for Richard Nixon in California during his first race for the House of Representatives and for Prescott Bush during his successful quest for a Senate seat from Connecticut, and he became a lifelong acquaintance of Nixon, Bush, and the latter's son George H. W. Bush. His orchestra played at inaugural galas for Dwight Eisenhower, Richard Nixon, and Ronald Reagan (as well as for Democrat Harry S. Truman). In 1981 Reagan held a White House concert featuring and honoring Hampton, who then received a Kennedy Center Honor the next evening.

Off of the bandstand Hampton was not shy about exploiting his government connections to advance a second career in real estate. His particular area was the development of public housing projects, a Great Society-era initiative which he easily reconciled with his conservative dedication to self-help in the black community. In the 1960s New York's Republican governor Nelson A. Rockefeller (for whom Hampton also campaigned) assisted the bandleader's first effort, the Lionel Hampton Houses in Harlem, and the state also helped to build the Gladys Hampton Houses (named after his late wife) in the same region. Again in the 1980s, Hampton frankly recalled, "with a Republican administration in the White House, I was hoping to get some federal money." He succeeded, and built the Hampton Hills housing project in Newark, New Jersey. Hampton served as a delegate to a few Republican national conventions as well.[6]

Among black jazz musicians, though, Lionel Hampton's story is striking in its uniqueness. From a very early age, Hampton's life moved forward on parallel sets of tracks, involving music and ideologically informed entrepreneurialism. While Hampton is certainly representative of a small black bourgeoisie that has remained loyal to Republican conservatism, he cannot be considered a politically influential force within jazz circles.

As we look at the issue of jazz and conservatism from the perspective of the early twenty-first century, it may seem that an ideological trend in jazz of more recent vintage may be detected in the assertion of "traditional" personal and professional values by some musicians and cultural critics, notably trumpeter/composer Wynton Marsalis and drummer/critic Stanley Crouch. Marsalis, for example, finds it "racist" when a European journalist asks him, "why don't you rap?" and describes his music as "an alternative reality to the prevalent stereotype." The musician also saw his sextet (now disbanded) as an alternative to the avant-garde and fusion movements in jazz. He sympathizes with fusion musicians who in the 1970s had to "accommodate" to the popularity of rock music, but laments their criticisms of his sextet. These musicians and other "social critics," in Marsalis's view, "were even threatened because we dressed up when we played, we tried to be clean." While the trumpeter is fully conscious of the legacy and persistence of racism, he accentuates the positive in American society: "there is a sense of struggle and energy, the energy of possibility, the energy of improvement and ascension." Crouch, similarly, argued in 1994 that antiracism has reached a critical mass of sorts in contemporary America, paving the way for positive African American role models in the ranks of new jazz musicians barely out of their teens:

> Nicholas Payton, Abraham Burton, Ali Jackson, and Kevin Hays don't walk around with their shoes untied, their pants falling off, caps sideways. Karen Farmer, Vanessa Rubin, and Renee Rosnes never give the impression they're turning tricks on the side. They represent a movement of young people who aren't trying to emulate the bad taste of pop stars and gangster rappers.

"They suffer no feeling of a generation gap" with older musicians—nor, Crouch implies, do they suffer from any of the restrictions imposed on other young black people in the Reagan-Bush era.[7]

Marsalis's and Crouch's scorn for post-1960 experimental jazz and its political messages and their championing of what they consider to be jazz's traditional bedrock values of self-discipline, respect for tradition, and dedication to professionalism have been associated by some commentators with political conservatives' calls for personal responsibility and individualism and their rejection of identity politics and of collective social action. The jazz traditionalism of the 1980s and 1990s has met with vociferous criticism from veterans of the 1950s and 1960s jazz scene. Avant-garde musicians complain strenuously that Marsalis and his colleagues have coopted all of the public attention and commercial opportunities from them. One critic of jazz traditionalism, the saxophonist Michael Zilber, goes as far as to label Stanley Crouch "the David Horowitz of jazz criticism" and Wynton Marsalis "the Ronald Reagan of jazz." The latter's tight control over Jazz at Lincoln Center, now the most prominent stage for jazz music in the nation, alienates partisans of "post-Coltrane" improvisation. One such partisan calls Marsalis a member "of the jazz world's right wing" and laments his "angry defensiveness" in response to critics, a posture which masks his power to deny avant-garde musicians access to the Lincoln Center stage.[8]

Neoconservative style and attitudes in jazz, of course, have a direct relevance to our topic. The association of jazz with particular social values, for better or worse, makes it a political tool. I will return to the content of these recent musical and social ideologies at the conclusion of this essay. First, though, it is necessary to explore the uses to which post-1960s politicians associated with the New Right—rather than musicians who happen to be politically or socially conservative—have put jazz, as both a symbol and as a beneficiary of their government policies.

First, the symbolism. The place to start is on 29 April 1969, during one of the most paradoxical evenings ever to transpire at the White House. On that night president Richard M. Nixon threw a lavish and joyous party for Duke Ellington, celebrating the composer and bandleader's seventieth birthday and awarding him the Presidential Medal of Freedom. For the first time, an all-star roster of jazz greats appeared at the nation's house: Earl Hines, J. J. Johnson, Clark Terry, Louie Bellson, Dave Brubeck, Gerry Mulligan, Paul Desmond, Billy Taylor, Jim Hall, and others. Willie the Lion Smith and Dizzy Gillespie were guests who later joined in jam sessions. Anecdotes of this evening abound: Ellington kissing the president four times, explaining that he was planting "one [kiss] for each cheek"; Vice President Spiro T. Agnew playing "Sophisticated Lady" on the piano; Ellington dancing with Nixon's secretary Rose Mary Woods, later of Watergate fame; Fatha Hines joining the president after the party in the upstairs quarters and swapping tales about boyhood piano lessons.[9]

The inspiration of the evening has been contested by historians and participants. Conventional chronicles of the Nixon years have labeled it an early, atypical, and characteristically cynical effort by the administration to feign Republican interest in African Americans. Nixon's actual disinterest, this version goes, was reflected in his alleged remark to H. R. Haldeman that all of the jazz greats should be invited—"like Guy Lombardo." In a scathing study of race and the presidency which he titled *Nixon's Piano*, Kenneth O'Reilly contrasts the Ellington evening with another White House social event less than a year later, the 1970 edition of the annual dinner held by the Gridiron Club (a Washington correspondents' group). On this night Nixon and Agnew, seated at baby grand pianos, played "Dixie" and engaged in southern-drawl banter (many thought it was mocking black dialect, a la *Amos 'n' Andy*) about a currently hot Beltway topic, the Administration's "Southern Strategy" for wooing white conservative voters away from the Democratic party.[10] Even before the Ellington evening, as O'Reilly and many others have shown, Nixon regarded average urban blacks with contempt and used code words in his speeches that stoked white voters' hostility to ghetto uprisings and the demands of civil rights activists. Nixon's main contact with African Americans, in fact, seemed to have been during White House *soireés*, when celebrity supporters such as Pearl Bailey, Sammy Davis Jr., Lionel Hampton, and James Brown hugged and traded kind words with the president. In this analysis, then, the Ellington evening is viewed negatively, as a damning exception to the general course of Nixon's (and conservatives') relationship with jazz and with African Americans in general.

However, alternative interpretations of the evening have been presented. One black musician in attendance exulted the next day that "Nixon did something no one else has ever done—this is the first time an American black man was honored in the White House." The most thoroughgoing and positive interpretation of Nixon's cultural politics has been presented by Leonard Garment, who variously served as the president's law partner, aide, and personal attorney. Garment, a Brooklyn native and Democrat who had dabbled in socialism as a youth and had once pursued a career as a reed musician—briefly playing with Woody Herman's orchestra in 1944—became a successful Manhattan attorney. In the mid-1960s he became Nixon's law partner and confidant. In early 1969, at the president-elect's request, Garment came to Washington as an informal advisor. In this capacity, as he recalls in his delightful autobiography, *Crazy Rhythm*, he was encouraged by Willis Conover, the jazz-loving music director of the Voice of America, to propose a birthday dinner for Ellington at the White House.[11]

Garment's recollections of the evening's planning and execution feature none of the cynicism and opportunism that other chroniclers have highlighted. Instead, he accentuates the positive: "it was one of the happiest, most relaxed public occasions of Richard Nixon's life." Garment's view of his own role as a Nixon advisor, though, is not free of cynicism; he called it "a job out of . . . the distant swamplands of Republican politics, such as civil rights, Jews, and cultural affairs, activities that no sane and reasonably ambitious person in my position would have touched in 1969." He became an official White House aide a few weeks after the

Ellington evening, acting as a counselor and fix-it man on a variety of issues. Later the president's personal attorney during Watergate, Garment saw plenty of the administration's dark side (and though his memoirs do not make the connection, the desperate unhappiness and eventual suicide of his wife of thirty-five years must have been exacerbated by the pressures of the Nixon era).[12]

Revealingly, though, Garment notes that Nixon largely showed him "his more admirable qualities, his resourcefulness, his flexibility, his curiosity and willingness to explore multiple perspectives of a situation." (Would that other Americans, even other members of the White House staff, had been able to witness these admirable qualities more often.) In Garment's view, the Ellington evening was a chapter in his own ongoing effort to stimulate the president's interest in jazz and in the other arts. In this pursuit he was strongly motivated by his perception that Nixon, in fact, "was a closet aesthete [who] had strong, traditional views about what was good or bad in painting, music, architecture, and writing."[13]

True as that may have been, a full study of Nixon's motives would undoubtedly show a wider array of influences that led him to endorse an unprecedented government promotion of jazz and other arts. Nixon certainly was familiar with precedents such as the State Department-sponsored international goodwill tours by the Dizzy Gillespie, Benny Goodman, and Louis Armstrong bands, which took place during the Eisenhower Administration, in which he served as vice president. In addition, Nixon's main Republican presidential rival in the 1960s, Nelson Rockefeller, had pioneered support of the arts in New York state by setting up a council and a budget for grants and arts promotion. Arts policy was one of a number of areas in which Nixon coopted Rockefeller's free-spending approach to problem-solving under the guise of a conservative "new federalism." The governor's chief arts administrator (and erstwhile mistress), Nancy Hanks, would also work in Washington for Nixon. Nixon's approach to arts policy reflected his unique brand of political deviousness. An activist by nature, eager to coopt initiatives and control from the largely liberal northeastern economic and cultural elites whom he despised, Nixon expanded and diversified the mission of the National Endowment of the Arts (NEA).[14] Leonard Garment was entrusted with the early stages of the task.

The NEA had been founded in 1965 as a minor appendage of Lyndon B. Johnson's Great Society. LBJ—whom no one ever accused of being a closet aesthete—ignored this particular creation of his, and the NEA grants program struggled along on tiny annual budgets of about $6 million. Beginning in 1969, Garment—guided by his well-connected fellow arts advocates, Michael Straight and Nancy Hanks—persuaded Nixon to double the NEA's budget, and then to double it again, and again—and again. Nixon's last budget, for fiscal year 1975, proposed $90 million in grants to artists, institutions, and promoters of the lively and stationary arts. By then Hanks, director of the NEA under Nixon and Gerald R. Ford, ruled over a small empire that dispersed over 5,000 grants a year. As Alice Goldfarb Marquis and other observers have argued, this ballooning government commitment to the arts had several roots: Nixon's desire to coopt and outmaneuver the left-leaning arts establishment and the Democrat-led Congress; Garment's lobbying abilities; and also the wild popularity of the grants in communities across the American "heartland," where enjoyable artistic byproducts especially gave the more affluent Republican voters in those areas a rosier view of government planning and spending. Nixon probably also earned some gratitude in the inner cities through his patronage of community arts, dance, and music in those areas (even though he made no use of that gratitude, and apparently learned nothing from it).[15]

Jazz's place in this rising tide of arts funding was not especially prominent, but it was secure. In a reversal of the usual practice in Washington (especially regarding the arts), the hard cash and Beltway influence Nixon bestowed on jazz far exceeded the lip service he paid to it (via such gestures as the Ellington evening). In 1969, at the behest of Leonard Garment and Willis Conover, a panel of critics and musicians (including Bill Evans and Milt Hinton) began to formulate an NEA jazz program. The result was a 1970 pilot project that awarded 30 grants—to individuals and school—totaling $20,050. This was a minuscule portion of the $2.5 million music program, which spent forty times as much on large grants to opera companies and even more on aid to symphony orchestras. (This fact may have demonstrated that Nixon's tastes were traditional indeed.) By 1972, though, the annual jazz program was dispensing over a hundred grants costing $242,925, ranging from small awards to composers and students to large ones for Antioch College's jazz department ($21,500) and the service organization Jazz Interactions ($21,300, much of which went to an oral history project that paid older musicians to tell their life stories).[16]

In the early 1970s, while Nixon publicly ignored jazz, the music's
future in the federal government was largely determined by struggles for
influence among the growing legions of NEA advisors and bureaucrats.
In 1973 jazz lost a battle, when all of the arts were lumped into a single
grants program that classified awards by recipient types (artists, universities, students, and organizations). The next year, though, the arts' distinct identities were reasserted. Jazz, "folk," and "ethnic" music were
given their own program, largely due to the lobbying efforts of the composer and academician Gunther Schuller and the jazz pianist and composer Billy Taylor. Taylor, meanwhile, was becoming jazz's most visible
lobbyist in Washington, as well as the promoter of the image of jazz as
"America's classical music."[17]

Bureaucratic momentum, rather than ideology, further advanced
jazz's fortunes at the NEA into the late 1970s, beyond the Republican
administrations of Nixon and Ford and into the Democratic era of
Jimmy Carter. In 1981, in Carter's last budget, jazz grant monies reached
a new high of nearly $1.5 million ($1,493,000, to be exact). In that year
performers received up to $15,000 in stipends, and the National Jazz
Foundation—a Washington-based promotion groups largely formed
to serve as a secondary, grass-roots dispenser of jazz grants—received
$121,000. The general explosion of government jobs programs in the
seventies provided other support for jazz musicians and other artists. As
Steven Dubin has shown, by the end of the decade the Comprehensive
Employment and Training Act (CETA, which became law in 1973)
supplied $200 million annually—nearly double the NEA's total grant
funding—for the training and employment of all kinds of artists.[18]

As Garment (who continued to advise the NEA), Alice Goldfarb
Marquis, and others have noted, the explosion in arts funding contained
the seeds of its own demise, as the sheer number of grants made the selection process increasingly indiscriminate. While the NEA's eclectic patronage of the arts scene won it wide grass-roots support, it also resulted in
grants to frivolous or intentionally shocking avant-garde projects that,
when publicized, threatened to undo the consensus for federal arts support. Thus, when Joan Mondale, wife of Carter's vice president, lobbied
for an even more comprehensive federal arts policy, she actually com-
pelled NEA administrators and interested members of Congress to admit
that the existing policy was already too intrusive, pouring money annually

into the pockets of increasingly regular beneficiaries and encouraging grant-application gamesmanship among artists and community groups. "Joan of Arts" (as one journalist dubbed Mondale) was stymied, and generally, an ideological argument against arts funding—later a key conservative weapon in the "culture wars"—began to form.[19]

No jazz grants particularly hurt the NEA's image, but it could also be argued, as Alice Marquis has put it, that it "appears questionable . . . whether the endowment's grants . . . have [particularly] enhanced the art form [either]." NEA leaders interviewed by Marquis apparently told her (she has no footnote to substantiate this paragraph) that the well-established "dense professional network" of jazz musicians and promoters functioned just fine without federal guidance and aid.[20] This conclusion begs the question of whether *better* government assistance would have helped jazz—which, despite Marquis's claim, has always been harmed by economic exigencies and public apathy and could have used some patronage, especially in the stagflation-wracked 1970s (which also saw much critical hand-wringing about the possible demise of jazz as an art form). More specifically, the highly inconclusive results of that decade's heavy funding of jazz suggest that no political faction—conservative, liberal, or otherwise—had been able to enlist jazz or to ally it with a larger ideological movement.

In the 1980s conservative politics triumphed, as Ronald Reagan was elected to two presidential terms and succeeded in implementing large components of the New Right agenda. While social and welfare programs suffered deep cuts early in his term in office, though, federal arts funding remained surprisingly steady. While the huge increases of the 1970s were halted, neither did conservatives' calls for the termination of the NEA become a reality. Its new director, Frank Hodsoll, did announce that the endowment's main role now would be to stimulate greater private patronage of the arts. Hodsoll also hoped to use it as a bully pulpit to exhort Americans to reduce their weekly television viewing and to visit museums and concert halls. While jazz in particular did not incur the wrath of conservatives in the early Reagan era, various NEA initiatives showed that the music was viewed as particularly problematic, and that it was a target for reevaluation. In 1983 the endowment spent $50,000 for special "on-site evaluation activity" of its own jazz program.

This evaluation resulted in some curious new trends. Funding for some longtime projects, such as the Jazz Oral History Project, was discontinued, while service organizations (which had many private contacts) received even greater support. In fact, monies for jazz actually kept growing, reaching an all-time annual high in 1984 of $1.777 million. Two new initiatives, though, gave hints of an imminent end to this generosity. First, Hodsoll (with Reagan's blessing) began to emphasize celebratory rituals, such as the annual honors bestowed on legendary performers by the American Film Institute and the Kennedy Center for the Performing Arts, the new National Medal of the Arts—and, beginning in 1983, "Jazz Masters" grants of $20,000 apiece to notable elders in the field. In this sense the Reagan administration was taking its cue from Nixon's Ellington evening, using the arts as a platform for celebrity homage and medal ceremonies. Second, Hodsoll revived the practice of reassigning elements of the jazz program into general categories that put it in direct competition with other genres, for example by putting jazz concert grants into the "festivals" category. In 1985 overall NEA funding began to decline for the first time, suggesting an ideological sea change. The next year Hodsoll sponsored a conference "to examine the field of jazz and consider its future," which resulted in a study that found an enormous and willing potential future audience for the music. Hodsoll's ultimate purpose became clearer, though, in the 1986 NEA annual report, in which he boasted that his recent jazz initiatives "[have] already resulted in new linkages between the commercial and not-for-profit sectors of the jazz world and [have] brought fresh media coverage to the field." In short, he argued that jazz would be able to win over its future mass audience without NEA funding.[21]

By this time almost all of the major jazz names that had helped guide NEA policy in the 1970s were no longer playing advisory roles. (By the end of the decade, Roscoe Mitchell could be considered the only significant jazz musician on the advisory panel, which was dominated by college-level jazz educators.) The jazz program was funded annually at about half a million dollars but seemed utterly adrift; the Jazz Masters program ambled on, seemingly as a sop to older African American musicians (and as of 2004, the awards have never been increased above their initial amount of $20,000).

The George H. W. Bush administration ushered in the troubled tenure of NEA director John Frohnmayer, who was staggered politically by the

Robert Mapplethorpe and Andres Serrano art-show controversies and never recovered. For conservative opponents of government support for the arts, the cultural battle over funding for avant-garde art dovetailed nicely with the tremendous success of Frank Hodsoll's privatization initiative for arts funding. The right-wing assault on the NEA reached its climax in 1995, after Republicans seized control of both houses of Congress for the first time in forty years. The Newt Gingrich-led congressional leadership slashed the endowment's budget by more than forty percent. Since then the NEA's jazz program has limped along, continuing to bestow $20,000 Masters grants with little publicity and aiding the music (as well as the other arts) through block grants to state arts agencies (which made specific federal support for jazz invisible). The present system is a manifestation of Richard Nixon's "new federalism" in classic form, displaying a blend of ideological commitment to ineffectively low funding[22] and pointless symbolic gestures that neither Nixon nor Reagan had dared to attempt in earlier decades. The saxophone-playing Bill Clinton, politically cautious and plagued by scandal, did not effectively reverse this conservative trend. In 1997 congressman John Conyers effected the passage of House Concurrent Resolution 57, which labeled jazz a "national treasure" and encouraged NEA funding that would provide jazz instruction in the nation's schools, but the resolution had no practical effect. The official neglect of jazz continues today under the administration of George W. Bush.[23]

As I mentioned at the outset, this diminution of jazz's governmental profile since the mid-1980s has been accompanied by the rise of a more general cultural assertion of a neoconservative approach to jazz history and performance. Stanley Crouch's celebration of tradition-minded, well-behaved young black musicians such as Wynton Marsalis, Marcus Roberts, and Christian McBride, along with Marsalis's homilies in favor of classic jazz and against avant-garde hip-hop and Ken Burns's heavily hyped traditionalist PBS jazz documentary, have seemed to suggest that America's quintessential outsider music has been coopted into a culture of private patronage, in which social criticism and protest have been muted and tradition-worshiping passivity has been encouraged. Crouch and Marsalis espouse no political affiliation, and the Republican party's continuing inability to win over black voters suggests that black cultural neoconservatism (of any kind) has not inspired an embrace by many blacks toward political conservatism. If anything, neoconservatism in jazz seems like yet another opening to black voters that Republicans have failed to exploit. No jazz factions have surrendered themselves fully to the conservative political agenda, and conservatives have not especially embraced jazz as provocatively as Richard Nixon embraced Duke Ellington on that April evening in 1969.

At the same time, though, the current total neglect of jazz in the arts policy debate and its neutral position in the public sphere also indicates the success of the privatization of jazz. The dominance of private funding is symbolized by Marsalis's sumptuous fiefdom, Jazz at Lincoln Center, which will soon be ensconced in a palatial new home in the AOL/Time Warner complex on Columbus Circle in Manhattan. Privatization, though, has had little impact to date on the public as a whole, which remains woefully ignorant of jazz traditions (despite even the impact of Ken Burns's well-intentioned boosterism) and disdainful of jazz CDs and radio broadcasts. The lack of any counterweight to the cruel effect on jazz of the mass-oriented private marketplace, as well as the neutralization of any public forum for socially conscious jazz artists, represents what is, for now, the true triumph of conservative arts policy.

Notes

1. See Elise K. Kirk, *Music at the White House: a History of the American Spirit* (Urbana: University of Illinois Press, 1986).

2. David Stowe, *Swing Changes: Big-Band Jazz in New Deal America* (Cambridge: Harvard University Press, 1994); Paul Lopes, *The Rise of a Jazz Art World* (Cambridge, U.K.: Cambridge University Press, 2000).

3. On Wilson see James Lincoln Collier, *Duke Ellington* (New York: Oxford University Press, 1987), 139–42; see also John Hammond with Irving Townsend, *John Hammond on Record* (New York: Ridge Press, 1977).

4. Lopes, *The Rise of a Jazz Art World*, 123–25; see also Stowe, *Swing Changes*, introduction, and Lewis A. Erenberg, *Swingin' the Dream: Big Band Jazz and the Rebirth of American Culture* (Chicago: University of Chicago Press, 1998), especially chapter 5.

5. Sidney W. Finkelstein, *Jazz: A People's Music* (New York: Citadel Press, 1948); André Hodeir, *Jazz: Its Evolution and Essence*, trans. David Noakes (1956; reprint, New York: Da Capo, 1975); Marshall W. Stearns, *The Story of Jazz* (New York: Oxford University Press, 1956).

6. For the preceding two paragraphs: Lionel Hampton and James Haskins, *Hamp: An Autobiography* (New York: Warner Books, 1989), 156, 167, 169 passim.

7. Wynton Marsalis and Carl Vigeland, *Jazz in the Bittersweet Blues of Life* (New York: Da Capo, 2001), 151–52, 181–82, 236; Stanley Crouch, *The All-American Skin Game, or, The Decoy of Race* (New York: Pantheon, 1995), 191.

8. Michael Zilber, "*J'Accuse*, Burns and Marsalis," [2002] <www.allaboutjazz.com/birdlives/bl-94.htm> (visited 29 March 2003); "Rant: Lincoln Center Redux," [1995] <junior.apk.net/~hoon/8cMuso.html> (visited 25 February 2004).

9. Leonard Garment, *Crazy Rhythm* (New York: Times Books, 1997), 171–73. In 1931 Ellington had visited the Hoover White House as part of a delegation of black celebrities, and during the Kennedy and Johnson administrations assorted jazz combos had performed at the mansion. In 2002 the soundtrack recording of the 1969 White House concert was finally released by Blue Note, #35249. See also Leonard Garment, "A New Revelation From the Nixon White House," *New York Times*, 25 August 2002, II: 23, 25.

10. Kenneth O'Reilly, *Nixon's Piano: Presidents and Racial Politics from Washington to Clinton* (New York: Free Press, 1995), 3–7, 322; H. R. Haldeman, *The Haldeman Diaries: Inside the Nixon White House* (New York: Putnam's, 1994), 31.

11. *Washington Post*, 1 May 1969, quoted in Stephen E. Ambrose, *Nixon: The Triumph of a Politician, 1962–1972* (New York: Simon and Schuster, 1989), 247; Garment, *Crazy Rhythm*, 146–49, 171; Garment, "A New Revelation," 23.

12. Garment, *Crazy Rhythm*, 151, 171, 325–33.

13. Garment, *Crazy Rhythm*, 163.

14. On jazz and 1950s cultural diplomacy see Alyn Shipton, *Groovin' High: The Life of Dizzy Gillespie* (New York: Oxford University Press, 1999), 266, 280–85, and Walter L. Hixson, *Parting the Curtain: Propaganda, Culture, and the Cold War, 1945–1961* (New York: St. Martin's, 1997), 115–19; Alice Goldfarb Marquis, *Art Lessons: Learning From the Rise and Fall of Public Arts Funding* (New York: BasicBooks, 1995), 42–43; Bruce J. Schulman, *The Seventies* (New York: Da Capo, 2001), 27–29.

15. Marquis, *Art Lessons*, chapters 2–3; Garment, *Crazy Rhythm*, 164–169, 213–16.

16. National Endowment for the Arts, *Annual Report* (Washington, D.C.: Government Printing Office) (henceforth *NEA Report*): 1970, 1972, n.p.; on the Smithsonian Jazz Oral History Project see Ron Welburn, "Toward Theory and Method with the Jazz Oral History Project," *Black Music Research Journal* 7 (Spring 1986): 79–95.

17. *1973 NEA Report*, n.p.; on Billy Taylor see Michael Mooney, *The Ministry of Culture: Connections Among Art, Money, and Politics* (New York: Wyndham, 1980), 77, 250.

18. *1981 NEA Report*, n.p.; Steven C. Dubin, *Bureaucratizing the Muse: Public Funds and the Cultural Worker* (Chicago: University of Chicago Press, 1987), 17–18, 52–54.

19. Marquis, *Art Lessons*, 106–30; Garment, *Crazy Rhythm*, 169; Mooney, *The Ministry of Culture*, chapter 2.

20. Marquis, *Art Lessons*, 122.

21. For the preceding two paragraphs: *NEA Reports*, 1983–1986, n.p.; *1986 NEA Report*, 3; Harold Horowitz, *The American Jazz Music Audience* (Washington: National Jazz Service Organization, 1986).

22. Total arts-agency spending by the fifty states peaked in 2001 at $447 million, but by 2003 appropriation had declined to $354 million, or average spending of $1.22 per capita. "State Arts Agency Legislative Appropriations Down," National Association of State Arts Agencies <http://www.nasaaarts.org/nasaanews/approp_down.shtml> (visited 9 April 2003).

23. John Frohnmayer, *Leaving Town Alive: Confessions of an Arts Warrior* (Boston: Houghton Mifflin, 1993); on the Clinton-Gingrich years see Jane Alexander, *Command Performance: An Actress in the Theater of Politics* (New York: Public Affairs, 2000). Conyer's resolution proposal, House of Representatives, 12 March 1997, is reprinted on <www.thomas.loc.gov> (visited 24 April 2004). In 2004 President George W. Bush proposed a 20 percent increase in the 2005 NEA budget to fund a carefully defined "American Masterpieces" initiative, "arts presentations and educational programming to introduce citizens to great works of art of all forms, including paintings, music, dance, and literature." Anne Marie Borrego, "Arts and Humanities Endowments Would Get Big Increases," *Chronicle of Higher Education* (13 February 2004), 5.

Progressive Ideals for the Opera Stage?

George W. Chadwick's The Padrone
and Frederick S. Converse's The Immigrants

CHARLES FREEMAN

Music scholarship has often treated American art music of the nine-teenth and early twentieth centuries as a poor stepchild to later, more overtly "American" classical idioms, such as the populist style of Aaron Copland, the jazz-inflected idiom of George Gershwin, or modernist styles of composers such as John Cage. Comments such as those found in the fourth edition of *A History of Western Music,* long a standard text for the teaching of music history, are typical. The body of composers active in the United States in the late nineteenth century is first faulted for not participating in the wave of nationalist musical composition exemplified by such composers as the Bohemian Antonín Dvořák or the Russian "Mighty Five" composers. Two composers of that generation, Horatio Parker (1863–1919) and Edward MacDowell (1860–1908), are discussed perfunctorily (notably, the MacDowell composition that is chosen for a closer examination is his so-called "Indian" Suite, the only one in which he makes use of American folk material) before the nar-rative hurries on to a more extended discussion of "the first important distinctively American composer," Charles Ives (1874–1954).[1]

By defining musical Americanism narrowly in terms of chronology and musical style, scholars are prone to overlook works that embrace an American identity in other terms. This essay examines two operas by composers George W. Chadwick and Frederick S. Converse, both asso-ciated with a Romantic generation of musicians active around the turn of the twentieth century. By examining Chadwick's *The Padrone* (1912) and Converse's *The Immigrants* (1914) in correlation with the history and politics of the American Progressive Era, the two operas are understood as thoroughly American works, each with a distinct response to a particular historical phenomenon.

Contemporaneity and Politics in Libretti

Both of these operas invite a particular scrutiny due to their contemporary settings. Chadwick's manuscript of *The Padrone* indicates that the story is set in the "summer of the present day," while Converse's manuscript indicates a setting in the 1910s (the opera was written mostly in 1912 and 1913).[2]

This choice of setting is quite unusual in opera, and particularly in American opera of the early twentieth century. From the earliest days of opera, plots tended to be taken from ancient mythology; only infrequently have composers and librettists chosen contemporary settings or subject matter. American composers were no different; typical plots were taken from ancient legend, such as John Knowles Paine's *Azara* (1901) or Horatio Parker's *Mona* (1912), or fantasy stories (Converse's *Iolan, or The Pipe of Desire*, from 1911). Some composers and librettists did choose subjects from American history, such as Victor Herbert's *Natoma* and Converse's *The Sacrifice*, both from 1911. Both, however, were set in the nineteenth century. *The Padrone* and *The Immigrants* were in fact unique in being composed and set in the same time period.

How did Chadwick and librettist David Stevens, or Converse and librettist Percy MacKaye, make these works contemporary? What markers of modern life and thought can be found in these dramas? The musicologist can only answer these questions with the aid of the historian's work. The plots of both works include elements—characters, ideas, institutions—that can be related directly to the America of the 1910s, when read against the backdrop of scholarship concerning the sometimes-troublesome period of American history known as the Progressive Era. This study will demonstrate this approach to the contemporaneity of these operas, identifying those plot elements that resonate with significant themes and subjects in Progressive Era scholarship.

The Padrone

The libretto of *The Padrone* was written by David K. Stevens (1860–1946), based on a scenario by Chadwick. The libretto was Stevens's first. He would later collaborate with Chadwick on *Love's Sacrifice* (1923), as well as with Victor Herbert (*The Madcap Duchess*, 1913) and Henry Hadley (*Azora, Daughter of Montezuma*, 1917).

Act I of *The Padrone* opens in an Italian restaurant owned by the padrone Catani. A padrone or "boss" was a person, generally male and usually an Italian immigrant himself, who acted as a broker for fellow Italians immigrating to the States.[3] Catani has made his fortune by brokering the passage of numerous Italians to the United States; the newly arrived immigrants are thereafter indebted to Catani and end up working for him many years, possibly even a lifetime, to pay that debt.

In the restaurant are a number of Catani's subjects employed in the restaurant, as well as many customers, including a party playing dominoes at one table. Francesca, a waitress, flirts with Dino, who, as he proudly announces, has already won "three games tonight," only to be reprimanded by Marta, her mother, who manages the restaurant for Catani. Unconcerned, Francesca lets slip to Dino that Marietta, her sister, is to be married. Dino questions Marta and finds out that Marietta is to wed Marco, her lover from the old country, as soon as his ship arrives the next day.

Francesca encourages Dino and the other customers to remain until Marietta arrives, in order to wish her well. Dino asks Francesca about Marco, and she reveals that she and Marco had been lovers in Trapani before his affections turned to Marietta. This revelation is cut short by Marietta's arrival.

Marietta has been in Catani's employ as a tambourine girl partnered with the organ grinder Giuseppe. Unbeknownst to Catani, she has been setting aside part of her meager earnings to pay Marco's passage to the United States, in order that he not be indebted to Catani.[4] As she enters, disposing of her tambourine, she sings wearily of the day's work and declares it her last. At this Marta scolds her, but Marietta is undeterred; her mind, heart, and soul are consumed with the wedding the next day. To the gathered customers she announces her wedding, and the crowd sings her a festive toast. Marta gathers up Marietta's earnings for the evening as Catani enters.

Catani is dumbfounded at mention of the wedding; he has had no inkling of Marietta's wedding plans, and has in fact been planning to take Marietta as his bride. Marta at last reveals Marietta's impending wedding, which provokes Catani to a rage. He checks himself, though, and orders everyone out of the restaurant; he wants to interrogate Marietta alone. Marietta rebuffs Catani's alternating threats and pleadings and then leaves, leaving Catani stunned and vowing to make Marietta his at any cost.

Francesca re-enters, and Catani presses her for information about Marco. Francesca reveals not only her past with Marco but also his recent imprisonment in Trapani. Catani hatches a plan to thwart the wedding by having Francesca reveal Marco's prison record to American immigration officials; Marco would then be forced to return to Trapani, leaving Catani free to claim Marietta as his own. He wins Francesca's reluctant cooperation by offering to pay for her return to Trapani to woo Marco.

Act II takes place at the dock, where Italian immigrants waiting for their arriving loved ones mingle with upper-class tourists, dock workers, and immigration officials. While Marietta looks for Marco, Catani arrives, bearing a letter that admits Marietta and her family to the immigration processing area, ostensibly the sooner for Marietta to greet Marco. Marietta is suspicious, but Catani claims to have accepted Marietta's decision. At last Marco appears, and the happy couple sings an extended love duet. Catani goads the jealous Francesca to betrayal. When Marco presents his papers (bearing an assumed name), Francesca steps forward and denounces him as a fraud and felon. Marco is apprehended and returned to the ship.

Remorseful, Francesca admits to Marietta that Catani provoked her betrayal. Marietta, stunned and somewhat maddened, takes a knife left behind by the chief immigration inspector and stabs Catani. He expires, calling for a priest, just before the wedding party returns with the priest who was to wed Marietta and Marco; the wedding party reacts to the scene in horror as the curtain falls.

The Immigrants

Frederick Converse's two final stage works, *Beauty and the Beast* and *The Immigrants*, were created in collaboration with the noted playwright and poet Percy MacKaye. The scenario was Converse's own, inspired by a scene he witnessed during a trip to Italy in 1909, according to Converse's daughter, Mrs. Junius S. Morgan.[5]

MacKaye sought out Converse as a collaborator in 1905, asking him to compose the music for MacKaye's play *Jeanne d'Arc*.[6] The pair eventually collaborated on two masque productions, *Sanctuary, a Bird Masque* and *The Masque of St. Louis*, and even on a film score, *Puritan Passions*, based on MacKaye's stage play *The Scarecrow*, in addition to the two operas.[7] MacKaye also adapted his earlier play *The Canterbury Pilgrims* (1903) into a libretto for Reginald DeKoven (also titled *The Canterbury Pilgrims*, 1917), and wrote the libretto for the same composer's *Rip van Winkle* (1920).

The plot of *The Immigrants* unfolds over three acts, in which the setting moves from an Italian peasant village to a ship bound for New York to a slum in New York City. In Act I, the villagers are celebrating a feast day, singing and dancing in the village square, while the American artist Noel works at his easel. The feast is interrupted by police, intent on collecting forty lire in taxes owed by the old peasant farmer Sandro. He cannot pay, and the carabinieri are about to carry him off to prison when Noel intervenes, giving the soldiers the money for Sandro's tax, plus enough for "drinks for two" as Noel scornfully says.[8] Sandro, his daughter Lisetta, and her lover Giuseppe express their gratitude to Noel, believing he must be a rich fellow, but Noel portrays himself as a poor artist who just sold a sketch. He shows them his current project; to their surprise, it is a painting of Maria, Sandro's older daughter, praying in the church for her betrothed, Giovanni, imprisoned for his debt. As the family goes into the church to see Maria, another American interrupts Noel; he is Scammon, the unscrupulous commission agent selling steerage cabin space to poor Italians seeking to go to America. Scammon sees Noel's portrait of Maria and steals it when Noel leaves. Maria appears, nearly crazed with grief, despairing that Giovanni has not come. Noel goes to the prison to obtain Giovanni's release. Meanwhile, Scammon puts on his show, a slightly ludicrous parade of donkey carts featuring trinkets of the Statue of Liberty and a float also depicting the Statue. Maria and the newly freed Giovanni, along with the rest of the family, are finally persuaded to leave Italy for America, despite Noel's warnings that all is not as rosy as Scammon claims. Scammon is even willing to provide the family's tickets for free. Act I ends in celebration as the family and many others make ready to leave for America.

Act II takes place on board a ship about to arrive at New York harbor. As the immigrants gaze out over the scene, Scammon reveals his true intentions to Maria. Since Giovanni has been in prison, immigration officials will not allow him into the United States. He then attempts to persuade Maria to stay in New York, in a luxurious apartment to be provided by Scammon; he can no longer conceal his desire for her, and kisses her forcibly. Noel appears and a struggle ensues, and a defeated Scammon leaves. Giovanni returns, having found out he will not be allowed into the country. Poisoned by Scammon's lies, Giovanni believes that Noel has plotted to steal Maria from him; only when he strikes Noel and Noel does not respond is he convinced of Noel's innocence. Noel plans to smuggle Giovanni ashore, but Scammon returns with a number of immigration officers who seize the two men as the fog lifts and all the immigrants prepare to disembark under the gaze of the Statue of Liberty.

Act III opens on a grim scene of urban decay, a grimy slum in New York, with a sweatshop in view to the left. Presently Giuseppe and Sandro enter, lamenting the long hours Maria and Lisetta are working in the sweatshop. The workers begin to come out of that building, with Maria supporting a swooning and obviously heat-sick Lisetta. Lisetta dreams deliriously of the fountain in their Italian village and sings of a boat that sailed the wrong way. The men leave to seek help from a nearby settlement house. While Maria tries to cool and comfort Lisetta, Scammon enters, inebriated. He taunts Maria by comparing their desperate lot with the posh life he had offered her. At last he offers her money to prove his love. Enraged and desperate, Maria stabs Scammon. As he lies motionless on the ground, Maria realizes that they can use Scammon's money to return to Italy. She turns to Lisetta, but the younger sister has died in the heat. Sandro and Giuseppe return, with two surprise companions: Noel and Giovanni, who had been assisted to freedom by the settlement residents. Maria tells of Scammon's advances, her attack on him, and Lisetta's death. Scammon, not yet dead, tries to rise; Giovanni kills him, but not before Scammon has called for police. One officer arrives, but seeing the size of the gathering crowd, he retreats to wait for more support. The crowd grabs for the money, and as the police converge, Giovanni delivers an impassioned speech to the crowd urging them to resist. A scuffle ensues, but ultimately the crowd is dispersed and Giovanni and Maria are led away by the police. As the opera ends, police stand guard over Scammon's body and Sandro prays dumbly over Lisetta. Noel, surveying the scene, concludes the opera with the lament, "O Liberty! When will you cease in darkness to destroy the souls that seek you?"[9]

The Operas and Their Histories

These two operas suffered a common fate: neither was performed in its time. Chadwick submitted *The Padrone* to the Metropolitan Opera in hopes of a performance during the 1913–14 season, but the opera was turned down by Giulio Gatti-Casazza, the artistic director of the Metropolitan, with a note stating that it "was not found suitable for production" there.[10] Music critic Henry E. Krehbiel told Chadwick that Gatti-Casazza disliked the portrayal of Italians in the opera and found the work "too true to life."[11] Andreas Dippel, an opera impresario in Chicago, also received a score of *The Padrone* in early 1913, but his resignation from the opera there ended any hopes of a Chicago staging. Chadwick's frustration with *The Padrone*'s fate is apparent in his diaries; upon completion of the orchestral score of the opera in June 1913, he penned the terse comment, "Glad to get that out of the way."[12]

Converse's opera *The Immigrants* was completed in early 1914. Hopes for a performance of the opera dimmed when the Boston Opera Company, of which Converse was vice president, went out of business that same year. Converse apparently submitted the work in a contest for a performance in Los Angeles, but to no avail. Though the opera was never performed, librettist Percy MacKaye (1875–1956) reworked his libretto into a stage drama, which was performed at the Moorhead State Teachers College (now Moorhead State University) in Minnesota in 1921.

The Padrone was finally performed in a concert version in Waterbury, Connecticut in September 1995 and staged in Boston, Massachusetts in April 1997. To this date, *The Immigrants* has not been sung.

Very few scholarly sources on opera mention *The Padrone* or *The Immigrants*. A pair of annotated catalogues of the operatic repertoire provides some basic information on these works. H. Earle Johnson's *Operas on American Subjects* gives a brief description of *The Padrone* and also acknowledges *The Immigrants*. Frederick Martens's *A Thousand and One Nights of Opera* includes a summary of *The Immigrants*. Martens not only recounts the plot in some detail but also describes the music as "distinctly 'twentieth century'" and even as "a 'jazz opera' in the sense that 'jazz' is occasionally employed as a valid 'American musical idiom.'"[13] Only one brief section of the music, sung by the villain Scammon in Act III, could be considered remotely related to a jazz idiom. Elise Kirk's *American Opera* acknowledges the inaccuracy of this designation, while acknowledging its distinctive subject matter, but attempts to label *The Immigrants* as a verismo opera, which fails to convey fully the uniquely American character of the story.[14]

As a result of the limited scholarly attention paid to these operas, as well as their lack of performance history, the incomplete perception persists that *The Padrone* and *The Immigrants* are purely "European" works, lacking any American character or content. Where musicology falls short, however, the work of historians and scholars of the Progressive Era illuminates these operas, highlighting how these works tap into issues and situations in American life and culture which were current in their time and that still attract scholarly attention today.

A Political and Social Context for the Operas

"Progressivism" and its related terms have proven particularly troublesome to scholars of the era. Nonetheless, as James Connolly has noted, "Like an unpleasant party guest, Progressivism refuses to go away."[15] Connolly also recognizes the discomfiture of scholars with that term, citing it as being too hazy or imprecise.[16] The word is still frequently used to describe the reform-minded political and social impulses of the early twentieth century.

Richard Hofstadter observes one simple reason for the difficulty of defining progressivism. He observes that "so many people could, at some time and on some issue, be called 'Progressive,'" citing the presidential election of 1912 as an instance in which all three major candidates attempted to portray themselves as progressive to some degree.[17]

The progressive impulse is identifiable in numerous movements, from crusades for housing improvements in cities to populist agrarian organizations in rural areas. Among those conditions in American society that provoked calls for reform were the consequences of American industrialization and the increasing power of corporations, the frequent conflict of labor and capital, changing immigration patterns and increasing American resistance, and economic class conflict. Of course, in many cases, these factors are inseparably intertwined.

These various progressive impulses were generated in response to the overwhelming changes in American society over the final third of the nineteenth century. The rapid industrialization of the American economy can be identified as a root cause of many of the changes that sparked calls for reform. Industrialization was accompanied by the emergence of the giant corporation, such as Standard Oil, an economic entity of unparalleled reach and scope that accumulated greater and more sweeping economic power and influence. Corporate policies and decisions affected not only the wealthy owners of business, but also managers, laborers, and consumers from the heart of the city to the remote countryside. Individuals both rich and poor found their economic conditions increasingly determined by the actions of corporate barons in faraway places, rather than under their own control or local influence. This was a frightening and unsettling situation for many Americans.[18]

Corporations and industry also changed the face of the American city. Population became increasingly concentrated in urban areas as workers congregated around the opportunities for employment offered by factories. Manufacturing work was in many ways a deadening experience. The drudgery of routine, dissatisfaction with boring or unfulfilling tasks, and the clock-driven routine of the workday had a numbing effect on the worker's psyche.[19] Urban conditions worsened as cities became more crowded. Persons of widely different backgrounds were thrown together in stressful and difficult situations, competing for jobs and clashing over cultural differences. City governments struggled and sometimes failed to provide the basic necessities of urban life.[20]

Economic downturns in the 1890s produced disastrous results. An economic depression in 1893–1894 threw millions into unemployment; many were homeless and hungry as well.[21] Strikes erupted into violent conflict and were frequently suppressed by government action. President Grover Cleveland ordered federal troops to put down strikers when the Pullman strike of 1894 disrupted rail service in several states.

The seeming breakdown in society and its institutions of the 1890s generated the beginnings of serious and coordinated urban reform. Reform-minded campaigners were able to bring together diverse coalitions to oppose municipal governments that were increasingly seen as corrupt or ineffectual.

Even after the economy began to improve after 1897, the effects of economic depression were not forgotten. Citizens had been troubled when federal and state governments did not act to relieve the worst effects of the economic downturn, and in some cases violently suppressed those who agitated for government intervention. In 1894 Jacob Coxey, an Ohio quarry owner, led an "army" of unemployed workers on a 36-day march from Ohio to Washington to demand a federal public works program. "Coxey's Army" was clubbed down as it approached the Capitol, and Coxey was arrested for walking on the grass.

Walter Rauschenbusch observed the inhumanity of the conditions under which many of the poorest and most oppressed members of society worked. Writing in *Christianity and the Social Crisis* (1907), he argued that the corporate-industrial complex that had come to prominence by the turn of the century made "property the end, and man the means to produce it." He further declared that "to view [people] first of all as labor force [was] civilized barbarism."[22]

Rauschenbusch, a Baptist theologian and minister, represents evangelical Protestantism, one of two spheres of belief and knowledge that Link and McCormick identify as inspiring progressive ideals.[23] The Social Gospel movement of the 1890s and 1900s urged that it was the Christian's duty to correct the ills of society generated by the rise of industrialism. The other body of thought cited by Link and McCormick was found in the social and natural sciences.[24] A number of reform-minded individuals from the fields of statistics, sociology, economics, and psychology brought to the progressive impulse a firm conviction that the investigation of facts concerning society's condition, the presentation of those facts to the citizenry of the United States, and the application of social-science principles to the analysis of those facts would inevitably facilitate the improvement of the human condition in American society.

One manifestation of the progressive urge to present facts to people in order to move them to action was the rise of so-called "muckraking" journalism. President Theodore Roosevelt first applied this name, borrowed from a character in John Bunyan's *Pilgrim's Progress*, to the particular brand of journalism that set out to expose and report the worst degradations of society, particularly pertaining to industrialization and corporate behavior. Journalistic muckraking thrived in the first decade of the twentieth century. Among the highlights of muckraking were Ida Tarbell's documentation of the business methods of the Standard Oil Company, John Spargo's angry denunciation of child labor in America, and Upton Sinclair's grisly muckraking novel *The Jungle*, a thinly fictionalized account of conditions in the stockyards of Chicago.[25]

Muckraking journalism also had an impact on later generations of artistic and literary realists. Stephen Crane and Theodore Dreiser both had experience as reporters, and John Sloan, George Luks, Everett Shinn, and William Glackens worked as newspaper illustrators early in their careers, which gave them exposure to the reality of city life as represented in newspapers and magazines.

Among the thornier issues facing the United States during the Progressive Era was immigration. The first decades of the twentieth century witnessed a rising tide of immigrants coming to the United States from Italy and Eastern Europe. For example, out of 488,000 immigrants into the United States in 1901, 269,386 came from those regions of Europe, compared to 93,000 from Great Britain, Ireland, and Scandinavia. This trend continued for most of the decade.[26]

With this wave of immigration came increasing objections to American immigration policy. Part of the outcry against this new wave of immigration stemmed from the fear of anarchism, regarded by many as a "foreign" doctrine.[27] That fear, which had been strong in the United States since the Haymarket bomb in the 1880s, was shockingly reinforced by the assassination of William McKinley in 1901 by Leon Czolgosz, an anarchist and a child of Eastern European immigrants.

Another argument put up against immigration was that immigrants were too often of low moral character. For example, it was claimed that immigrants drank too much.[28] Since the scourge of the saloon was a favorite target of some progressive-style reformers, restriction of immigration became tied up with the drive for prohibition. In the minds of some Americans, immigrants were also inextricably linked to the system of political bosses and party machines that were widely believed to be corrupting American politics in the early twentieth century.[29]

Jane Addams, among others, observed a connection between the poor conditions and low pay of young women and lax moral conditions in their communities, frequently immigrant communities. She wrote trenchantly of the exhausting labor necessary in many cases to maintain a minimal standard of living: "for thousands of them the effort to obtain a livelihood fairly eclipses the very meaning of life itself."[30] When presented with the opportunity to make four times as much money in prostitution as in factory work, Addams noted, it should hardly be shocking that so many uneducated young women from desperately poor families turned to the former.[31]

Progressives were of mixed impact concerning immigration. Some progressives, for the reasons noted above and others, advocated restrictions on immigration. Proposals such as quotas and literacy tests, which had been introduced as early as the 1890s, began to appear in Congress with greater frequency during the 1910s. President William Howard Taft vetoed a literacy test requirement for immigrants in 1913, the year after George Chadwick completed *The Padrone*, and President Woodrow Wilson did the same in 1915, but the law finally passed over Wilson's veto in 1917, three years after Frederick Converse completed *The Immigrants*.[32] More severe immigration controls, including quotas, were passed in 1921 and 1924.

On the other hand, some reformers were repulsed by calls for immigration restriction. In particular, many progressives who participated in the settlement house movement around the turn of the century were determined to make common ground between immigrants and native-born citizens. Hull House, the pioneering Chicago settlement founded by Jane Addams and Ellen Starr, was only one of many establishments that brought young, middle-class citizens, particularly college students, together with the urban poor, frequently including immigrants. Groups of students and others moved into the poorest areas of cities and provided social aid, artistic opportunities, and educational services to the residents of the neighborhood.[33]

The pinnacle of influence of the settlement movement may well have been in 1912, the year in which Chadwick and Stevens completed *The Padrone* and Converse and MacKaye began work on *The Immigrants*. That was also the year of the formation of the Progressive Party and Theodore Roosevelt's Progressive campaign for the Presidency.

The political platform of the Progressive Party was heavily influenced by such organizations as the National Conference of Charities and Correction, whose "Social Standards for Industry" draft document provided the basis for much of the platform.[34] That draft document in turn reflected the experiences of such settlement leaders as Hull House founder Jane Addams and Henry Street Settlement resident Florence Kelly, general secretary of the National Consumers' League.

One of the more insidious and dehumanizing institutions against which the settlement workers and other reformers struggled was the sweatshop. Numerous accounts were produced during the progressive era of the unsafe and unhealthy conditions, grueling hours, and numbing labor for insufficient pay that characterized garment factories and other industrial facilities. Some of the accounts were written by women of middle- or upper-class standing who actually took jobs in such factories to encounter the conditions firsthand and later report them as accurately as possible. Marie van Vorst took a job cleaning shoes at a factory to observe the conditions in which workers toiled there. She reported standing for five hours straight in one stretch, having cleaned over one hundred shoes, and earning twenty-five cents.[35] Alzina Stevens, a Hull House member, had worked in a textile mill at age thirteen and lost a finger on one hand while working there.[36]

Child labor in particular galled many reformers, and some of the most vocal and determined reform efforts were directed at curbing the hours and improving the conditions in which children worked. The ultimate goal was the abolition of child labor.[37] Progress in this area was frustratingly slow and unsteady. Settlement workers were key players in the campaign against child labor; Julia Lathrop, a Hull House resident, was appointed in 1913 as the first director of the Children's Bureau, a federal department charged with overseeing child labor issues.[38]

Working conditions in the city also provoked concern and calls for change. Concern about working conditions in factories grew exponentially in the aftermath of the Triangle Fire. That 1911 disaster, in which 146 women perished, exposed unhealthy conditions and unsafe practices that were not unique to the Triangle Shirtwaist Factory and led to new factory safety laws, fifty in New York State alone, for which progressive reformers had long campaigned.[39] Even so, the enforcement of such laws was sometimes weakened or severely curtailed by business interests.

Though facing daunting tasks, progressives as a rule were optimistic, though not without some anxiety. Richard Hofstadter observes the underlying hopefulness of some important book titles of the period, such as *The Old Order Changeth*, *The New Democracy*, and *The Promise of American Life*.[40] This optimism stemmed primarily from a strong conviction that the problems faced by American society could be solved, once those problems were studied, analyzed, and understood, and once people were convinced of the need for change. As a result, progressive reform methods were typically characterized by thorough study and analysis of a problem, with the application of modern techniques of sociology, psychology, and statistics; the dissemination of the information so gathered and the exhortation of the citizenry to action; reliance on the expert solutions proposed by trained professionals; and, eventually, the execution of reform through governmental action.

The progressive impulse for gathering information is most grandly exemplified by the Pittsburgh Survey, a massive study of the living and working conditions of the citizens of that city. Published in six volumes between 1909 and 1914, the Pittsburgh Survey laid out in minute statistical detail the difficult facts about the poor living conditions, dangerous work conditions, insufficient wages, and rampant disease problems faced by an alarming number of Pittsburghers.[41] Such projects were carried out both by private interests, as was the Pittsburgh Survey, and government initiatives. The overwhelming statistical documentation of such social ills as the costs of workplace dangers and the insufficiency of wages for women sparked numerous reform initiatives and also spurred similar surveys of other cities.

With the information gathered in such surveys and studies, progressives were quick to turn to the media to disseminate to the American people their well-documented calls for reform. Books flowed from the pens of reformers, but magazine and newspaper articles also put forth unflinching exposés of the most sordid and inhumane conditions in which many urban dwellers lived. Informing the American public was crucial to any drive for reform; the progressives trusted that the citizenry, armed with the facts and figures concerning social ills, would naturally and instinctively be motivated to action to right those wrongs and improve society as a whole.

The Progressive Party's defeat in 1912 and the onset of World War I contributed to the dissipation of the most vital period of progressive influence in American society. Nonetheless, the influence of some progressive ideals and methods continued through the 1920s and into the New Deal policies of the 1930s.

The work of Hofstadter and Link and McCormick represents only a tiny fraction of the scholarship that can inform the curious musicologist exploring the Progressive Era. Allen Davis's *Spearheads for Reform* illuminates the history of the settlement house movement, an outpost of which figures into the lives of Converse and MacKaye's desperate immigrants.[42] A scholarly volume that also merits mention is David Shi's *Facing Facts: Realism in American Thought and Culture*, which brings scholarship on Progressivism to bear in consideration of contemporary American art and literature, providing a model for the concordance of historical and artistic scholarship.[43]

The Operas in Political and Social Context

George Chadwick's opera is not dotted with speeches, slums, sweatshops, settlements, or strikes. No calls for reform are advanced, and no riots break out. The moment at which it advances closest to political comment, the remarkable opening scene of Act II featuring the mingling of immigrants and tourists at the steamship pier, is presented with only subtle revelations of the immigrants' views of America and no overt political comment. Nonetheless, there are elements in *The Padrone* that suggest the influence of progressive arguments and themes of discourse.

One such element is Marietta's assertion of herself as a "maid" or "maiden," noted in part 1. When viewed in the context of the characterization of immigrants as morally lax, an attitude which drew Jane Addams's comment on poor working conditions and poverty as root causes of immorality, Marietta's self-characterization becomes more pointed and significant.

Marietta is a young and attractive woman in the employ of a man who, she knows, wants her for his own. She works as a tambourine girl, partnered with an organ grinder, playing on the streets of the city, a task she describes as "bold coquetting."[44] Negotiating the dual pitfalls presented by her employer, who lusts after her, and her job, which exposes her to the unwanted advances of strangers, she has preserved her purity and proudly presents herself to Marco as an unblemished bride. This fervent defense of her reputation flies in the face of the stereotype of the morally lax immigrant.

Catani's apparent influence with the immigration officials in Act II is politically ambiguous. He is able to gain access to the immigrant processing area for himself, Marietta, Francesca, and Marta by presenting a letter to an immigration official. The audience member is not privy to the contents of the note. How has Catani come to such a position of influence? It is left unclear whether he holds such sway by reason of his financial resources, or simply because of his position in the community. If his financial clout has brought him this power, it suggests the unpleasant possibility that these immigration officials are somehow beholden to the wealthy and can potentially be bought for the right price. If his social status gains him entry, the suggestion of greater cooperation with the socially important is still an unpleasant one. A third possibility is that his record as a sponsor of immigrants motivates his ready admission to the processing area.

Catani is, of course, the title character of *The Padrone*. While his portrayed role as employer and implied oppressor of Maria and others is central to the opera's action, the history and role of the padrone in American society is one more clue as to how up-to-date Chadwick and Stevens's plot is.

A padrone was typically a contractor or broker who found employment for new immigrants in return for a fee. By reputation, the padrone also provided the fare for passage to the United States, and charged exorbitant fees, such that the immigrant would be indebted to the padrone for a very long time, and therefore under his control. Indeed this provides an important element of *The Padrone*'s intrigue; Maria is determined to bring her lover Marco to the United States without Catani's aid or influence.

Such scholars as Luciano Iorizzo and Humbert S. Nelli, however, challenge the prevailing view of the padroni as consistent exploiters and oppressors of their compatriots. Nelli, in particular, strongly argues that the padrone seldom functioned as more than a labor agent.[45] Most telling for this study is Nelli's citation of the 1911 report of the Dillingham Commission that the padrone system was, for all practical purposes, defunct in the United States.

The opening scene of Act II also merits mention, if only for its juxtaposition of the new and the old in American life. The scene holds some political and philosophical significance for its suggestion of what immigrants seek in the United States: an escape from troubles in the old country and material wealth in the new. Here it is appropriate to remember that *The Padrone* is the creation not of immigrants, but of two native-born American citizens from families that had been in America for many generations.

Although most of the politically charged content of *The Immigrants* is found in the final act of the opera, there are scenes in both Act I and Act II that suggest political dimensions within the drama. The Italian soldiers, or carabinieri, and the prison portray a corrupt and oppressive society, one whose cruel and crushing treatment of its citizens drives the most desperately oppressed into the arms of anyone who promises something better. Act II, in which Scammon executes his scheme to separate Maria from Giovanni, suggests the ease with which the greedy and corrupt can take advantage of governmental authority.

A politically telling scene occurs early in Act I, when the kindly artist Noel intervenes to prevent Sandro from being jailed. Even as Noel is paying off Sandro's debt, along with extra for the soldiers' trouble, another scene is being played out silently to the side.

Page 15:

A Contadino with a hamper strapped to his back is stopped by two of the soldiers. They make him unstrap the hamper, open it, and reveal bottles of wine.

Page 16:

FIRST SOLDIER: *(to peasant) Your license!*

The Peasant stares in fright, searches his coat and brings forth a paper, which the soldiers take and examine, winking at each other.

Page 28:

The soldiers by the peasant with the hamper have helped themselves to his case of wine. One of them now lugs it off, while the other turns to the peasant and tears up his license paper, before his scared face.

The peasant retreats forlornly among the commiserating bystanders. The soldier rejoins his companions, gaily.[46]

In this scene, two soldiers harass a hapless peddler and confiscate his goods, leaving him broke, empty handed, and dejected. Even if Noel's intervention has caused a happy result for Sandro and his family, the audience is reminded that such good fortune is all too rare, and that there are far too few Noels available to stand between the people and corrupt authority. Here is a first suggestion of the conditions that drive Sandro and his family to accept the opportunity to flee to America.

As more is revealed about the family, particularly about Giovanni's imprisonment for debt, the true oppressiveness of life in this village becomes apparent. Even after Giovanni is released from prison, the futility of their existence hangs over him; he realizes he still faces "once more the taxes. And once more no hope to pay."[47] It is little surprise that America, as portrayed by Scammon, becomes an attractive alternative to life in the village.

One common element in the three acts of the opera is the appearance of the Statue of Liberty, a national emblem that was less than forty years old at the time. In Act I the Statue is depicted in Scammon's slightly ludicrous show for the Italian townspeople, his sales pitch to entice them to emigrate. Scammon's hat is decorated with little trinkets, replicas of the Statue of Liberty, and the donkey-drawn float that ends his little parade bears a larger replica of the Statue. Late in Act I Scammon tosses his little statues to the crowd. His description of the image as he does so is instructive; he calls the image "Santa Liberta! . . . the little Saint who comes from America!"[48] The next example contains his description of this "saint" and her offerings to those who seek her. The villagers, enraptured by Scammon's motion pictures and festive trappings, echo its final line in chorus:

> Luck and opportunity, liberty, immunity
> All may have who pray to her,
> Simply shout: Hurray to her! Ha! Ha! Ha! Santa Liberta! [49]

Giovanni, newly freed from prison, has a different reaction. The image of the Statue eerily coincides with "the great Madonna" of Giovanni's dreams, a vision he saw constantly associated with "liberty" and "opportunity," the hopes with which he sustained himself in prison. Seeing Scammon's mock statue so soon after his release, Giovanni comes to equate the image with that of the Virgin Mary of his visions, the "pitiful Madonna of the poor!" His vision of a mighty hand holding aloft a torch in the mist is fulfilled at the emotional pinnacle of Act II.

> *Beyond those walls I walked and walked:*
> *Always I said two words; over and over—*
> *Awake! Asleep! Two words! Liberty, Opportunity!*
>
>   . . .
>
> *But in the lonely silence and the dark, I dreamed of her,*
> *I dreamed—and from the dark She came.*
> *The great Virgin: Maiden and mighty mother—pitiful Madonna of the poor!*
> *My prison walls were mist, and all the floor like ocean fog,*
> *And thou and I were kneeling in the night,*
> *And millions more with bundles on their backs were huddled round us there.*
> *But soon the dark burst, and a mighty hand came through the mist. . . .*[50]

Another voice is raised in Act I over the Statue image. Noel interrupts Scammon at the climax of his final sales pitch, denouncing him and his scam and offering his own vision of America. Adopting the female personification of America implied by the Statue, Noel attempts to warn the immigrants against false hopes, but his jeremiad is too little and too late to dissuade the disillusioned Giovanni from seeking his "liberty and opportunity" there:

> *That land you mock, America,*
> *Is dear to me, my motherland:*
>   *And I, who love her, know too well*
> *Her bitter fight with prowling greed*
>   *And hungry want by her own hearth,*
> *To save the children at her knees;*
>   *Yet they who clamor round her doors*
> *She welcomes still, but not unwarned.*
>   *Come with your sorrows, come, she cries,*
>   *But come not blinded to the truth;*
>   *The woes you fly await you still.*
>   *Not mine, not mine the promised land,*
>   *Beyond it lies for all who seek to follow still afar!*[51]

These three disparate views of America as represented by the Statue, are at the heart of the opera's dramatic conflict. Scammon uses it for personal gain; Giovanni sees it as a hope for the hopeless; and Noel sees it with all its flaws and shortcomings.

The Statue of Liberty itself appears in Act II; as the immigrants' ship arrives in New York harbor, Giovanni's vision of a hand bearing a torch through the mist is realized. As he and Maria see his vision fulfilled, they slowly sink to their knees as if in prayer. Scammon's plot to have Maria for his own soon shatters the young couple's hopes. Immigration officials apprehend Giovanni even as the other immigrants take up the "Santa Liberta" refrain from Act I. Scammon has somehow deceived an immigration official into aiding in his scheme.

In a time when official corruption was targeted by reformers, the ease with which Scammon manipulates this anonymous official was a dismaying reminder of the ease with which persons in positions of power or influence could turn officials or agencies charged with upholding the public good. Though the analogy to corrupt political officials is far from precise, the theme of the law being used for the benefit of the wealthy resonates with Scammon's actions here.

In Act III the appearance of the Statue image is a cruel mockery of the hopes and dreams it earlier embodied. Looming over the grimy slum in which Act III takes place is a neon sign, advertising "LIBERTY Storage Vaults," displaying to all an illuminated outline of the Statue. Giovanni observes the image with bitter irony in his final speech to the people; pointing to the sign, he cries:

Santa Liberta! Behold her there!
Pray to your saint, my people,
My people wandering in the Promised Land.
Is she not glorious on this summer night?[52]

Act III, the only act of *The Immigrants* that takes place in the American city setting, portrays a New York slum populated with despairing Italian tenants dreaming of home and lamenting their fate. We quickly learn through fragments of dialogue of Lisetta and Maria's sweatshop employment, the helpful settlement house nearby, the homesickness of the immigrants in general, Giuseppe's increasing desire to take violent revenge on their oppressors, and the severe heat wave affecting the city. An earlier version of the libretto even included a reference to a strike at the sweatshop that had been broken by management.[53]

Pages 6–8:

SANDRO: *Here, 'Seppe, sit, our girls are late tonight.*

GIUSEPPE: *Lisett' is working overtime, she said.*

SANDRO: *Too sick she is.*

GIUSEPPE: *This heat is hell.*

SANDRO: *T'was forty more died yesterday.*

GIUSEPPE: *Hardly my wages pay the rent to house us in that rotten hole.*
            O God, if I could kill something to save Lisett.

SANDRO: *And poor Mari!*
            They work too long, my little girls.

Pages 36–37:

MARIA: *She is asleep.*
            We'll let her sleep out of doors. She needs the air!

GIUSEPPE: *I'll go and see the good folk yonder in the settlement*
            And ask if they will let her sleep upon their roof.

MARIA: *That's right. Go with him, Papa.*[54]

Giovanni's Act III speech to the agitated crowd sums up the plight of all of the immigrants on stage. His words were no doubt intended to resonate with the oppression felt by many of the poorest members of modern society. The slain Scammon is then identified with those who run the "roaring soul machine" in the second part of the speech.

You begin to feel, and think
But who are you, are we, to feel and think?
You are not men, with hearts and minds and passions.
You are cogs and wheels,
Cogs, wheels, and levers in the great machine,
The roaring soul machine America.

        . . .

If God is prisoned in a poor man's heart,
Who is it makes a cog and wheel of him?
Who is it mocks the eternal God

And tries to crush his lifeblood in a blind machine?
Who made you what you are of what you were
And put you in this slum to rot in soul and die in body here?
Scammon—and I killed him. Did I do well?[55]

This scene lays bare the immigrants' plight, an age-old story of inhumanity by the powerful toward the powerless, written in the mechanistic imagery and turbulent rhetoric of "modern" America. The rhetoric and the impassioned indictment of the corrupt echo frequent themes in the political discourse of the Progressive Era.

The libretto of *The Immigrants* frequently and clearly echoes themes found in the politics of its time. If the theme of the opera were not clear enough, the final words of the libretto make plain the sympathies of its creators. After Giovanni and Maria are arrested and carried away, policemen stand guard over the slain Scammon, and Sandro prays over Lisetta's lifeless body. Noel, surveying the scene, eyes the neon sign with the Liberty image and sings a final indictment of America's treatment of its immigrants. The broadly worded charge against "Liberty" makes clear that the fault for the fate of those who seek America cannot be confined to Scammon and his ilk; it is borne by all Americans. The end of the opera is a call to action for justice.

In misery together!
O Liberty!
When will you cease in darkness to destroy those that seek you?[56]

Clearly, these two operas approach the subject of the immigrant very differently. Converse and MacKaye have filled *The Immigrants* with references to their contemporary culture and political time, to a far greater degree than Chadwick and Stevens in *The Padrone*, which actually appears dated by comparison when the current state of padronism in the United States is considered. The two operas may cover similar stories, but they do so in very different fashions.

The work of scholars of the Progressive Era illuminates *The Padrone* and *The Immigrants*, setting these operas apart from musicological relegation to the dustbin of outmoded non-American works. Further, incorporating these historical insights into evaluation of these works challenges musicologists to reconsider how a musical work is defined as "American" or "non-American," refuting the notion that musical Americanism is restricted to references to selected popular American musical styles. *The Padrone* and *The Immigrants* only make sense as American stories, clearly identifiable with a specific time and place. To overlook such works when constructing a history of American music cannot be justified when the work of the historian is joined to the work of the musicologist.

Notes

1. Donald Jay Grout and Claude V. Palisca, *A History of Western Music*, 4th ed. (New York and London: W. W. Norton, 1988), 785–6.

2. Manuscript copies of both operas are held in the Harriet M. Spaulding Library, New England Conservatory of Music, Boston.

3. *Webster's Ninth New Collegiate Dictionary* (Springfield: Merriam-Webster, 1983), 846.

4. Victor Fell Yellin, *Chadwick: Yankee Composer* (Washington and London: Smithsonian Institution Press, 1990), 212.

5. Mrs. Junius S. Morgan, interview with Robert Garofalo, 28 May 1968, cited in Garofalo, *Frederick Shepherd Converse (1871–1940): His Life and Music* (Metuchen: Scarecrow, 1994), 60 n.60.

6. Garofalo, *Frederick Shepherd Converse*, 20.

7. Garofalo, *Frederick Shepherd Converse*, 30 n. 71.

8. Frederick S. Converse, *The Immigrants*, Act I, 27. This and following quotations from the libretto are from the manuscript score of *The Immigrants* held in the Spaulding Library.

9. Converse, *The Immigrants*, Act III, 179.

10. Yellin, *Chadwick, Yankee Composer*, 210–211.

11. Yellin, *Chadwick, Yankee Composer*, 211.

12. Cited in Steven Ledbetter, "George W. Chadwick: A Sourcebook," (Boston: 1983), [n.p.]

13. Frederick Martens, *A Thousand and One Nights of Opera* (New York: Appleton-Century, 1938), 251–2.

14. Elise Kirk, *American Opera* (Urbana and Chicago: University of Illinois Press, 2001), 223–4.

15. James J. Connolly, "H-SHGAPE Bibliographical Essays: Progressivism" <http://www.h-net.msu.edu/~shgape/bibs/prog.html>, 1.

16. Connolly, "H-SHGAPE Bibliographical Essays: Progressivism."

17. Richard Hofstadter, "Introduction," in *The Progressive Movement 1900–1915*, ed. Richard Hofstadter (Englewood Cliffs: Prentice-Hall, 1963), 3.

18. Arthur S. Link and Richard L. McCormick, *Progressivism*, The American History Series (Arlington Heights: Harlan Davidson, 1983), 11.

19. Link and McCormick, *Progressivism*, 11.

20. Link and McCormick, *Progressivism*, 12.

21. Link and McCormick, *Progressivism*, 18–19.

22. Walter Rauschenbusch, *Christianity and the Social Crisis* (New York: Macmillan, 1907), 370.

23. Link and McCormick, *Progressivism*, 22.

24. Link and McCormick, *Progressivism*, 22.

25. Ida M. Tarbell, "History of the Standard Oil Company," *McClure's*, 1902; John Spargo, *The Bitter Cry of the Children* (New York: Macmillan, 1906); Upton Sinclair, *The Jungle* (New York: Doubleday, Page and Company, 1906).

26. Lewis L. Gould, *The Presidency of Theodore Roosevelt* (Lawrence: University Press of Kansas, 1991), 36.

27. Gould, *The Presidency of Theodore Roosevelt*, 36.

28. Link and McCormick, *Progressivism*, 102.

29. Kendrick A. Clements, *The Presidency of Woodrow Wilson* (Lawrence: University Press of Kansas, 1992), 20.

30. Jane Addams, *A New Conscience and an Ancient Evil* (New York: 1912; microfilm New Haven: Research Publications, 1976), 56.

31. Addams, *A New Conscience and an Ancient Evil*, 57.

32. Link and McCormick, *Progressivism*, 101–102.

33. Link and McCormick, *Progressivism*, 73. A recent dissertation by Shannon L. Green examines the musical activities of Hull House: Shannon L. Green, "Art for Life's Sake: Music Schools and Activities in U. S. Social Settlements, 1892–1942" (Ph.D. dissertation, University of Wisconsin at Madison, 1998).

34. Allen F. Davis, *Spearheads for Reform: The Social Settlements and the Progressive Movement, 1890–1914* (Oxford: Oxford University Press, 1967: reprint New Brunswick: Rutgers University Press, 1984, 1991), 194–197.

35. Mrs. John Van Vorst and Marie Van Vorst, *The Woman Who Toils: Being the Experiences of Two Gentlewomen as Factory Girls* (New York: 1903; microfilm New Haven: Research Publications, 1976), 102.

36. Davis, *Spearheads for Reform*, 103.

37. Davis, *Spearheads for Reform*, 133.

38. Davis, *Spearheads for Reform*, 132.

39. Link and McCormick, *Progressivism*, 83.

40. Hofstadter, "Introduction," 5.

41. Link and McCormick, *Progressivism*, 77.

42. Davis, *Spearheads for Reform*.

43. David E. Shi, *Facing Facts: Realism in American Thought and Culture, 1850–1920* (New York and Oxford: Oxford University Press, 1995).

44. George W. Chadwick, *The Padrone* (libretto by David K. Stevens), Boston, 1913, 54. The composer's original manuscript orchestral score is located at the Spaulding Music Library.

45. Humbert S. Nelli, "The Italian Padrone System in the United States," *Labor History* 5:2 (Spring 1964): 154.

46. Converse, *The Immigrants* (libretto by Percy MacKaye), Act I, 15–28.

47. Converse, *The Immigrants*, Act I, 165.

48. Converse, *The Immigrants*, Act I, 205.

49. Converse, *The Immigrants*, Act I, 205–209.

50. Converse, *The Immigrants*, Act I, 166–168, 172–176.

51. Converse, *The Immigrants*, Act I, 234–239.

52. Converse, *The Immigrants*, Act III, 143–145.

53. Percy MacKaye, *The Immigrants*, typescript draft copy (incomplete) of libretto contained at Spaulding Library, New England Conservatory of Music, [n.p.]

54. Converse, *The Immigrants*, Act III, 6–8, 36–37.

55. Converse, *The Immigrants*, Act III, 148–161.

56. Converse, *The Immigrants*, Act III, 178–179.

PART III

CRITIQUES OF MUSIC AND HISTORY

The Perspective of Cultural Studies

Fictions of Alien Identities
Cultural Cross-Dressing in
Nineteenth- and Early Twentieth-Century Opera

SANDRA LYNE

"None of these 'women in Puccini's operas' can be understood without history."[1]

An Anecdote

In 1996, the State Opera of South Australia's ladies' chorus was dressing for a performance of Puccini's *Turandot*.[2] This opera was first performed in 1926, one of many European operas of the "long nineteenth century" to be set in Asia.[3] Covering skins that varied from pink to olive with white-yellow face make-up, elongating Caucasian eyes with black eyeliner, and scooping individuality into formal hats and identical white robes, Australians of European background metamorphosed into 'ancient' Chinese Imperial court women. Moving with small steps in formations that characterised Asians as indistinguishable clones and members of a populous "herd," we sang Italian lyrics first heard almost a century ago in Europe and America. We were walking metaphors of cultural hybridity, projections of a desiring Western imagination, sponsored by Boral Industries and Southern Television Corporation.

This discussion enlists the perspective of an operatic performer and utilizes the lens of cultural studies to investigate the interplay of culture and ideology in the performance of "Asianess," particularly female Far-Eastern Asian-ness, in nineteenth-century Grand Opera.[4] It interprets some codes of racial signification that structured Puccini's operatic spectacles, *Turandot* and *Madama Butterfly*,[5] operas that were performed before Europeans (particularly Victorian Britons), and it concentrates on the stereotype of the "exotic Asian woman," who was usually played by a European in "cultural cross-dress." [6] Shifts in the staging structure of a 1996 production of *Madama Butterfly*[7] can be construed as a response to social values that have changed outside the operatic theater's "time warp" over time (nearly a century after the opera's first performance).

William Weber, in *Beyond Zeitgeist*, envisions musical history as something other than a coherent progression of distinct musical ages dominated by their canonical "great" composers.[8] Such a concept, Weber posits, has forced musical history into literary and philosophical categories, such as "Baroque," "Classical," and "Romantic," that emerge from and are energized by an underlying universal master plan. According to Weber, music's historians and scholars have invested faith in the transcendent nature of this historical vision, so that musical history functions as a type of totalizing belief system rather than a flexible, multi-faceted method of documentation and interpretation that addresses the multiplicity of motivations, contexts, and expediencies that constitutes "history." Music's actual development, from Weber's viewpoint, has been discontinuous and non-teleologic.

Anthropological historian Henrika Kuklick, in *The Savage Within*,[9] observes that in the nineteenth century, increasingly secularized Europeans (particularly in Britain) were eager to find new systems of universal structure and theories of function that would explain (and justify) their own (preferably superior) position in an expanding world. Europe's bio-racial theories, and Marx's totalizing system based on workers' relations to the means of production, are examples of this impulse toward total coherence and control. The dominant Victorian British model for all human growth and change, including progress in art and music, was based on evolutionary patterning. Infusing an Enlightenment secular rationality with biological science, this model assumed the existence of an upward, progressive impetus in humanity's development that was driven by our ability to think and to order society in a rational manner. (It also allowed for the idea of *some* decay.) This Utopian assumption, that embraced all areas of human endeavor, never recovered from the impact of World War I and the ongoing breakdown of European territories and racial hierarchies. It is surprising that, in spite of the general disillusionment, musical history was still viewed as a coherent, ascending system evolving from within an exemplary, rational civilization.[10] Grand opera, the paradigm of European culture that reached its zenith in the nineteenth century, reflects much of the irrationality and psychic anxieties of this era.

In the recent past, opera's adherents have behaved as though the art form provided a refuge from the tyranny of analytical and social critique, and as if the emotionally charged experience of opera was set apart, and, according to a "common liberal humanist assumption . . . shorn of history and beyond or outside of power relations."[11] However, over the last decade, it has been subject to the analytic attentions of scholars from a variety of disciplines that have not traditionally been aligned with musical history. The unabashed interdisciplinarity of cultural studies has offered musicologists and historians multiple channels through which to examine music's historical and social contexts, as it incorporates a variety of interpretive strategies from disciplines including the social sciences, film theory and anthropology. Motkus maintains that "culture and cultural products, such as the arts, must be studied within the social relations and system through which culture is produced and consumed," thus highlighting the contingency of cultural studies to the study of society, politics and economics.[12]

In *Beyond Zeitgeist*, Weber focuses on musical output as cultural product when he states that economic exigencies and systems of desire and its satisfaction had more to do with the development of musical styles than composers' sensitivities to the prevailing *Zeitgeist*. In his opinion, Mozart's responses to the demands of patronage determined his style, rather than his sensitivities to the "Spirit of the Age." Stressing the importance of "everyday business" to the emergence of musical styles, Weber also suggests that the *frottola,* the light genre of the sixteenth century, was developed mainly in deference to the request of a Mantuan patroness.[13] Likewise, in the nineteenth century, composers such as Puccini and Verdi wrote Grand Operas to appeal to a paying public, creating musical and visual fantasies to please and entertain, but not to politically challenge the dominant ideologies of its privileged audiences, who were beset by fears of social disorder emanating from working class discontent, and the problems of retaining global power.[14] The use of European languages and only passing pentatonic references to Asian musical forms cocoons the Asia of nineteenth-century opera within the European imagination, as a fantasy construction. This fantasy is not, however, disconnected from the politics and ethics of the real world: the psychic satellite of opera orbits the everyday economic planet, and each exerts a profound influence on the other. Audiences and their desires create an interlocking system of supply and demand.

Reception theories from literary studies are useful tools with which audience reactions and perceptions, a vital part of a musical work's cycle of construction/performance/reception/reconstruction, may be examined, and film theory demonstrates how creative production is inevitably situated within economies of desire.[15] Film theory is of particular use in analysing racialized images in opera, as the two art forms both depend on a synthesis of actors, music and dialogue (libretto).[16] The original creative material of both movies and opera is subject to the interventions and interpretations of producers and directors. Film's interpreters share their focus on the audience's desires and "ways of seeing" with anthropologists, who investigate the meanings generated by public displays of racialized image. In the nineteenth/twentieth centuries, anthropologists developed displays of ethnological photographic records as evidence of "backward" and "advanced" races and engineered ethnic displays at museums and world fairs.

A brief investigation of the central assumptions that framed nineteenth-century middle and upper class perceptions of Asia on the stage indicates that operas from that era were profoundly inflected with a priori ideas of Caucasian superiority. "We can learn about the obsessions of [nineteenth century Europe] . . . by studying the cultural clichés that make it onto the operatic stage for public consumption."[17]

In order to address opera in its cultural and ideological contexts, the impact of scientific racism on its nineteenth-century audiences, and their sensitivities regarding class structure, should be considered.[18] It was the Victorians who naturalized and institutionalized the concept of race, elevating it from an idea to an objective reality.[19] Racism in nineteenth-century opera was partly a symptom of the transformation of race studies into a science.[20] In the second half of the nineteenth century, the Anthropological Institute and the Anthropological Society of London institutionalized theories such as biological determinism and comparative anatomy. Their professional middle-class members claimed for themselves specialized authority in racial matters. These theories were based on the writings of Knox, Gobineau, Darwin, and others, the photographic typologies of A. H. Keane, and the observations of travel writers, and were not immune to mythologizing impulses. Both anthropological institutions abandoned the idea of a humanitarian, ethical approach to science, claiming that such attitudes were inappropriate, sentimental and an impediment to "objectivity," a stance that facilitated Britain's management of Empire and its recruitment of the cheap labour required to maintain its industries.

"Colored" (non-white) races were fixed in place by their physiological characteristics, for their coloring, features, and build supposedly determined their psychology, temperament, and moral character. In terms of nineteenth-century ethnology, the lighter-skinned Japanese and Chinese were evaluated differently by Europe's elites than were darker-skinned races. Although not seen as equal to Europeans, Far Easterners were higher up the nineteenth-century racial hierarchies than were their Middle Eastern and African counterparts. The Japanese were higher than the Chinese, but they were never the equals of Europeans (in the latter's own opinion)[21]: their "extraordinary and surprising" technological developments in the late 1800s were considered by the influential ethnologist, A.H. Keane, to be due to "their capacity for at least imitating the features of foreign institutions."[22] It was Keane's "scientific" opinion that the Japanese and Chinese could not be trusted, although the Japanese were:

> on the whole of a kindly and lovable disposition, especially when compared with the Chinese and other branches of the Mongolian family . . . beneath many genial and amiable qualities there is often betrayed a spirit of treachery, suspicion and revenge, which will for years pursue its victim under the cloak of the most seemingly cordial friendship. A mercenary disposition and unbridled licentiousness are also amongst the darker shades of [the] picture. . . .[23]

Japan and China's ancient governmental hierarchies and sophisticated art forms were acknowledged by the new sciences as civilized, if regressive, societies that were more irrational than Western cultures that had benefited from the Enlightenment. Members of nineteenth-century European/American opera audiences did not constitute an ideologically

homogenous group, although they were of the upper and the upwardly
mobile middle classes that consumed the masses of new scientific books
and journals flooding the market with emerging racial theories. These
readers were heavily influenced by prevailing ideas of biological determinism and similar hierarchic theories that created a void between
themselves and non-European cultures. Reaching deeply into its art
forms of opera, theatre, visual art and photography, Europe's newly
institutionalized racism both demeaned and aestheticized Asians, especially women. It positioned them as exotic, Oriental, and Other in static,
ancient cultures that provided lavish spectacles for the enjoyment of
the rational, progressive, if somewhat less colorful, European self.[24] The
Other's biologically determined capricious cruelty, despotism, and irrationality heightened the drama, the challenge and the romance for the
"outsider" protagonist who usually found himself alone among an alien
land and people.

Operatic tales of love, death and betrayal in Asia and the Middle East
circulated through major European cities, the self-acknowledged centers
of high art, in French, English, German or Italian.[25] Opera was a part of
a wider addiction to "ethnicity as spectacle" that gave nineteenth- and
early twentieth-century Europeans a window through which they could
inspect their world and its inhabitants at a comfortable distance. They
also frequented the ethnic sections of museums, traveling Indian shows,
and circuses, but most of all, the International Exhibitions of Britain,
America, France, Holland, Austria, and Germany that displayed people
and customs, crafts and every aspect of foreign cultures. Beginning in
1851 with London's Crystal Palace Exhibition, these massive events fostered commerce and were meant to promote Europe's status as an
empire-builder. Supported by Anthropological Societies, who wanted to
reify their new theories of race, they were also held in large grandiose
structures, that contextualized and dwarfed the exhibits.

Throughout Europe, lavish opera houses were built, refurbished, and
redesigned, in the major centers of culture: Vienna, Frankfurt, Munich,
Paris, Moscow, Barcelona, Leningrad, New York, Buenos Aires, New York,
Prague, London, and Beyreuth. Opera's luxuriant musical composition
required that it be performed in equally sumptuous spaces that could
accommodate a large stage and orchestra, and elaborate seating for the
very wealthy. Chandeliers, paintings and sculptures, ornate costumes,

and stage effects, and the audience's jewels, furs, and grand apparel reflected opera and its patrons' status. Marbled white opera halls of fine design framed the actors and the drama within a visible European Empire that pursued and drew its wealth from much of the rest of the world. Grand framing structures signified the audience's relationship to this world, partly real and imagined, affirming hierarchy.

Opera's entrepreneurs, librettists, and composers were themselves a part of this system: their job was to supply the type of product that was required by the patrons. David Levin, in *Opera through Other Eyes*, reflects that operatic plots of the nineteenth century reflected "certain anxieties about consolidating aesthetic and social wealth [and] . . . marshalling huge aesthetic resources in a massive display of massive display."[26] He also observes that they reclaimed "lost cultures and epochs" evoking Empire, by focussing on ancient themes, justifying their own "claims to mammoth, imposing political power."[27] According to Levin, opera was a "cultural hand-me-down of the elite . . . [an] orderly transfer of the cultural trappings of power from one generation of the 'entitled' to the next. The violence that underlies this transfer is often displaced to the stage. . . . [These operas] feature a struggle for accession to political and social power."[28]

Beige-colored Europeans sang the roles of their exoticized "Others": non-whites were never used, even to represent themselves, partly because Europeans disapproved of the public display of real "mixed-race" love relationships.[29] The dark side of the dream was that many aspects of opera became an enactment of racial and class inequality, what music scholars William Ashbrook and Harold Powers refer to as an "unconscious manifestation of racial arrogance."[30] Of the several classificatory modes by which European groups and individuals assessed each other in the latter half of the nineteenth century, race and class were pre-eminent, especially in Britain. However, race proved to be a more acute determinant than class: Asians and Caucasian-Europeans of comparable rank were not recognized as equals even if they were dressed in similar clothes. Commentators of the time variously described Japanese nobles' adoption of Western dress as "aping," "disfiguring," and "unseemly and comical."[31]

This type of demarcation of difference between an inside and an outside group is a central process in the structuring of racial stereotypes. Most scholars of operatic history would have to admit that Opera has repeatedly used racial (as well as class and gender) stereotypes in its fantasies. Many theories may be used to investigate the machinations at work in the formation and application of these stereotypes.[32] Social psychologists have conducted extensive research into racial stereotyping and prejudicial behavior, seeking to understand the mental and social processes that make it possible to regard others so completely alien that violent or exploitative action against them is "justified." Stereotyping has played its part in the major tensions and conflicts of the twentieth century: white/black racism in America, ethnic atrocities in many parts of the world, Nazism and the Holocaust, racially-based terrorism, rejection of refugees, and domestic and sexual exploitation of Asians, particularly women.

In the last thirty years, anthropologists have been keen to reveal and dismantle the effects of ethnic bias in anthropological theories that justified racial domination and oppression. In *Myth and Stereotype*,[33] Rosemary Breger defines not only the structure of racial stereotypes, but also a method that describes their function in different cultural contexts. This approach is based on Foucault's theories of discourse as a public mode of presenting and structuring an object and its social space, as outlined in *The Archaeology of Knowledge*.[34] At certain points over time, these statements intersect and agree with each other, as in the nineteenth century, when literature, travel and historical accounts, memoirs, and evolutionist theories concerning both women and Asians intersected and concurred with performative representation of Asian women. The stereotype is ostensibly accepted as truth when it appears in several discourses, and is repeatedly projected in the public domain. Opinions, ideas and impressions, sheer fantasies and mistakes become tangible, knowable things: "The more often something is said by an ever-larger group, the more it is accepted as 'true.'"[35] This agreement among the in-group gives rise to a sense of secure identity and of control over the out-group.

Gilman, a social psychologist, has indicated in *Difference and Pathology* that stereotyping in itself is a necessary process by which individuals and groups make sense of the world, and justify status within it.[36] Negative stereotypes usually contain a minimum of fact, and, when competition from an out-group threatens the status, resources or security of an in-group, the process can become pathological, and generate stereotypes that legitimize the denial of others' rights, power, autonomy and identity. A representational, psychic mode by degree impacts on the material world, and an out-group's image is either idealized or demonized, its differences rendered homogenous, and its diversities simplified. In Gilman's words, "[W]e create images of things we fear or glorify. These images never remain abstractions; we understand them as real world entities. We assign them labels that serve to set them apart from ourselves. We create 'stereotypes.'"[37]

A process of aestheticization occurs when an insider group tries to deny that an outsider group is similar to itself, and thus renders that group fantastic, unreal or innocuous. In so doing, it concentrates on superficial and trivial aspects of another culture and people, obsesses with artifice and artefacts, and sees outgroup members as fantasy beings, fetishised things that will absorb lack and satisfy desire. For example, in the mid-nineteenth century, Western travel writers construed Japan as a "fairyland," and Western males habitually described Asian women as "dolls" (pretty, small, and easy to control) or benign elves. Such stereotypical Asian images, in the context of Western Empire, connect with and influence international relations. In *Foreign Bodies*, David Napier sees this interaction in terms of microcosm and macrocosm:

> [T]he microcosmic symbol stands in sympathy with the larger phenomena that constitutes what we call "reality": the symbol becomes the basis for other sympathetic relations, so much so that the actions occurring in the real, actual or architechtonic world may be inseparable from their symbolic content.[38]

Asian Dolls and Demons

Since the nineteenth century, when Europe dominated large sections of the world economically and politically, Asian women have been assessed and described by European onlookers, mainly male travellers, diplomats, and traders confined to areas such as treaty ports, as simplified beings who behave in predictable ways: they are deferential, erotically available, and self-sacrificing, or inscrutable, lethal and cruel. These evaluations feed the dynamics of subordination and power in European grand operas that are biased towards the creators of the boundaries, who choose the structures within which images are defined.

In the lexicon of Imperialism, the domination of a nation was often equated with sexual access to its women. In much the same way as World War I propaganda used to depict nations as women, and nineteenth-century political cartoons encapsulated philosophical ideas and emotions in female form, opera's lead female singers embodied racialized exoticism, and were also metaphors for national identity. Puccini's protagonists Madame Butterfly and Turandot project Western stereotypes of Asian women that respectively aestheticize and demonize Asia.

In *Madama Butterfly*, Puccini and his librettists seem to dignify Asian women, departing from the stereotype by positioning a European man unfavorably in contrast to an Asian woman. Captain Pinkerton is ostensibly an anti-hero, inviting audience disapproval for his heartless exploitation of a sweet, young Japanese girl, and Butterfly is the heroine, by virtue of her sensitivity, loyalty, and long-suffering endurance. While audiences sympathise with Butterfly, she is depicted like most Asian women in the literature of the time, as an idealized racial stereotype. Butterfly is associated with heightened, almost cultish eroticism; the geisha-face was designed to "float" like the moon in the dimness of the teahouses. "Real" geisha were the least accessible women to European men in Japan, contrary to the popular Western myths in which every teahouse woman or courtesan in a kimono was a "geisha." Not only an ex-geisha, Butterfly was also childish, simple, occupied with trivia, gullible, and grateful for the attentions of a European man. Sacrificing her religion in spite of familial disapproval and rejection, Butterfly suffers, waits for years, cares for Pinkerton's Amerasian child, and ultimately loses both husband and child. She ends her life via *seppuku*, a ritual practiced by the Samurai class to restore honor in extreme circumstances, as a symbolic punishment for miscegenation.[39] The status-quo intercultural order is restored as Pinkerton and Kate claim the child (who rarely looks Japanese in most operatic productions) to raise and educate as an American, and Pinkerton has a "real" marriage to Kate. The audience is made aware that nothing good can come from interracial sexual fraternization as it was against the scientific "natural order."[40]

Puccini's Imperial princess Turandot, before Prince Calef's conquest, creates havoc as she overrides "nature" and forswears the company of men. She is possessed with the avenging spirit of her ancestor, Lou-Ling, a virgin princess who was raped and killed centuries before. Turandot not only isolates herself from potential suitors, but murders them if they fail her three-part questionnaire. She is thus cast as an extreme stereotype, the monstrous, castrating goddess-woman, the sibyl or sphinx. In another sense, she represents China's reported insularity, cruelty, and despotism to outsiders.

According to public officials Ping, Pang, and Pong, Turandot's disinterest in men was clearly against the natural order, bringing disaster to the land. China had been peaceful before her strange behavior, they say, but now "China is finished!" Spring does not come, and the snow does not thaw. The villagers beg her to "come down," that is, abandon her virginity and become sexually active. Turandot was desirable but not docile, approachable, or sexually available, and disinterested in giving life. She is instead identified with the solitary yet erotic moon, the lover of the dead, shining coldly on graveyards. Her light is a "deathly glow," and her kiss is of death and blood.[41] She is "white as jade, cold as ice, the beautiful Turandot." Her refusal to give up her lofty virginity spurs droves of international would-be lovers to risk the death penalty by answering her triple-trick questions.

Turandot does, of course, eventually descend, as Calef answers all three questions correctly. Her continuing coldness is overcome as he finally thaws her "frigidity" with a kiss, a thinly disguised metaphor for sexual intercourse, or perhaps invasion by another nation. "She was ice, now she is aflame!"[42] Calef, as the Prince of Tartary, represents the invader who easily answers her questions, wins the kingdom, and both defeats and wins the unruly woman.[43] As the Chinese apparently could not manage it by themselves, Chinese national disorder is put right by a rational outsider. This opera expresses anxieties about disordered society and also affirms Imperialist scenarios of rational male (the West) conquering and ordering the feminine, mystic East.

Turandot was the last major Grand Opera to deliver Orientalist spectacles about Asia. Film took over opera's role, beginning with early black and white films and progressing to modern-day epics like *The Last Emperor*.[44] In the late 1930s, idyllic representations of the Japanese became negative, as "The Yellow Peril" images became particularly virulent.[45] Stereotyped or caricatured images were powerful tools in controlling fears of Japanese aggression. Later, the Chinese communist revolution and Japan's trade wars and industrial development triggered a similar reaction, illustrating Gilman's point that "[s]tereotypes arise when self-integration is threatened . . . [they are] ways of dealing with the instabilities of the world. This is not to say that they are good."[46]

From 1941 until 1952, Hollywood produced anti-Japanese feature films, and pseudo documentary films. As Europe lost its colonies and territories in Asia, America took over its imperialistic role. Due to American engagement in World War II, and the Korean and Vietnam Wars, widespread serviceman/prostitute/local encounters (after an initial silence) spawned an ongoing rush of literature and film in the West that portrayed Asian/American relationships of desire, bringing in their wake a new wave of racialized female stereotypes that associated Asian women with a conquered people, servility and hyper-sexuality. The old stereotypes reappeared in a new context, indicating that "stereotypes are inherently protean, not rigid, and that they pass from one discourse to another."[47] Over time, they are often repressed, and lie dormant, but reappear in another context, giving the impression that they are indestructible. These enunciative modalities build on, reinforce, and comment on the messages and images portrayed in the other. Throughout the twentieth century, numerous novels featured Butterfly-like Asian women.[48] Films, theatre, and television repeatedly screened reproductions, in various forms, of stereotypical Madame Butterflies who were loved, impregnated, left to die, but nostalgically remembered by her faithless Western lover.

Operas about Others Today

Supported by the development of large-scale global operatic spectaculars, both *Turandot* and *Madama Butterfly* enjoy undiminished popularity in contemporary times, and often sell better than more recent works. Opera's audiences have changed since the nineteenth century: they are no longer culturally homogenous: globalization, multiculturism, and actual or tele-travel has ensured that public experience of other cultures has expanded greatly. As opera's expensive staging and personnel demands keep ticket prices high, a large proportion of opera's audiences are still from the middle and upper classes, including the ruling elites who create foreign policies and set immigrant quotas. Ethical and political questions arise about the implications of perpetuating fetishized Asian images replete with the value judgements and obsessions of their creators, out of context and out of time.

Racial insult is easily elided during an operatic performance, as opera works by the entrapment and ravishment of the senses and emotions, as audiences escape into the magnificence of music, singing, and the spectacle of a highly-charged, sensual event, willing to forgive all just to hear a favorite aria sung with splendor. Simply getting Asian directors and singers to replace Europeans in appropriate roles apparently does little to change opera's Orientalist ideology: the actors become complicit within Orientalist structures for financial and career advancement. Increased contact with and awareness of the complexities of other cultures does not seem to greatly lessen the West's desire for the East as a site of alternative site of fantasy: Orientalism finds new outlets in video games and martial arts films, and glossy international magazines project images of Eurasian femininity and fashion. Some global entrepreneurs and artists, from both East and West, widen the gaps between "self" and "other" and make use of sophisticated technical expertise and equipment, international commercial communication networks, and international demands for large operatic spectacles, to mount Orientalist extravaganzas unmatched in the nineteenth century. A wealthy international audience pays generously for the thrill of viewing major global productions in a variety of different locations. In 1997, director Zhang Yimou staged Puccini's *Turandot* in Florence, Italy. In 1998, he directed it again in Beijing.[49] Sean Metzger observes that this latter $15-million production drew 4,000 people, mostly from overseas, for its opening night. This was mainly because the ticket prices excluded the locals: "the top ticket price for the night was U.S. $1,250, nearly half the national per capita income that year."[50] Metzger comments that Yamou's production "manipulated old stereotypes," and was structured around "an intercultural aesthetic that hinged not only on Orientalist visions of race and national culture but also on certain fantastic expectations of excessive sexuality."[51]

Yamou added brilliant and accomplished elements of Chinese culture to the production: "the drum corps that opened *Turandot* in the Forbidden City attempted to replicate a Ming-dynasty convention in which percussion preceded court events."[52] Authentic costumes, dances, fabrics, and an executioner proficient in martial arts contributed only a superficial, aesthetic splendor to the production. Chinese nationals were represented by large numbers of dancers and non-singing artistes not integral to the opera's dramatic heart. Radical re-thinking of opera's stereotypical representations is required if this paradigmatic art form is to deliver more than entertaining spectacles and nostalgia for grand despotic regimes and oppressive lifestyles, both supported by wonderful music and glorious singing.

It is possible to escape from the signifying racial codes of nineteenth-century Eurocentric philosophy, ideology and scientific hierarchism. The destabilization of universalities and meaning of the twentieth century has made it theoretically possible for directors and designers to think outside of the identity systems that emphasize the binarisms of self and other, in-group and out-group, and that connect behavior to race, and race to fixed hierarchy. The semiotic concept that any sign (signifier) engages in an ambiguous relationship with many possible referents (signifieds), is useful in imagining an embodied operatic character (the sign) disconnected from a hierarchical, stereotypical racial identity (the signified), located in a geographical place, (Japan, China), but not within imposed hierarchies of race. A staged presence does not have to signal a prescribed menu of behavior, if that neutrality is signalled cleverly: signs can attach to many possible referents. In *Empire of Signs*, Barthes indicates that an actor's (or singer's) presence can be negated, and replaced by a "pure sign."[53] He uses the example of a fifty-year old male Kabuki actor, in the mask and costume of a young woman, who does not imitate or represent a woman, but absents his own identity, becoming a pure signifier of the idea of woman. This application of the Zen concept of inner void is reflected in conventions of the Japanese language that treats characters in novels as inanimate objects, unlike humans and animals.

> [T]he fictive characters introduced into a story (once upon a time there was a king) are assigned the form of the inanimate; whereas our whole art struggles to enforce the "life," the "reality" of fictive beings, the very structure of Japanese restores or confines these beings to their quality as products, signs cut off from the alibi referential par excellence; that of the living thing.[54]

The non-specific, abstracted nature of signs, and the referential ambiguity of Barthes's Zen approach is one way to sidestep self-conscious appropriations of Asia and Asians (at the visual level at least: words and music need to remain intact in order to preserve the artwork's cohesion and integrity).[55] Buddhist and Taoist ideas of interconnectedness, the inner void and the fluid self, when used to stage an opera such as *Madama Butterfly*, can undercut biologically time-warped oppositions between an irrational Other and a rational Western self by negating and absenting the racialized body.

Some contemporary artistic directors and producers have demonstrated an awareness of the dissonances generated by racially deterministic, performative representation by re-shaping opera's visible ideologies and structuring philosophies, and by visualizing opera through different eyes. Moffatt Oxenbold's 1999 Adelaide production of *Madama Butterfly* for State Opera of S.A. partially evaded entanglement in ideological, semiotic structures common in the nineteenth and early twentieth centuries, and diluted the essentialism mixed with desire that fixates Japan and its people within ancient stereotypes. Oxenbold did not attempt to create "real" Japanese scenes, but employed devices from Japanese drama, such as black-garbed stage assistants (Koken), whose interventions abstracted and alienated the action from reality. A body of water separated the stage from the audience, and thus symbolically from the "real" world, emphasising a retreat from geographical location to the imagination. Oxenbold's production added a degree of dignity to an opera in which Japanese society has been mocked with dubious stage mimicry of "old Japan," unlikely looking Japanese singers, and tawdry sets. The audience was not denied visual beauty of color or design, but it was refused the type of staging that has traditionally, and painfully, replicated the Japan of fans and teapots. Structured according to principles of Zen, the stage arrangements, sets, costumes, and design were reduced to bare essentials. Kabuki and Noh theatrical elements and stylized movements directed attention to the opera's artifice. Minimalist make-up signified racial ambivalence, and the singers' bodies became signs relating to elusive and mobile referents: Butterfly, not encased in "yellow-face," was racially indeterminate. Clad in garments that suggested the idea of kimono rather than replicated it, she did not sport painted, slanted eyes and did not move in an exaggerated manner that

Westerners had in the past been careful to emulate as an "Oriental" way of moving (small steps, hurried gait). This lack of mimicry decentred the protagonist's ethnicity, giving the impression that the opera's emotional and dramatic themes could have happened anywhere. The sign "Butterfly" only ambiguously adhered to Japan.

For a European audience, the production's tragedy was potentially more shocking: there was no secret relief that such bad things happened to someone who was securely "Other" and not to one of "us." The events could not be safely relegated to "over there," raising the following questions: how would an audience react if the cultural roles were reversed? What if this was a European woman exploited by a Japanese man? Would the opera's plot still seem "exotic," or racially provocative, or just tawdry?

The ingrained bitterness of a racist past may be permanently ingrained in opera's structure. However, directors and producers who attempt to remodel the art form at least begin to imagine alternatives to racially based power relationships and stereotypes. Modifying opera's visual forms may be nothing more than band-aid therapy, but audiences are thereby informed that times have changed, and that music is to be held accountable for its complicity in social oppression.

Opera's richness has grown from the grubby soil of commerce, ideology, and public sensibility, and is grounded in the social realities from which audiences may hope to escape. By its ability to lift the spirit, Opera seems to transcend all of that. Its virtuosity inspires us with hope and implores exemption from the everyday scrutiny of critics who would spoil the fantasy. This essay asked the question, "Whose fantasy?"

Notes

1. Catherine Clement, *Opera, or the Undoing of Women*, trans. Betsy Wing (Minneapolis: University of Minnesota Press, 1988), 20.

2. Giacomo Puccini, Giuseppi Adami, and Renato Simoni, *Turandot. An Opera in Three Acts.* La Scala, Milan, 1926. The Australian Opera's production of *Turandot* was presented by the State Opera of South Australia, Adelaide Festival Theatre, Adelaide, 1996.

3. Although Puccini's opera was produced in the twentieth century, his life, work, and ideas (especially concerning women, Asia, and Orientalism) reflected themes prominent in the nineteenth century; *Turandot* was his last, unfinished work.

4. "Far Eastern" is of course an extremely Eurocentric term. As Derek Scott observes, in *Orientalism and Musical Style*, the East is, "far from *us* and therefore the word relies

on a metageography for its meaning." See Derek B. Scott, "Orientalism and Musical Style," *The Musical Quarterly* 82, no. 2 (1988): 323.

5. Giacomo Puccini, Giuseppi Giacosa, and Luigi Illica, *Madama Butterfly. An Opera in Three Acts.* First performed, La Scala, Milan, 1904.

6. As discourses about Southern and Middle Eastern Orientalism use different codes of signification from that of their Far Eastern counterparts, this discussion does not engage with operas such as *Samson and Delilah* or *Aida*. The latter operas project images of a different fantasy landscape and people: Madame Butterfly and Turandot are not mythologized in the same "belly-dancing" mode as Salome or Delilah. They represent erotic dynamics of females from two different fantasy landscapes: in the (masculine) gaze of visual art, Asian women were usually painted inside their kimonos and not naked as were countless Middle Eastern or Turkish women.

7. Giacomo Puccini, Giuseppi Giacosa, and Luigi Illica, *Madama Butterfly. An Opera in Three Acts*, La Scala, Milan, 1904.

8. William Weber, "Beyond Zeitgeist," *The Journal of Modern History* 66, no. 2 (1994): 321–45.

9. Henrika Kuklick, *The Savage Within: The Social History of British Anthropology, 1885–1945* (New York: Cambridge University Press, 1991).

10. Weber considers that music's interpreters persisted with approaches that were not tolerated in other fields (from which they were isolated) *because* of the widespread disillusion and fragmentation of the twentieth century, as the arts became a refuge of unity and heroic fantasy: "The intense intellectual passion for this mode of thought is spiritual in nature: its popularity stems from a need to perceive a higher unity within an increasingly disunified and desacrilised culture" (Weber, 323).

11. Dorinne Kondo, *About Face: Performing Race in Fashion and Theater* (New York: Routledge, 1997), 230.

12. Heidi Tolles Motkus, "The Art of Cultural Studies," *Phi Kappa Phi Forum* 83, no. 13 (Summer 2003): 8.

13. Weber's information on the *frottola* is found in William Prizer, "Lutenists and the Court of Mantua in the Late Fifteenth and Early Sixteenth Centuries," *Journal of the Lute Society of America* 13 (1980): 4–34, and Isabella d'Este Lorenzo da Pavia, "Master Instrument Maker," *Early Music History* (1982): 87–127. Weber cites Zaslaw's idea that Mozart's choices of composition were chiefly determined by their economic viability: the composer abandoned pieces for which he did not have a patron or audience: in other words, his "daily professional activities" were a part of the system "through which culture is produced and consumed." See Neil Zaslaw, "Mozart as a Working Stiff," in *On Mozart*, ed. James Wood (New York: Woodrow Wilson Center Press), 1994.

14. Sean Metzger observes that like Carlo Gozzi's Persian-inspired play of 1761, Puccini's *Turandot*, emerged from a "series of uneven cultural exchanges and unabashedly orientalist fantasies." In a letter to one of his librettists, Puccini encouraged his wordsmith "to find a Chinese element to enrich the drama and relieve the artificiality of it." See Giuseppe Adami, ed. *Letters of Giacomo Puccini* (London: Harra, 1974), 272, quoted in Sean Metzger, "Zhang Yimou's Turandot," *Asian Theatre Journal* 20, no. 2 (Fall 2003): 209–9.

15. Gina Marchetti has given a particularly clear analysis of the ways in which Asian female images have been projected in motion pictures. See Gina Marchetti, *Romance and the "Yellow Peril": Race, Sex, and Discursive Strategies in Hollywood Fiction* (Berkeley: University of California Press, 1993).

16. The libretto was the starting point of operatic musical composition. Operatic music is a vehicle of narration and is mostly subordinate to the libretto's demands; however, it may diverge from and intensify the drama and dominate the production. Delays in librettists Adami and Alfano's output probably contributed to Puccini's failure to complete *Turandot*.

17. Linda Hutcheon, *Opera, Disease, Death* (Lincoln: University of Nebraska Press, 1996), 11.

18. The Victorian British craze for Japonisme and Chinoiserie was also a powerful determinant of racialized meaning at the time, but space presently available does not permit its discussion.

19. Shearer West, *The Victorians and Race*, 2nd ed. (Aldershot and Vermont: Ashgate, 1998), 2.

20. For much of the information in this paragraph, I am indebted to D. Lorimer, "Race, Science and Culture: Historical Continuities and Discontinuities, 1850–1914," in West, *The Victorians and Race*, 1998.

21. According to Keane's *Ethnology*, the Chinese possessed pronounced Mongolian characteristics, but the Japanese were only "slightly tinged with it." "The Mongols" were classified as beneath Caucasians.

22. See A. H. Keane, *Ethnology: The Primary Ethnical Groups*, 2, 2nd ed. (Cambridge: Cambridge University Press, 1896), 479.

23. Keane, *Ethnology*, 479.

24. The term "Other" is well-worn and due for a change: in the absence of another term as compact and accessible, I use it as a form of shorthand.

25. In Italy, where most operas popular in Europe were composed, people from all classes attended the opera (perhaps because of its large outdoor venues such as the Arena di Verona), but in most other Western countries, opera halls and after-show dinner parlours were dominated by the upper and middle classes.

26. David J. Levin, ed., *Opera through Other Eyes* (Stanford, California: Stanford University Press, 1993), 14.

27. Levin, *Opera Through Other Eyes*, 14.

28. Levin, *Opera Through Other Eyes*, 14–15.

29. There are undocumented reports that a Japanese woman sang operatic arias in late 1800s in Britain, but this was an exception to the rule that continued through the first half of the 1900s.

30. William Ashbrook and Harold Powers, *Puccini's Turandot: The End of the Great Tradition* (Princeton: Princeton University Press, 1991), 11.

31. Toshio Yokoyama, *Japan in the Victorian Mind* (Hampshire and London: Macmillan, 1987), 107. See also Liza Dalby, *Kimono* (London: Vintage, 1993), 95–96.

32. Daniel Bar-Tal, *Stereotyping and Prejudice: Changing Conceptions, Springer Series in Social Psychology* (New York: Springer-Verlag, 1989); Simon James Beal, "Stereotype Knowledge, Personal Beliefs, and Racial Prejudice in Children" (Honors thesis, University of Adelaide, 2000); Richard Dyer, *The Matter of Images: Essays on Representations* (London and New York: Routledge, 1993); J. F. Dovidio, "Racial Stereotypes: The Contents of Their Cognitive Representations," *Journal of Experimental Social Psychology* 22 (1986): 22–37; Sander L Gilman, *Difference and Pathology: Stereotypes of Sexuality, Race, and Madness* (Ithaca: Cornell University Press, 1985).

33. Rosemary Breger, *Images of Japan in the German Press and in Japanese Self-Presentation* (New York and Paris: Peter Lang, 1990).

34. Michel Foucault, *The Archaeology of Knowledge* (London: Travistock, 1972).

35. Breger, *Myth and Stereotype*, 5.

36. Gilman, *Difference and Pathology*, 16.

37. Gilman, *Difference and Pathology*, 15.

38. David A. Napier, *Foreign Bodies: Performance, Art, and Symbolic Anthropology* (Berkeley: University of California Press, 1992), xviii.

39. Butterfly's honor would not have been particularly compromised by such a desertion in Nagasaki in the late 1800s: these types of transactions of economic expediency were common at that time, and were regarded pragmatically by the populace. It is more feasible to conclude that a "broken heart" and the alienation from her family would have precipitated the suicide, rather than honor. However, European playwrights, librettists and novelists loved to include a "hara kiri" (an incorrect term) scene in tales of Japan.

40. In the racially obsessed climate of the late 1800s, miscegenation was frowned upon. It was held that inter-marriage with other races lower on the hierarchy would lead to the degeneration of the Caucasian races.

41. Giacomo Puccini, "Turandot." *Esso Nights at the Opera*, State Theatre of the Victorian Arts Centre, dir. Graeme Murphy (Melbourne: ABC television and Australian Opera, 24 November 1991).

42. Giacomo Puccini, *Esso Nights at the Opera*, Act 3.

43. As the Tartars were Turkish-Mongolians, Calef was thus "Chinese" enough to avoid intimations of miscegenation.

44. Mark Peploe and Bernardo Bertolucci, *The Last Emperor,* dir. Bernado Bertolucci, prod. Jeremy Thomas, Tokyo, Columbia Pictures, 1987.

45. See Phil Hammond, *Cultural Difference, Media Memories: Anglo-American Images of Japan* (London and Herndon, VA: Cassell, 1997). For a Japanese perspective, see Japan Photographer's Association, *A Century of Japanese Photography* (New York: Panthenon, 1980), 325–356.

46. Gilman, *Difference and Pathology*, 16.

47. Gilman, *Difference and Pathology*, 18.

48. Examples of "Butterfly" literature include: Richard Setlowe, *The Sexual Occupation of Japan* (New York: HarperCollins, 2000); James Webb, *The Emperor's General* (London: Penguin, 1999); Graham Greene, *The Quiet American*, 1952, (Hammondsworth: Penguin in association with Heinemann, 1962). See also a "Butterfly" musical: Claude-Michel

Schonberg, Alain Boublil, and Richard Maltby, *Cameron Mackintosh Presents Miss Saigon: A Musical* (London: Wise, 1990).

49. Zhang Yanou, *Turandot in the Forbidden City*, Working People's Cultural Palace, Beijing, September 1998.

50. Henry Chu, "A great wall comes Down: Puccini's "Turandot" Makes Its Long Awaited Debut in China," *Los Angeles Times*, September 7 (1998), sec. F, 1.

51. Sean Metzger, "Zhang Yimou's 'Turandot'" *Asian Theatre Journal* 20, no. 2 (Fall 2003): 215, 209.

52. Sean Metzger, *Asian Theatre Journal*, 210.

53. Roland Barthes, *Empire of Signs* (New York: Hill and Wang, 1970).

54. Roland Barthes, *Empire of Signs*, 5.

55. Derek B. Scott discusses Orientalist musical signifiers that permit the "immediate comprehension of musical allusion." These include tunes based on a pentatonic scale, "perfect fourth and fifth intervals moving in parallel motion," gong crashes and dissonance. According to Scott, the "final eleven tragic Orientalist measures of Madama Butterfly" provide a paradigmatic model of the Far Eastern Orientalist "sound" used by Western composers. See Scott, *Orientalism and Musical Style*, 327.

Judge Harsh Blues
Lynching, Law, and Order in the New South[1]

MICHAEL A. ANTONUCCI

The blues emerged as a form of American popular music during the last quarter of the nineteenth century. With its layered African polyrhythms, syncopated call-and-response patterns, and distinctive I-V-IV chord progression, the blues catalogues a range of experiences shaping African American life during the rise of the New South. In this way the music enters into a conversation with the climate of terror and racialized violence that enveloped the United States from the end of slavery through the renewal and consolidation of white Southern political and economic power. The blues, therein, exhibits a singular capacity for recording what novelist and critic Ralph Ellison describes as "incongruous juxtapositions" forming "the territory" of "American unwritten history."[2] By mapping this terrain, the blues constitutes a deep repository of evidence, supplementing received notions about African American experience and American history at large. Firmly rooted in the expressive culture produced by enslaved Africans and their descendants, the music bears witness to historical events and conditions shaping African American life during the dismantling of the Reconstruction goals and implementation of Jim Crow segregation. As such, the blues makes visible marginalized, overlooked portions of the American historical record.

The interaction between Black music and African American historical experience is explored at length by LeRoi Jones in *Blues People* (1964). Throughout his foundational study of African American culture and history, Jones maintains that form and content in Black music always reflects developments in African American social history. To ground his argument, he claims that established patterns governing African American life in the antebellum American South were entirely transformed by the economic, legal, and social practices that emerged within the New South. According to Jones, during the Reconstruction and post-Reconstruction periods, freedmen and their descendants were set into a new "life of movement from farm to farm or town to town." As a result of these "more complicated social situations," he writes that "the music of [Black people] began to reflect these social and cultural complexities and change."[3] In this way, Jones maintains that as it replaced the hollers, shouts, spirituals, and work songs that defined Black music within the institution of slavery, the blues becomes the enduring African American cultural product, reflecting the cultural and political landscape of the New South.

Throughout *Blues People* Jones argues that this Africanized form of American folk music comprises a record of historical conditions shaping African American life. Identifying this dimension of the music, Jones speaks to the ability of the blues to both store and present African American culture and history. For Jones, the blues and blues rooted musical forms become a steady ostinato, marking the historical experience of African Americans and the United States at large. He thereby recognizes the music as a means of accessing details about African American historical experience, particularly those events and elements obscured by what Ellison, his critical interlocutor,[4] refers to as "historical amnesia." In this sense Jones sees the music as working to revise and complicate simplistic notions about Black people and African American culture in the United States. In this respect, he joins Ellison in a larger project recognizing the blues as an engaged, multi-valent document that interrogates circumstances and attitudes relevant within African American life.

While Jones works toward these ends in *Blues People*, Ellison's efforts emerge through a series of essays on music that appears in *Shadow and Act*. This collection includes "Remembering Jimmy," a review which considers the vocal stylings of bluesman Jimmy Rushing. In the piece, Ellison draws on his familiarity with Rushing's blues, which dates back to Ellison's youth in Oklahoma City, bringing a measure of context to Rushing's body of work. He asserts that even before the singer became known as "Mr. Five-by-Five," Rushing was "not just a local entertainer." Ellison supports his claim, suggesting that Rushing's performances with the legendary territory bands, including the Blue Devils Orchestra, the Benny Moten Big Band, and Count Basie Orchestra, express "a value, an attitude about the world for which [black] lives afforded no other definition."[5] In this way, Ellison's "Remembering Jimmy" presents the blues as being underscored by "more profound implications," that, ultimately, provide listeners a "corrective." He submits that Rushing's vocals are "not simply a matter of entertainment; they also tell us who and where we are."[6]

Ellison, like Jones, recognizes the blues as delivering an extended critique of what he describes in a later essay as "American mythic history." Both writers see structural elements and lyric content of the blues as engaging in a call-and-response dialogue with the peculiar conditions that confronted African Americans in the New South throughout the Jim Crow era. In their own ways, they claim that through their capacity to worry, expand, and explore a simple riff or vocal line, blues musicians effectively penetrate and encounter unspoken truths within the American historical record. As such, despite their well-publicized differences, Jones and Ellison understand and promote the blues impulse as pushing limits and extending boundaries that implicitly challenge aspects of a white-dominated power structure. Their foundational work in this area, thereby, provides a structure for investigating how the blues impulse, at once, speaks to and is shaped by the social and political realities of the New South and the United States at large.

Throughout the 1880s and 1890s, fallout from the Hayes-Tillden Compromise eroded political and legal rights African Americans were supposed to have secured with passage of the 13th, 14th, and 15th amendments to the United States Constitution. During the final decades of the nineteenth century, black Southerners saw their Reconstruction era gains swept away in an environment of escalated hostilities, which were ultimately sanctioned in the establishment of a legally codified second-class citizenship, as sanctioned by the 1896 *Plessey v. Furguson* decision. This systematic subversion of African American political needs and social concerns extended well into the twentieth century. In addition to being, at once, ignored and vilified as a group, African Americans were consistently degraded and dehumanized throughout American popular culture. These developments ultimately coincided with and were largely underwritten by a program of violence and extra-legal activity.

In the preface to *Trouble in Mind* (1997), Leon Litwack explains that "violence and the fear of violence helped to shape black lives and personalities . . . the extent and quality of the violence unleashed on black men and women in the name of enforcing black deference and subordination cannot be avoided or minimized."[7] Litwack goes on to state that while its details make for "unpleasant reading," the realities of this racialized violence are impossible to separate from the social fabric of the New South. As he writes at the outset of his comprehensive study of Black life in the New South, "young blacks underwent the rites of racial passage in a variety of ways. But the specter and threat of physical violence—'the white death'—loomed over nearly every encounter. If they themselves were not the victims, the violence fell on members of the family, friends, and neighbors, almost always with the same intent—to remind black men and women of their 'place.'"[8]

By virtue of developing within this climate and because of its strong connections to the fabric of African American life, seemingly, the blues provides an ideal vehicle for gaining insight into the New South's "unwritten history." Yet, despite the frequent occurrence of lynchings and other forms of racialized violence while blues and blues-rooted music grew in popularity, blues scholarship has not looked to connect these two prominent features of the cultural landscape during Jim Crow. In fact, as Albert Murray does in *Stomping the Blues* (1976), some take pains to distill and remove the blues from its historical context. This is seen when Murray writes, "But even when blues lyrics address themselves directly to the economic, political and judiciary circumstances, far more often than not the main emphasis is going to be placed on the victim's love life." He continues his ahistorical portrait of the blues by stating:

> The pseudo-folk lyric currently so dear to the hearts of avant-garde nightclub patrons and self-styled revolutionary revelers blame the crooked judge, but traditional folk lyrics are about the damage to a love affair. . . . In fact in the 160 available recordings of Bessie Smith, a few notable exceptions such as "Washer Woman's Blues" and "Poor Man's Blues" notwithstanding, the preoccupation is clearly not at all with hard workmasters, cruel sheriffs, biased prosecutors, juries and judges but with aggravating papas, sweet mistreaters, dirty nogooders and spider men.[9]

However, Dwight Andrews points out in "Black into Blues" that there is a great deal to be said about the oppositional dimensions of the blues, especially when its use and application of African musical retention, such as sonic stacking, manipulations of rhythmic pulse, and stressed accents, is given consideration.[10] Even so, the investigation Andrews undertakes in "Black into Blues" does not treat another subversive or oppositional impulse the blues deploys through the use of lyric and musical signification (signifyin'), as Sam Floyd discusses in "African American Modernism, Signifyin(g) and Black Music."[11] Bringing these dimensions into account, it becomes clear that blues musicians consistently staged and performed acts of resistance to the repressive social, political, and economic conditions present in the New South. In this way the music complicates and expands dominant historical accounts of the New South. Yet, despite the formal opposition, described by Floyd, Andrews, and others, the most compelling manifestation of blues resistance is found, perhaps, in the "attitude" that the music exhibits in its frank discussions of human behaviors and emotions.

This attitude becomes particularly evident in the way that blues lyrics engages "difficult" issues not readily broached in the dialogue of a social structure defined by the numerous "taboo subjects" that comprise the race line. This impulse is seen in the music's treatment of issues such as gender roles, sexuality, money, labor, love, power, jealousy, and loss. In these issues, the blues seems to seek, even demand, that a truthful attention be brought to bear on the subject at hand. "Telling it like it is," "breaking it down," or even "getting to the nitty-gritty," are, to a greater or lesser extent, blues clichés. At the same time, however, through these attempts to interrogate the complexities of a situation, the blues asserts the "corrective" alluded to by Ellison in "Remembering Jimmy." Given the contradictions and incongruities that shaped the New South's race relations and race rituals, any concerted efforts to privilege "the whole truth" or uncover pervasive myths underwriting its social, legal, and political structures, assumes a particular type of significance.

Understood in light of the hazards inherent to African American life in the United States during the Jim Crow era, the impact of such a project becomes doubly compounded. As such, these blues correctives effectively inscribe the field of African American historical experience within the context of the "both/and" propositions that inform the music's harmonic structure and lyric content. Rooted in these ambiguities, the blues point of engagement with its audience and subject matter is ultimately manifest in the sonic collisions and shifts of meaning. An example of this is seen in Mississippi John Hurt's "Ain't No Telling" when he sings:

> *The way I'm sleeping, my back and shoulders tired*
> *The way I'm sleeping, my back and shoulders tired*
> *The way I'm sleeping, my back and shoulders tired*
> *Gonna turn over, try it on the other side.*
> *Don't you let my good girl catch you here*
> *She might shoot you,*
> *may cut and stab you too*
> *Ain't no telling what she might do.*[12]

On one level, these lines treat themes of deception, power, and violence within a romantic relationship. At the same time, these themes are easily applicable to context of unfair labor practices and the extra-legal, radicalized violence Litwack describes in *Trouble in Mind*. The indeterminate meanings and multiple contexts in which these lines may be accessed through Hurt's use of a rhetorically ambiguous, double-negative—"Ain't No Telling What She Might Do"—as both the title and tag-line of the song. Framed within this contingent, "both/and" prospective, "she" may be either an unpredictable lover or stand for the hair-trigger volatility of the social landscape of the New South.

Yet, even while the blues is steeped in an ambiguity, opening limitless interpretive possibilities, the form does not have room for ambivalence or equivocation. For instance, regardless of the interpretation Hurt's audience takes from the smooth vocals in his "Ain't No Telling," the song's lyrics bear witness to violence and possibilities of violence, thereby speaking tangibly to African American lives set within the limits of Jim Crow segregation and the New South. This dynamic effectively illustrates the blues at work, strategically deploying indeterminacy, as a means of confronting contradictions and injustices present in everyday life.

Describing living conditions present in the New South, Litwack writes, "the consensus in the white South over the need to establish a rigid color line and maintain racial supremacy allowed for little dissent. And since whites were prepared to punish dissent, most blacks might have been expected to accept quietly and passively the restraints imposed on their lives."[13] The historian goes on to point out that, as a group confronting these circumstances, African Americans had few channels for seeking recourse. Largely disenfranchised and facing an unjust legal system and the ever-present threat of extra-legal activity, conventional political and legal methods for redressing grievances were untenable. Litwack is quick to add that even when faced with these conditions, African American resistance to the white supremacist agendas advanced in the Jim Crow South was evident, particularly if one listened closely to the blues.[14]

In *A Festival of Violence* (1995) Tolnay and Beck point out that between the years 1884 and 1905 at least 1,374 African Americans were lynched by white-mobs. This figure represents nearly three-quarters of all lynchings that occurred during this twenty-year period. Based on these figures, during the period, on average, white mobs lynched 70 black people per year, which translates to an average of more than one lynching per week.[15] The absence of a blues commentary on a practice as prevalent as lynching becomes especially surprising in light of the demonstrated willingness of blues musicians to engage subjects that lay beyond the limits of polite discourse in the New South. In this respect, the music's perceived silence on incidents of racial violence—particularly lynchings—seems to contradict that fundamental blues impulse that does not allow for equivocation or the possibility of backing-away from the self-evident truths in a given situation. However, as W. Fitzhugh Brundage argues in "The Roar on the Other Side of Silence," the struggle to control "the production of and limits of social meaning" is central to the conflicts between dominant and subordinate social groups. In his exploration of black resistance to white violence in the American South, Brundage argues that African Americans worked to "undermine the legitimacy of white rule by invoking a language of dissemblance."[16] The blues makes a major contribution to this project.

"Snitchin' Gamblers' Blues" provides an example of this blues impulse toward delivering "correctives" to both white domination in the New South and dominate versions of the American historical record. This tune, attributed to an anonymous song writer and recorded by the Memphis Jug Band, does so by delivering an account of the post-Reconstruction era in terms that gives a vivid illustration of why historian Rayford Logan calls this period the "nadir of American race relations." As played by the Memphis Jug Band, "Snitchin' Gamblers' Blues" delivers an up-tempo chronology, documenting the rise of Jim Crow segregation. Its thinly veiled lyrics provide a demonstration of Brundage's "language of dissemblance" while offering an account on the changes African Americans experienced and witnessed within the dynamic political, social, and legal landscape of the late nineteenth century in the American South. This interpretation of the song becomes exceedingly apparent when the "snitching people" are understood as a reference to Southern whites determined to undermine the political gains of African Americans guaranteed by the 13th, 14th, and 15th Amendments to the United States Constitution.

The song opens with the lines, "Now its eighteen hundred and its ninety-one/that when the snitching people just begun."[17] Significantly, 1891 was a year in which the number of reported lynchings of African Americans in the United States exceeded one-hundred persons for the first time, rising from eighty-eight in 1890 to 127.[18] The anonymous blues artist who wrote these lyrics extends his critique of deteriorating social and political conditions of African Americans in the United States at the last decade of the nineteenth century in this verse's next two lines, "Now its eighteen hundred and its ninety-two/the snitching in town: Lord they just won't do."[19] Here, "Snitchin' Gamblers' Blues" focuses on a year in which the number of reported white mob lynchings of Black men and women reached an all time high, 155, according to figures collected by the National Association for the Advancement of Colored People.[20] Connections between these lines and the escalation of racialized violence in the last decade of the nineteenth century becomes particularly apparent when they are understood as originating in Memphis, Tennessee and the Mid-South region.[21] The reference to "snitching in town" has a particular resonance with a triple lynching that took place in Memphis on 8 March 1892. This was the first documented lynching to take place in a major Tennessee population center. Prior to 1892 all Tennessee lynchings recorded by the NAACP occurred outside this state's three largest cities, Memphis, Nashville, or Chattanooga.[22]

The second verse of "Snitchin' Gamblers' Blues" continues to treat issues pertaining to law, order, and lynching in the New South while, interestingly, shifting from its year-by-year chronological account. 1893 and 1895, years in which the reported number of African Americans lynched by white mobs modestly declined, are not mentioned in the lyric. This focus of the verse, again, remains on years when African Americans suffered losses at the hands of "snitchers," who deprive black Southerners of their inalienable rights to life, liberty, and property.

> Now it's eighteen hundred and its ninety-four
> The white people load me in the workhouse door
> Oh it's eighteen hundred and its ninety-six
> that when the snitchers thought all their snitching was fixed.[23]

Arguably, the singer of this blues is fortunate to have been "Load(ed) in the workhouse door" when he came into the hands of "the white people" in 1894, a year when the number of reported lynchings rose to 128 people.[24] With the next two lines, the unnamed blues lyricist(s) who wrote "Snitchin' Gamblers' Blues" reveals the tune's underlying political orientation and historical consciousness. When these oblique references are brought into dialogue with the events of 1896, a double-edged irony emerges from the lines. This becomes apparent when it understood that while the number of reported white-on-Black lynchings declined in 1896, it was also the year when the *Plessey v. Furguson* decision legalized Jim Crow segregation in the United States. In this way, "the snitchers" are only too pleased to think that their "snitching was fixed."

Where the Memphis Jug Band's "Snitchin' Gamblers' Blues" addresses the consolidation of an unjust social and political climate in the New South, Furry Lewis, another Memphis-area bluesman, delivers an equally frank assessment of the Southern judicial system with "Judge Harsh Blues." In this tune, Lewis sings and strums out an account of the arbitrary and unjust structure of the Southern judiciary. His critique begins with a simple declaration of innocence when he sings,

> They arrested me for murder
> I ain't never harmed a man.
> Arrest me for murder and, Lord, I ain't harmed a Ma-a-an.
> Woman hollered murder and I ain't raised my hand.[25]

Lewis continues, underscoring the idea that random arrests on trumped up charges were a common occurrence for African Americans throughout the Jim Crow-era. This is seen as he attempts to console a female figure, distressed by her failure to raise a sufficient amount of bail money to secure the singer's release. Addressing his "woman," Lewis tries to reassure her by singing, "Baby, I'm arrested please don't grieve and moan/ 'Cause I'm arrested, please don't grieve and moan/Penitentiary seems like my home."[26]

The singer extends this critique by continuing to address "Judge Harsh," who has turned a deaf ear to his pleas for leniency. In the song's final verse, Lewis offers an ambiguously worded, but clearly pointed, blues corrective indicting the structure and function of the Jim Crow legal system. He sings, "Judge, the people hollerin' 'bout what in the world will they do/Lots of people had justice, they'd be in the penitentiary too."[27] With these lines the singer speaks to the criminal inequities within the Southern judicial system's treatment of African Americans. As such, "Judge Harsh Blues" contributes to a blues' archive documenting of the lives and experiences of a people traditionally marginalized by conventional renderings of the American historical record. Understanding this song becomes possible when it is remembered that Lewis lived his life as a Black man in West Tennessee during the high tide of white mob violence against people of African descent.[28] A similar act of resistance is performed in the lyrics of Blind Lemon Jefferson's "Hangman's Blues." Again, the blues explores events and circumstances that Ellison describes as "American unwritten history." This becomes particularly apparent when this song is recognized as the work of an African American singer-songwriter who traveled extensively throughout the United States and spent time in jail in the early part of the twentieth century. As such Jefferson's "Hangman's Blues" clearly enters into conversation with the final stanza of "Judge Harsh Blues," gesturing to the prevalence of legal and extra legal executions of African Americans in the New South. This becomes evident when Jefferson sings, "They crowd around the courthouse : and the time is growing fast / Soon a good for nothing killer : is going to take breath his last / Lord I'm almost dying : gasping for my breath."[29]

The blues engagement with lynch law and racialized violence in the New South is further underscored by comments that Texas bluesman Sam Price made to musicologist Paul Oliver in an interview from the mid-1960s. In a subsection of Oliver's *Conversation with the Blues* titled "They

Burned Him," Price describes two lynchings that occurred when he was a youth in East Texas. This passage begins when the musician states:

> When I was a boy I lived in Texas and it was pretty rugged. I'll never forget the first song I ever heard to remember. A man had been lynched near my home in a town called Robinson, Texas. And at that time we were living in Waco, Texas—my mother, brother and myself. And they made a parody of this song and the words were something like this:

> *I never have, and I never will*
> *Pick no more cotton in Robinsonville,*
> *Tell me how long will I have to wait,*
> *Can I get you now or must I hesitate?*[30]

Price, whose career spanned sixty years and included performances and recording sessions with the legends, including Big Joe Turner, Trixie Smith, and Cow Davenport, explicates these lyrics when he continues and states:

> Now what that meant by that song was that he would never pick any more cotton in Robinson—Robinsonville—because a man had been lynched there. And shortly after that they lynched a man in Waco, Texas. I was in the public school you know as a kid. And we had to run home and close the door and then they lynched this man and then they burned him and sewed up his ashes in a little cloth and sold these ashes to the people.[31]

In this account, Price presents information all too familiar to people working with lynching narratives. Like other witnesses to a lynching, the bluesman speaks to the way that the impulse to lynch could infect a region and move from one community to the next. In this respect Price's description of being sent home from school and kept behind closed doors during the lynching is a typical part of these narratives. Even his recollections of the celebratory rituals of desecration conducted after the event are repeated elsewhere. However, through the explication of a seemingly banal song lyric, Price's narrative assumes a particular significance, providing an important set of insights into the relationship between blues and lynching.

The structure of the Price/Oliver interview leaves room for speculation about the origin of what the blues man calls "the first song that [he]
ever heard to remember." As it appears on the page, Price's description
of this song leaves readers wanting to know what the song was and, perhaps more importantly, who was singing it at the time he learned the
tune. The ambiguity surrounding the origins of the song allows for several interpretations. It is possible that Price's tune is a blues of some kind
or another that "they"—again it is unclear whom this might be, but presumably a group of black musicians—worked up as what the piano
player describes as a "parody." In this case, it becomes possible that the
parodied song was one that was written by white musicians to com-
memorate the Robinsonville lynching, the type of "lynching ballad"
that Bruce E. Baker explores in his essay from Brundage's *Under Sentence
of Death* (1997), "North Carolina Lynching Ballads."[32] When read in
this way, Price's tune stands as an illustration of the blues' capacity to
respond directly to the culture of lynching and racial violence.

These lyrics also may be taken simply at face value. When approached
in this way, they appear to provide a very direct blues-rooted commentary about hard working conditions and the need for their singer "to
move on" to a better situation. The singer begins by proclaiming, "I
never have, and I never will/Pick no more cotton in Robinsonville." He
continues by questioning the wisdom of remaining in this Texas town
when he asks: "Tell me how long will I have to wait/Can I get you now or
must I hesitate?" With this line it is possible that Price's song is actually
a riff on Reverend Gary Davis's "Hesitation Blues."[33] Even if this is the
case, through Price's explication of these lyrics, the song becomes contextualized in a way that permits listeners from outside of the African
American community of McLennan County, Texas to gain a greater
grasp of this song's significance. Ultimately, Price's recollections about
the first song he "ever heard to play" reveal that in their own elliptical,
cryptic way, black musicians and the blues were anything but silent in
their treatment of issues related to racial violence and lynching.

In his interview with Oliver, Price offers an important set of insights
into the ways that the blues comment on these issues. Through his narrative the Texas bluesman clearly indicates that during the lynching era,
Black music served as a recognizable vehicle for public discourse about
a full-range of issues concerning African American listening groups,

including lynching and racial violence. At the same time Price's comments also suggest that what keeps this dialogue from being recognized and widely understood is that this commentary is frequently obscured by veiled references and ambiguous signification, such as those present in the Robinsonville song lyric.

The Price commentary, which he reiterates and expands upon in his autobiography *What Do They Want?* (1990), points to the need for a reassessment of prevailing assumptions and received notions about the blues and its dialogue with the American cultural and historical landscape.[34] Price reminds critics and scholars that when they encounter the blues, they are ultimately entering a portion of American cultural space that is "chaotic and full of contradictions."[35] Accordingly, entering this terrain demands that audiences, particularly critical and scholarly ones, reorient their ears to the possibility that even "the most obvious" and accepted interpretations may be revised by these blues correctives. In this way, Price's narrative maintains a fundamental resonance with a comment on the American historical record poet Michael S. Harper delivers in his poem "American History" when he writes:

> *Those four black girls blown up*
> *in that Alabama church*
> *remind me of five hundred*
> *middle passage blacks*
> *in a net, under water*
> *in Charleston harbor*
> *so redcoats wouldn't find them.*
> *Can't find what you can't see*
> *can you?*[36]

Like Harper does in "American History," Pierce directs his readers' attention to the deep gaps separating the lived experience of African Americans from an American historical record largely underwritten by notions of national exceptionalism, progress, and essentialized identities. By doing so, Price's narrative effectively expands an important aspect of the conversation about American race relations and race rituals. In addition, and perhaps more importantly, the Price/Oliver interview helps to identify the blues' engagement with African American culture and the American culture at large in a way that allows tunes like "Snitchin' Gamblers' Blues" and "Judge Harsh Blues" to be recognized as recording and accessing events from "American unwritten history." By making these kinds of connections, dominant understandings of the blues as a good-time music that offers simple entertainment give way to a more completely contextualized version of blues possibilities. When these possibilities are more fully recognized, the blues stand in as an archive of African American experience capable of reclaiming and explicating submerged and sublime aspects of black life in the New South. The music, thereby, offers a way for elements of the Jim Crow era's violent legacy to be retrieved and reconsidered.

From this perspective, Price's recollection of the Robinsonville lynching provides a dynamic illustration of the blues' capacity to access the past, summarized by Ellison in an frequently quoted passage from "Richard Wright's Blues" where he describes the blues as "an impulse to keep the painful details of a brutal experience alive in one's aching consciousness, to finger its jagged grain and to transcend it."[37] When the music is considered with respect to its historical context, what begins to emerge is a sharper understanding of the complex relationships binding the blues, its production, and its audiences. Ultimately, this conversation between the blues and American history "historicizes the blues" as much as it "blues history," revealing this dynamic mode's function as both transmitter and receiver of a richer and more complete American historical record.

Notes

1. I wish to extend a special thanks to Suzanne Flandreau and Andy Leach in the library and archive of the Black Music Research Center at Columbia College. Their assistance and attention have been crucial to writing this piece.

2. Ralph Ellison, *Shadow and Act* (New York: Quality Paper Books, 1994), 128–131.

3. LeRoi Jones, *Blues People* (New Jersey: Morrow, 1964), 62.

4. Ellison and Baraka (Jones) fired salvos at each other verbally and in writing on several occasions. The most famous of these exchanges, however, revolves around the subject of the blues. In his review of *Blues People* Ellison quips, "The tremendous burden of sociology which Jones would place on this body of music is enough to give even the blues the blues."

5. Ellison, *Shadow and Act*, 242.

6. Ellison, *Shadow and Act*, 246.

7. Leon Litwack, *Trouble in Mind* (New York: Alfred A. Knopf, 1998), xvi.

8. Litwack, *Trouble in Mind*, 12.

9. Albert Murray, *Stomping the Blues* (New York: Da Capo, 1987), 66.

10. Dwight A. Andrews, "Black into Blues," *Black Sacred Music* 6:1 (Spring 1992): 51–52.

11. Samuel A. Floyd, Jr., *The Power of Black Music* (New York: Oxford University Press, 1995), 87.

12. Eric Sackheim, *The Blues Line* (New York: Ecco Press, 1993), 232.

13. Litwack, *Trouble in Mind*, 241.

14. Litwack, *Trouble in Mind*, 260–261.

15. Stewart A. Tolnay and E. M. Beck, *A Festival of Violence* (Urbana, Illinois: University of Illinois Press, 1992), 271. These figures are drawn from table C-3 of *A Festival of Violence*. I have chosen the start and stop years simply because they represent the two years from the Jim Crow era in which the number of blacks lynched by white mobs were equal. The total number of blacks lynched by white mobs during this period is 1,374; the total number of people lynched during this period is 1,768.

16. W. Fitzhugh Brundage, "Black Resistance and White Violence in the New South 1880–1940," in *Under Sentence of Death*, ed. W. Fitzhugh Brundage (Chapel Hill, North Carolina: University of North Carolina Press, 1997), 275.

17. Michael Taft, *Blues Lyric Poetry: An Anthology* (New York: Garland Publishers, 1984), 274–275.

18. National Association for the Advancement of Colored People, *Thirty Years of Lynching in the United States* (New York: Negro Universities Press, 1969), 29.

19. Taft, *Blues Lyric Poetry*, 274–275.

20. NAACP, *Thirty Years of Lynching*, 29.

21. I am making this assumption here because although Taft credits the tune to an anonymous song writer, chances are that the it did not travel far when it came into the repertoire of the Memphis Jug Band, which featured, at various times, Will Shade, Charlie Piece, Memphis Minnie and others. These musicians were fixtures on the Memphis music scene through the 1920s and 1930s, in part because of their association with Memphis political boss E.H. Crump.

22. NAACP, *Thirty Years of Lynching*, 29. On 8 March 1892 three black men, Calvin McDonnell, Thomas Moss, and William Stuart, were accused of murder and lynched in Memphis, Tennessee. Later in 1892 an anonymous black man, listed by the NAACP as "A NEGRO" was accused of rape and lynched in Nashville. These were the only recorded lynchings in either city ("in town") until 1917 when E. Person, accused of "alleged rape and murder," was lynched in Memphis.

23. Taft, *Blues Lyric Poetry*, 275.

24. NAACP, *Thirty Years of Lynching*, 29.

25. Sackheim, *The Blues Line*, 254.

26. Sackheim, *The Blues Line*, 254.

27. Sackheim, *The Blues Line*, 254.

28. Walter Furry Lewis was born in Greenwood, Mississippi between 1893 and 1900. He came to Memphis during the second decade of the twentieth century where he

contributed to the first great awakening of American blues in the 1920s. With the exception of a short period of time in Chicago, Lewis spent most of his life in Memphis and the Mid-south region until his death in 1981.

29. Taft, *Blues Lyric Poetry*, 132.

30. Paul Oliver, *Conversation with the Blues* (New York: Horizon Press, 1965), 34.

31. Oliver, *Conversation with the Blues*, 35.

32. Bruce E. Baker, "North Carolina Lynching Ballads," in *Under Sentence of Death*, ed. W. Fitzhugh Brudage (Chapel Hill, North Carolina: University of North Carolina Press, 1997), 219–245.

33. The Hesitation Blues is a traditional blues for which the Reverend Gary Davis is sometimes given credit for composing numerous verses. An example of one of these verses is: "I woke up this morning, 'bout half past four,/Miss hesitation was knocking on my door. /Tell me how long do I baby have to wait?/Can I get you know, why must I hesitate."

34. Sammy Price, *What Do They Want? A Jazz Autobiography* (Urbana, Illinois: University of Illinois, 1990).

35. Ellison, *Shadow and Act*, 124.

36. Michael S. Harper, *Songlines in Michaeltree* (Urbana, Illinois: University of Illinois Press, 2000), 19.

37. Ellison, *Shadow and Act*, 78.

PART IV

Methodological Approaches

Henry Purcell and *The Universal Journal*

The Building of Musical Canon in the 1720s

WILLIAM WEBER AND DONALD BURROWS

Surprising though it may be, England can be credited with having been the first country where a canon of musical classics emerged. Music had little such tradition until the eighteenth century. While the names of some of the most highly renowned musicians remained in memory, little of their music was actually performed. The main places in the early modern period where old music was honored in canonic fashion were the Sistine Chapel, where Palestrina's works remained in the repertory regularly after his death, and a few English cathedrals and chapels, where service settings and anthems by Byrd, Tallis, and other sixteenth-century composers seem to have continued in use, surviving even the hiatus in Anglican practice during the Commonwealth period. After the term "ancient music" arose in England around 1700 to denote music of the sixteenth century, a set of repertories of old works developed that by 1780 were thought explicitly to serve as canon. By then works by Henry Purcell, Corelli, Handel, and a variety of other composers were also regarded as "ancient" and during the early nineteenth century they were included in the new denomination, "classical music."[1]

Little was written upon this extremely important development until well after the middle of the eighteenth century. It is of considerable significance to find a new and earlier source, and one that raises a profound question: why, by tradition, had musical culture had no classics? The subject of "Old Stile" music was treated in a series of three pieces that appeared in 1724 in *The Universal Journal*, a weekly magazine that seems to have been almost as little known then as it is today.[2] The articles include a eulogy to Henry Purcell that is remarkable at that date for the canonic nature of its thought. They suggest strongly that a remarkable breadth of thinking then existed in England concerning the very new idea that music from the past might be preserved as a corpus of great works.

The Universal Journal appeared between 11 December 1723 and 29 August 1724. It was a general interest periodical, one of the many imitations of the spectacularly influential *Spectator* and *Tatler* that had been published in the previous decade. The items that concern us were published in the issues of 27 May, 11 and 25 July 1724.[3] The first is a leading article, presumably by the editor; the second, printed on p. 3 and headed "From my own Apartment," has a similar style[4] but includes a poem by a colleague; and the third is a letter to the editor.[5] The first two pieces and the poem formed part of a rich journalistic literature that existed between 1705 and the 1730s on the subject of Italian opera, which had excluded British composers and (to a large extent) British singers from the stage of the King's Theatre, Haymarket.[6] Here the issue of who was to sing opera went hand-in-hand with issues about the export of British wealth, and with religious-cum-political resentments about the Roman Catholic background of the Italian performers.

Who, then, wrote the three articles? The first question we must ask is where the journal stood in the political spectrum of the time. *The Universal Journal* did not direct its attention upon politics as specifically as did many other periodicals, focusing instead upon the theatre. In its opening issue it declared that "the pulpits and the theatres we shall consider as the Medicines of Instruction; We shall not therefore suffer the One to be seditious, nor the Other to be immoral" (11 December 1723, pp. 1–2). The periodical offered no criticism of the Walpole regime such as was becoming widespread, eventually almost obligatory, in the literary community, as resentment grew over his refusal to serve as patron to men of letters. By abstaining from such commentary, the journal took a moderate Whiggish stance. Repeated attacks upon astrology and superstition in general resonated with the "enlightened" tone of that party's thinking. Early partisan associations did not inhibit canonization, and some of the composers referred to presented complex situations: Henry Purcell's reputation encompassed both strong Tory loyalties and his work for William III, while that of William Byrd delicately balanced loyal court service with fervent Catholic recusancy.

The 1724 texts provide some hints as to their author. A passage in the final one offers a pair of promising candidates, Ambrose Philips and

Leonard Welsted, when it declares, "Let our Dablers in Poetry therefore learn of *Philips* or *Welsted* to prize *Milton*."[7] Philips and Welsted took similar intellectual directions as their careers progressed, and collaborated in editing the journal *The Free-Thinker* in 1718–21. Philips (?1675–1749) seems the most likely of the two to have edited the magazine. He was a loyal Whig throughout his career: in Samuel Johnson's words, "Philips was a zealous Whig, and therefore easily found access to Addison and Steele."[8] He entered into a major dispute with the rising Alexander Pope between 1709 and 1714 when his recently-published books of pastorals were favoured by a commentator over those of Pope: Pope responded with a harsh satirical rejoinder and accusations that Philips was part of a cabal of Addison's supporters formed against him.[9] Since Pope was then a Tory, the two squared off over political partisanship: an edition of Philips's works published in 1799 claimed that "it was said he used to mention Pope as an enemy of the government."[10] In tracing the history of the episode, Annabel Patterson states that the conflict "disrupted literary friendships for a generation and led, on Pope's side, to the renunciation of pastoral as a viable mode of expression, and its deliberate sabotage by the parodies of Gay and his followers."[11] Pope's reputation grew far more than Philips's, and the two authors became irreconcilable enemies. The fact that *The Universal Journal* was discontinued on 29 August 1724 is a further important indication of Philips's role as editor. An article in the final issue— "The History of the Universal Journal, with the author's Last Will and Testament, Published by a Friend"—gives no reason why the series was to be ended, but it does make clear that the editor was going on to other things. In November 1724 Philips left England to become secretary to Hugh Boulter, a major contributor to *The Free-Thinker*, who in 1719 had become Bishop of Bristol and in the autumn of 1724 was translated as Archbishop of Armagh, primate of the Anglican church in Ireland.[12]

Leonard Welsted (1688–1747) was thirteen years younger than Philips but emerged within the same literary milieu. He seems to have owed a good deal to Philips, since the issues of *The Free-Thinker* represented his first major publications, and his aesthetic essay published in 1724 includes highly complimentary words toward his colleague.[13] Welsted conflicted with Pope, just as Philips did: in 1730 he charged the great man of contributing to the death of a lady, and Pope answered with an accusation that Welsted manipulated his patrons shamelessly. Most important of all for our purposes, Welsted married the daughter of Henry Purcell, Frances

Purcell, daughter of the composer and his wife Frances (nee Peters). She was born in 1688, married Welsted in 1706, became the executrix of her father's estate at her mother's death that same year, and was placed in charge of her young brother Edward.[14] The strongest evidence that Welsted wrote the letter of 25 July is a passage revealing intimate knowledge of family matters about the estate: "it must be owned a great Misfortune, that his Works were not corrected by himself, but that after his Death all Copies were called in from private Hands, and a Collection [i.e., *Orpheus Britannicus*] made with a View more to the Bookseller's Advantage, than the Author's Honour."[15] That his wife had died in 1724 makes it all the more likely that Welsted wrote the article, perhaps as a kind of memorial. Welsted may even have had some part in the first two articles, since there is other evidence of his opposition to Italian opera in London. In an article in *The Free-Thinker* in 1718 he had made the interesting comment that since opera performances were "Entertainments for a Select Audience" they could not be called "public shows."[16] In 1721 he published a Prologue to a play that had been delivered at Lincoln's Inn Fields Theatre (and was accompanied by an Epilogue by Steele on the same occasion) that included some of the earliest satirical commentary upon the Royal Academy opera company.[17] Welsted may very well have written some of the anonymously published satires about Italian opera at this period. Indeed, his discussion of the opera, the South Sea Bubble and the country's moral *malaise* in 1718 resembles greatly the treatment of the same subjects in a poem by Henry Carey that was included in the first of the three articles in *The Universal Journal*.

The early proponents of older music were associated chiefly with the "ancients" in the great Quarrel of the Ancients and Moderns that began in the 1690s.[18] While publications of that time did not address themselves to music, the term "ancient music" came into use inconspicuously around 1700 to denote works in the old polyphonic style as practised in the sixteenth and early seventeenth centuries. Henry Aldrich, Dean of Christ Church, Oxford, who figured significantly in the Phalaris dispute, became the main proponent of ancient music through his close involvement in the musical program at the Cathedral and as host of private meetings in his college rooms for singing Elizabethan and contemporary music. He and his colleagues were predominantly Tory high churchmen who championed old music as part of their critique of the Whig government. Arthur

Bedford contributed the most important ideological construct of their point of view in his attack on the commodification of musical life in *The Great Abuse of Musick.*

During the 1720s it was men of letters, most of them opposition Whigs associated with the "moderns," who came to the fore in discussions of old music. The pieces in *The Universal Journal* grew out of the critical methodology that figures such as Richard Bentley had marshalled against the unprofessional thinking that they found in contemporary writing on the classics. Their historical philology questioned the veracity of classical artefacts and demanded that the whole nature, and indeed authority, of ancient culture should be reconsidered.[19] Ambrose Philips and Leonard Welsted followed in this iconoclastic path in their approach to poetry and aesthetics, a bold posture in their time. Philips's book of pastorals focused upon rustic instead of classical models, English instead of ancient Greek or Roman, and in so doing mounted a critique of writers who he thought showed excessive reverence for antiquity.[20]

The presence in *The Universal Journal* of articles on the pastoral from that very point of view strongly indicates Philips's authorship. Welsted followed much the same modernist path in his poetry and his aesthetic writings, arguing that genius was to be found in a variety of times and places, and did not necessarily follow classical models.[21] One suspects that he was influenced by Bentley during his career at Trinity College, Cambridge. The article of 11 July offers a pithy example of the robust, iconoclastic mentality of the "moderns," stating a common intellectual assumption and calling it into question. After urging a greater unity between words and music, the author points out that great musical works had not been kept in perpetuity in the same way as great poems: "*David* touched a Harp so divinely, that he even charmed Evil Spirits; yet are his musical compositions dead with him, whilst his *Psalms* remain the Standard and just Model of all spiritual Hymns"—and much the same applied to Homer and Sappho.

It may seem paradoxical that, for all that they distrusted conventional thinking about literary classics, the "moderns" helped to build a musical canon. They did so because such a project furthered the rethinking of the classical tradition in literature, since it could help to establish canon independent of ancient models and free from the rigid principles by which it had been defined. A similar outlook can be found in William

Hogarth. Though a critic of academic canons such as were established by conservatories in the 1730s and 1740s, he joined the Academy of Ancient Music, the London society where works of Tallis, Byrd, Marenzio, and Palestrina were performed.[22] The unpresumptuous, workman-like character of Elizabethan polyphony must have appealed to him; he would have found a simplicity and an honesty in it that contrasted with the pretentious values he would later see in the ideas and the institutional leadership of Sir Joshua Reynolds.

The letter of 25 July to *The Universal Journal* goes farther than the preceding two articles, taking a broad perspective in suggesting a canonic status for Purcell and his music. The piece opens with the simple assertion that "*Purcel* was a *Shakespear* in Musick," but what follows has much greater depth and significance. The author attacks the assumption that had hitherto been basic to musical taste, that music in "Old Stile" was "out of Date, and therefore ought to be kick'd out of Doors." He puts the question in comparative terms, asking why similar principles do not apply in painting or literature:

> We have doubtless many good Painters now living; must therefore *Rubens*, *Vandyke*, *Lilly*, and *Kneller* be forgot? Must *Spencer*, *Milton*, *Shakespear*, and *Addison* be never read because there are writers of a later Date? And must *Corelli*, *Bird*, and *Purcel* never be sung, because they are Old Stile?

He then calls upon his colleagues to honor great figures in music as they do in their own field:

> In Musick we have many Great Masters now living, to support the Dignity of that heavenly Science; but it is the worst Complement any one can pay them, to make Blockheads of *Corelli* and *Purcell*. I am confident they would receive it with as much indignation as Mr. *Pope* or Mr. *Philips* would hear a Reflection on *Shakespear*, tho' never so much intended in their Favour. No, 'tis only the noisy Vulgar who set up idols, and demolish the Shrines of the Ancients.

The letter stands among the fullest prose eulogies to Purcell that were published in the century after his death. The most important previous tribute had been the publication in 1698, three years after the composer's death, of *Orpheus Britannicus*, a collection of his vocal works in both sacred and secular idioms.[23] It is indicative of the composer's unusually high reputation among men of letters that prefatory poems were contributed to the publication by John Dryden and Nahum Tate as well as by Purcell's brother Daniel, the organist Henry Hall, and "a person of quality." But no upsurge in performing Purcell's music followed, and it was virtually neglected in the period of the *Universal Journal* articles. None of his major theatre works were revived in London between 1717 and 1729, and *The London Stage* records the only occasional introduction of seven of his songs (on eighteen occasions) into other performances at the London theatres.[24] His famous *Te Deum and Jubilate* was still presented from time to time in church services for which orchestrally accompanied music was appropriate, such as that for the annual feast of the Corporation of the Sons of the Clergy, but even so it naturally shared the honors with works by contemporary composers, and Handel's settings of the *Te Deum* largely supplanted Purcell's in the 1730s.[25] As far as publication of Purcell's music was concerned, only the *Te Deum and Jubilate, Orpheus Britannicus*, and selections within anthologies of catches enjoyed sufficient demand from the purchasing public to remain in print.[26] Nevertheless, these publications meant that the more serious musicians and amateurs could become acquainted with Purcell's music, indeed rather more than was possible for music of the great majority of composers from the seventeenth century. In the long run, the continuing use of his *Te Deum and Jubilate* at festival events (in London and the provinces) served an extremely important function as the foundation of a practice upon which Handel's English works eventually remained in performance. But it was not until the 1760s that performance of Purcell's songs, theatre music, and sacred works became at all frequent.

What is particularly impressive about the letter of 25 July 1724 is that it is focused so substantively upon musical rather than literary or political agendas. Most citations of Purcell during the first half of the century invoked his name to promote the cause of English writers against foreign competition; in most cases his music itself was not of principal interest.[27] All of which is a tribute to the daring of the authors of the three pieces in *The Universal Journal*, most likely Ambrose Philips and Leonard Welsted. We can admire the originality of their contribution, even though they both ended up on the margins of the literary world. Little research or critical study has recently been done on either of them, but they attract a growing respect among scholars of the period for their willingness to question entrenched ideas and to do battle with Alexander Pope.

A comment made in the letter of 25 July deserves particular scrutiny: "if every man had the same value for *Purcel*, as the wonderful *Hendel* has." The historical perspective suggested here was quite unusual for the time. Although there would no doubt have been many people in London who could have remembered Purcell himself in 1724, his music had gone into eclipse after his death, especially after the arrival of Italian opera in London. That, after all, followed ancient convention in musical culture. Not only had there been a shift towards a different sort of theatrical entertainment from that to which Purcell had contributed, but also, as the first article in *The Universal Journal* noted, this movement had been accompanied by a new harmonic and melodic style, involving different principles of musical declamation. At a later period, and indeed into the twentieth century, it has been common to compare Purcell's musical treatment of the English language with Handel's, usually to the detriment of the latter. But no English composer in the 1720s would have been writing according to Purcell's manner, which by then was not merely "Old Stile" but was in a style that could not be recaptured after the musical influences from more modern Italian styles had been absorbed throughout Europe. Comparison of Purcell with Handel seems an unlikely topic during this period in any case, since Handel's treatment of the English language in "song" only became publicly audible with his introduction of English works of the oratorio type into his opera seasons in the 1730s. The sole area in which direct comparison would have been possible in 1724 was church music, and in particular through the two composers' settings of the Te Deum and Jubilate.[28] While Purcell's "St. Cecilia" settings in D major from 1694 remained in print thirty years later, Handel's "Utrecht" version from 1713 still awaited publication, and comparison could only have been made by people who had access to manuscript copies circulating privately, or who had listened attentively at performances of the music.[29]

There was accordingly little reason in 1724 to draw a link between the two composers on historical grounds, such as we may do today. One explanation for the phrase in the article might be that the author actually knew of discussions with Handel that gave testimony to his high regard for Purcell's music. As a man chiefly of the theatre, Handel mingled with the entrepreneurs and musicians who had succeeded Purcell's colleagues. It would appear that the respect that Purcell had achieved in the literary world—far higher than that of any other composer of his time—persisted an unusual length of time. A possible second explanation might be that the writer was referring in more general terms to an impression that Handel's music preserved some elements of the "Old Stile" with its figural and contrapuntal approach, when compared, for example, to that of Giovanni Bononcini, the other leading Royal Academy composer of the period. It is possible that the author, having heard Handel "Utrecht" music a decade before, could have formed the opinion that Handel's music was a logical extension of Purcell's "grand" style for English church music—even though in fact a comparison of the two works serves mainly to emphasize the stylistic gulf between the two composers.

A third possible explanation for the link that was drawn between Purcell and Handel derives from the notion of the "master composer." The passage occurs in a context where the author is stressing how great masters in painting and literature honored their forebears, and it was useful to his argument to say that Handel, by far the most important composer in London at the time, did so to Purcell. Links between master composers of past and present were to play a major role in the evolution of the idea of the musical canon during the eighteenth and nineteenth centuries. The canonization of a recently-deceased composer often came about in close relationship with the honouring of a rising contemporary musician; a symbiosis occurred between them that made each one seem all the more a master in the same genre. This was seen in the "succession" perceived between the concertos of Corelli and Handel (especially after the publication of Handel's Op. 6 in 1740), and onwards to those of Charles Avison and Francesco Geminiani after that. A further parallel existed in the interaction between the musical reputations of Haydn and Mozart, on one hand, and the ageing Beethoven, on the other, in Vienna during the 1810s and 1820s.

It is interesting to find the authors of the articles struggling to find a word by which to denote old music in their discussion of the "Old Stile." No generic term had as yet developed to identify music from the preceding generations. "Ancient music" was still in 1724 a term restricted to works written before about 1625, and only in the 1770s was it broadened to include any works that were several decades old. In any event, writers among the "moderns" such as Philips or Welsted would probably have avoided the term, since they were by instinct suspicious of the language by which classical texts had conventionally been discussed. It is all the more remarkable to find "Old Stile" being used to denote composers as diverse as these three: "And must *Corelli, Bird,* and *Purcel* never be sung, because they are Old Stile?" Pieces by the three composers had established themselves in quite different social and intellectual contexts: William Byrd's services and anthems were performed in the cathedrals and the Chapel Royal, Corelli's concertos in London and provincial music societies, Purcell's *Te Deum and Jubilate* in church services associated with annual festivals, and his songs (occasionally) in theatre and concert programs. Once again we find the author of the letter remarkably percipient, since an omnibus conception of old music was at least fifty years away.

Appendix

1) 27 May 1724, p. 1

> *Spite of Fashion let some few be found*
> *Who value Sense above an empty Sound.*
> —Prologue to the 2d Part of *Henry IV.*

Every Art and Science has in every Age had its particular Admirers and Followers; but *Musick* since its first Invention has met with general Applause: It has been universally received and encouraged; and to that and its Sister, *Poetry,* are attributed every Good of Life: To them we are said to owe the Names of Rational Creatures, they having brought the Generality of Mankind out of the Savage State in which they lived, to inhabit Towns, and to form regular Societies: The Stories of *Orpheus* and *Amphion,* are too well known to need repeating on this Occasion.

The works of our ancient and modern Poets are every where filled with the Praise of Musick: I will not quote particular Passages; they are so very numerous, that of themselves they would swell my Paper beyond its usual Length. I would rather chuse to admire the Improvements that have been made in it of late Years in our Nation; and indeed they are such, that we may venture to affirm they have brought that Art to the very Height of Perfection.

But I am grieved to say, that as Musick has improved, Sense decayed; and that this has been reduced to the lowest Ebb it possibly could be, whilst the other was attaining that Summit of Perfection. It was a custom amongst our Fathers, first to compose a Song, and then to set it to Musick; but their wiser Sons despise this old Fashion, and have quite inverted it. They value nothing but the Tune, which therefore they make it their Business to compose first, and then set Words to it, no Matter for the Sense, provided they are soft, and run smoothly to the Notes.

How many Examples will both Sacred and Profane History furnish us with, of eminent Musicians and Poets, who carefully cultivated the Sister Arts; yet thought that if they must incline to either Side, they ought to have the greater Regard for their Poetical Compositions. *David* touched a Harp so divinely, that he even charmed Evil Spirits; yet are his musical Compositions dead with him, whilst his *Psalms* remain the Standard and just Model of all spiritual Hymns. *Homer* sung from Door to Door the Wrath of *Achilles*, the Fall of *Troy*, and the Adventures of *Ulysses*; and tho' his Musick doubtless was good, yet is that perished, whilst his Songs connected form the noblest Epick Poems that ever were wrote. The beauteous *Sappho* the *Lesbian*, is mentioned by several Writers, as having excelled her Co[n]temporaries in Musick; and those Fragments of hers which are handed down to us, at the same time shew that she excelled them in her poetical Compositions. But this is a Truth so universally acknowledged, that more Instances of this Kind must be reckoned impertinent. Amongst our Moderns, *Purcell* was justly esteemed a great Master; and if we carefully read him, we shall find that he had as much Regard to the Song it self, as to the Air he composed for it.

But whether the Nation, to whom we owe our Improvements in this Art, be not so well furnished with sound Judgment as their Neighbours, or whether they have so entirely devoted themselves to the one, that it is impossible they should have any Attention left for the other, I will not say; but to our Sorrow we find, that a *Mio Caro* quavered and repeated half a Dozen times, is equivalent to all the soft and easy Things *a Suckling* or a *Prior* could have wrote.

I know not whether these warbling Gentlemen ever look forwards; but I am certain, that, were I in their Case, and capable of thinking, I should dread the Downfall of Musick in this Kingdom. All earthly Things are liable to the greatest Vicissitudes; and every thing is unstable. If Musick be at its Height amongst us, and that like all Things here below it cannot be fixed, of Necessity it must fall. How lately do we remember Wit in its full Bloom of Glory, when we were every Day blest with the Converse and Writings of an *Addison*, a *Garth*, a *Pope*, a *Prior*, a *Steele*, and several others, the Pride of the Age, and the Darlings of *Helicon*; but Death summoned some away, old Age overtook others, and the rest, for want of Company, are retired, and have left us to bewail the sudden fall of Wit, and the great Decay of Sense in so short a Time.

But there are Men still left in the World, whose Ears may indeed awhile be charmed with an *Italian* Voice, or Violin, but who will soon recover from that Lethargy into which they have been lull'd; and who, seeing the Frothiness of what they have admired, will be ashamed of owning that they even were Lovers of Musick, when it apears that for its Sake only Wit and good Sense have been banished the Commonwealth.

That the Fall of Musick is near at Hand, seems to me undoubted; I had my self a tolerable Opinion of *South Sea* Stock about four Years ago; but when Subscriptions began to run so prodigiously high, I foresaw its Fate. The Case is the very same here: Musical Subscriptions have been taken in at a very extravagant Rate, and frequent Calls made upon them; and if I am not misinformed, the Jobbers in that Way would fain get rid of what they have in that Fund; and I am told that even at this Present a Man might buy Opera Stock at a very considerable Discount.

I am led into this Way of thinking, by reading over my Friend *Saturnio*'s Observations upon the late Eclipse; wherein, amongst other things, he has particularly threatened Musick: As I have no great Faith in Prophecies, I was willing to account for its approaching Ruin from natural Causes; for I take for granted that its Downfall is near. Mean while some of my Readers will perhaps be much better pleased with Prophecy than Reason, and therefore I shall give 'em *Saturnio*'s own Words.

'The Position of the Heavens, at the Time of this Eclipse, is of dire portent to Musicians, but sheds a benign Influence upon Poets and Writers: The two Arts are here represented by the two great Luminaries; the strong and dazzling Rays of *Phœbus* being a just Emblem of Poetick Fire, whilst the Lunar Globe is a Representative of Harmony, which receives its Light from the other's bright Numbers: The Moon's intercepting the Rays of Light, and the Clouds gathering round the Sun, shew us the Decay of the one, by our too great Attachment to the other, and our being guided by the clouded

Imaginations and Fancies of some. But notwithstanding the Calculations made by the best Astronomers, the Eclipse was not total, which denotes that good Writing shall not be entirely rooted out of our Land. The Sun suddenly appeared again, and by its superiour Brightness eclipsed the Moon, whose Body then we could not discern; so shall Poetry shortly re-assume its pristine Glory, and so dazzle us with its recovered Beauty, that we shall not be able to discover any Charms in Musick: which shall then be so contemned and neglected, that our Children's Children, passing thro' the *Hay-Market*, shall look with surprize upon the ruin'd *Opera House*, and enquire, what Service that decayed Pile of Building was intended for.'

N. B. Saturnio at the same time made several other curious Observations; but they relating to **** and *** cannot be safely communicated at present; but the Author intends to take some more convenient Opportunity of letting the World know what they were.

2) 11 July 1724, p. 3

From my own Apartment.

The prodigious Encouragement which Foreign Professors of every Art and Science meet amongst us, whilst our own Countrymen are brow beaten and despised, has been so very often complained of, and so little taken notice of, that I do not repeat it in hopes of making many Converts; but I must own that I cannot, without being shock'd, meet with any particular Instance of it. Our Extravagance has no where shewn it self more conspicuously than in the Case of the *Italian* Singers, whilst our own Masters are despised and forgotten; and yet I have often heard Men of very good Sense, and who perfectly understand Musick, acknowledge, that among the Latter there were now as great Hands as any Age had produced; but this Acknowledgment they made in private, and at the same time owned they did not dare say such a Thing publickly, for fear of being laughed at, and reckoned meer Idiots in Musick.

A few Days ago I went to visit an Acquaintance whose Compositions I have always been old fashion'd enough to value, and who has obliged the Publick with several of 'em; I saw the last Work that he had publish'd lye upon his Table, and turning it over I found the following Lines written on the Reverse of the Title-Page in my Friend's own Hand; some Business

shortly after calling him out of the Room, I took a Copy of 'em on purpose to make 'em publick; I hope he will forgive my doing it without his
Knowledge. For fear of being thought partial I will not praise them; but
thus much I'll venture to say, That there is more good Sense in them than
in all the *Italian* Songs and Operas I ever saw, put together.

Resign they Pipe, thy wonted Lays forego,
The Muse is now become thy greatest Foe:
With taunts, and Jeers, and most untimely Wrongs,
The flouting Rabble pay thee for thy Songs.
Untuneful is our Native Language now,
Nor must the Bays adorn a British *Brow:*
The wanton Vulgar scorn their Mother-Tongue,
And all our British *Bards have bootless sung.*
Ev'n Heav'n-born Purcel *now is held in Scorn;*
Purcel! *who did a brighter Age adorn.*
That Nobleness of Soul, that manly Fire,
That did our British Orpheus *once inspire*
To rouse us all to Arms, is quite forgot:
We're, now, for something soft—We know not what.
Our ancient Bluntless [Bluntness] and Sincerity
Is alter'd to Grimace and Flattery;
Effeminate in Dress, in Manners grown,
We now despise whatever is our own.
A false Politeness has possest our Isle,
And ev'ry Thing that's English *is* Old Stile.
So Rome, *when famous once for Arts and Arms,*
Betray'd by Luxury's enfeebling Charms,
Sunk into Softness, and its Empire lost.
We may be as refin'd too—to our Cost.
Then break thy Reed; for ever close thy Throat,
Nor dare to pen a Line, or sing a Note;
For what would have been priz'd in former Days,
Will now but Envy and Derision raise:
Go court Retirement, learn to be obscure;
The Man who's least observ'd, is most secure.
Do'st thou write ill, then all against thee join;

Dost thou write well, they swear 'tis none of thine:
If they applaud, it is but for a Day;
But they condemn for Ever and for Aye.

3) 25 July 1724, p. 3

To the Author of The Universal Journal.

SIR,

As you seem, by some of your Writings, to bear Respect to the Memory of the late famous Mr. *Henry Purcel*, it has revived my Veneration for that wonderful Man, and stirr'd up a little Resentment in me against the modern Fops, who seem resolv'd to tear the Laurel from his Brow, and lay his Memory low in Oblivion.

I shall not vindicate him at the Expence of any Musician now living, tho' I hope I may without Offence, say, That *Purcel* was a *Shakespear* in Musick; and tho' we have had many great Poets since *Shakespear*, yet as none have exceeded, may I not say equal'd him; so tho' Musick has been improved almost to a Prodigy since *Purcel*'s Time, yet those Lines of Mr. *Hall*'s may be very well apply'd.

Sometimes an Hero in an Age appears;
But scarce a Purcel *in a Thousand Years.*

Now that this Great Man's Fame should dye, nay worse, that his incomparable Works should be made a Jest of by ignorant Coxcombs, who praise and condemn but by Example, and for Fashion's Sake, is enough to raise Resentment in any, who have the least Regard to the Honour of their Country, or Concern for true Merit.

The first and chief Reflection they cast on his Musick, is, that 'tis Old Stile: I grant it; (all the World knows it was not made Yesterday;) but I cannot comprehend these Gentlemens nice Distinction of Old Stile and New Stile, unless they would infer that the three Sister-Arts never flourished 'till now, or that the Musick, Painting and Poetry of the last Age is Old Stile, (*i. e.*) out of Date, and therefore ought to be kick'd out of Doors.

We have doubtless many good Painters now living; must therefore *Rubens, Vandyke, Lilly, and Kneller* be forgot? Must *Spencer, Milton,*

Shakespear, and *Addison* be never read, because there are Writers of a later Date? And must *Corelli*, *Bird*, and *Purcel* never be sung, because they are Old Stile?

In Musick we have many Great Masters now living, to support the Dignity of that heavenly Science; but it is the worst Complement [sic] any one can pay them, to make Blockheads of *Corelli* and *Purcel*. I am confident they would receive it with as much Indignation as Mr. *Pope* or Mr. *Philips* would hear a Reflection on *Shakespear*, tho' never so much intended in their Favour. No, 'tis only the noisy Vulgar who set up Idols, and demolish the Shrines of the Ancients. It is from our present Great Men I would have our *petits Maitres* silenced.

I defy any Person living to have a greater Veneration for *Raphael*, *Rubens*, and *Vandyke*, than *Richardson*, *Dake*, or *Vandebank* have for those glorioius Ancients. Let our Dablers in Poetry therefore learn of *Philips* or *Welsted* to prize *Milton*: And had every man the same value for our *Purcel*, as the wonderful *Hendel* has, I had never set Pen to Paper. In Co[n]temporaries indeed Emulation may eclipse the Merit of great Men in each other's Opinion: But the Grave throws all Blots aside; and there can be little Merit, where there is not Generosity enough to have Respect to the good Works of our Ancestors.

Purcel was our great Reformer of Musick; he had a most happy enterprizing Genius, join'd with a boundless Invention, and noble Design. He made Musick answer its Ends (*i. e.*) move the Passions. He expres'd his Words with a singular Beauty and Energy; there is a Manliness of Stile runs through his Works; and were *Italian* Words put to some of his Airs, they would not be found Old Stile, nor need any of our modern Composers be ashamed of them.

His Recitative is gracefully natural, and particularly adapted to the *English* Tongue. There is a Solemnity in his Songs, which at the same time awes and pleases; and when they do not, the Fault is too frequently either in the Singer, who consults not the Intention of the Author; or in the Hearer, who is determined to condemn whatever is *Purcel*'s.

Had that great Man lived till now, he had doubtless made yet greater Improvements in Musick; and it must be owned a great Misfortune, that his Works were not corrected by himself, but that after his Death all Copies were called in from private Hands, and a Collection made with a View more to the Bookseller's Advantage, than the Author's Honour.

There are doubtless many Songs in *Orpheus Britannicus*, which *Purcel* never intended for the Publick; little Occasional Pieces, done in his Juvenile Years, which he never designed to transmit to Posterity. But then, on the contrary, there are in that very Book (and of those a great many) such bright Originals, as will outlive the Malice and Ignorance of this fantastick Generation, and shine to the latest Posterity; when the Memory of that glorious *Englishman* shall again flourish, and when Musick and Reason once more be united.

Notes

1. See William Weber, *The Rise of Musical Classics in Eighteenth-Century England: A Study in Canon, Ritual and Ideology* (London: Oxford University Press, 1992); Weber, "The Intellectual Origins of Musical Canon in Eighteenth-Century England," *Journal of the American Musicological Society*, 43 (1994): 488–520; and Weber, "The History of Musical Canon," in *Rethinking Music*, ed. Mark Everist and Nicholas Cook (Oxford: Oxford University Press, 1997).

2. Among the numerous bibliographies of eighteenth-century periodicals, it is cited only in *The New Cambridge Bibliography of English Literature*, ed. George Watson (Cambridge: Cambridge University Press, 1969–77), vol. 2, col. 1325.

3. Issues nos. 25, 31 and 33. The journal announced that it was "To be continued Weekly," but there was a 10–day gap after No. 25, when the publication day changed from Wednesday to Saturday. The articles were first discovered by Donald Burrows in 1979, and reference to that of 11 July was included in Donald Burrows, *Handel and the English Chapel Royal during the reigns of Queen Anne and King George I* (Ph.D. dissertation, Open University, Milton Keynes, 1981), vol. 1, 107; see also the references in Weber, *The Rise of Musical Classics*. The letter of 25 July 1724 was reprinted in Michael Burden, ed., *Purcell Remembered* (London: Faber and Faber, 1995), 135–8.

4. The heading "From my own apartment" was used regularly in *The Universal Journal* for the second article, which was presumably also written by the editor.

5. Correspondence was explicitly solicited in the wording of the imprint at the end of each issue: "*LONDON*: Printed for T. Payne, near *Stationers Hall*; where Letters and Advertisements are taken in." Musical topics occurred fairly often in *The Universal Journal*, suggesting that the editor had friends among London musicians. Notices of the Festival of the Sons of the Clergy appeared twice, once including the text of Maurice Greene's festival anthem "Open the gates of righteousness" (see 11 December 1723, 6; and 18 December, 3). Concern for the needs of English musicians and actors is a theme of numerous articles that began in May 1724. The first (6 May), a discussion of benefit performances, includes an attack upon the large fees paid to opera singers.

6. See Donald Burrows, *Handel* (Oxford: Oxford University Press, 1995), 113–15; and Lowell Lindgren, "Critiques of Opera in London, 1705–19," in *Il melodramma italiano in Italia et Germania nell'età barocca: Atti del V Convegno internazionale sulla musica*

italiana nel secolo XVII, Loveno di Menaggio, Como, 1993, ed. Alberto Colzani, Norbert Dubowy, Andrea Luppi and Maurizio Padoa (Como, 1995), 143–65.

7. We are indebted to Professor Maximilian Novak for originally suggesting these two figures as possible authors and editors.

8. Samuel Johnson, *Lives of the English Poets,* ed. G. B. Hill (Oxford: Clarendon Press, 1905), vol. 3, 313.

9. See John Barnard, ed., *Pope: The Critical Heritage* (London: Routledge, 1973), 9; Charles Kerby-Miller, ed., *Memoirs of the Extraordinary Life, Works, and Discoveries of Martinus Scriblerus* (New York: Oxford University Press, 1988), 16, 221–2; Peter Quennell, *Alexander Pope: The Education of Genius, 1688–1728* (London: Stein and Day, 1968), 61–3, 110; George Sherburn, *The Early Career of Alexander Pope* (Oxford: Clarendon Press, 1934), 124–5, 137, 151–4, 303.

10. "The Life of the Author," in *The Poetical Works of Ambrose Philips,* from *Bell's Edition of the Poets of Great Britain* (London, 1799), vi.

11. Annabel Patterson, *Pastoral and Ideology: Virgil to Valéry* (Berkeley: University of California Press, 1987), 195. See also John M. Aden, *Pope's Once and Future Kings: Satire and Politics in the Early Career* (Knoxville: University of Tennessee Press, 1978), 118–191, 127, 137–8, 140, 142; and W. L. MacDonald, *Pope and His Critics: A Study in Eighteenth Century Personalities* (London: Dent, 1951), chapters 1–2.

12. *Dictionary of National Biography,* vol. 15, 1058–9; *Letters Written by His Excellency Hugh Boulter, Lord Primate of London* (2 vols., London, 1770), vol. 1, 83; vol. 2, 106.

13. *Epistles, Odes, &c. Written on Several Subjects, With a Translation of Longinus's Treatise on the Sublime* (London, 1724), li.

14. See Franklin B. Zimmerman, *Henry Purcell, 1659–95, His Life and Work* (London: Melbourne, 1967), 314, 316, 383.

15. The letter of 25 July criticizes the collection for including early songs, which indicates that the writer had unusually extensive knowledge of Purcell's music and perhaps access to unpublished portions of it. The assessment that Purcell did better later suggests that the author was someone knowledgeable in both music and criticism.

16. *The Free-Thinker: or, Essays on Ignorance, Superstition, Bigotry, Enthusiasm, Craft, &c.* (3 vols.), 14 November 1718, vol. 2, 59–60.

17. *A Prologue to the Town, as it was Spoken at the Theatre in Little Lincoln's-Inn-Fields and Epilogue on the same occasion by Sir R. Steele* (London, 1721). Welsted's early relationship with Steele is evident in his *Epistle to Mr. Steele, on the King's Accession to the Crown* (London, 1714).

18. See Joseph M. Levine, *The Battle of the Books: History and Literature in the Augustan Age* (Ithaca: Cornell University Press, 1991).

19. Joseph Levine, "Ancients and Moderns Reconsidered, *Eighteenth-Century Studies,* 15 (1981): 72–89; Levine, "The Battle of the Books and the Shield of Achilles," *Eighteenth Century Life,* 9 (1984): 33–61; and Levine, *The Battle of the Books.*

20. See his *Pastorals* (London, 1710), and *The Poems of Ambrose Philips.* See also Christine Gerrard, *Walpole and the Patriots: Politics, Poetry and Myth, 1725–1742* (Oxford:

Clarendon Press, 1994); Patterson, *Pastoral and Ideology*, 195, 206; and Aden, *Pope's Once and Future Kings*, 118–19, 127, 137–8, 140, 142.

21. See his "Dissertation Concerning the Perfection of the English Language, the State of Poetry, &c.," in *Epistles, Odes, &c.*, l-lvii.

22. Ronald Paulson, *Hogarth* (New Brunswick: Rutgers University Press, 1991–3), vol. 1, 334. On his relationships to the academies, see vol. 1, 104–9, 331–4.

23. *Orpheus Brittanicus, A Collection of All the Choicest Songs, for One, Two, and Three Voices. Compos'd by Mr. Henry Purcell* (London, 1698).

24. *The London Stage, 1660–1800*, Part 2, 1700–29, ed. Emmett L. Avery (Carbondale: University of Southern Illinois Press, 1960), vol. 2, 490, 492, 730. Two songs (three performances) are recorded at Lincoln's Inn Fields Theatre in 1718: most of the rest were performed by Richard Leveridge and Thomas Salway at the same theatre between 1726 and 1728. For Purcell himself, see Curtis Price, *Henry Purcell and the London Stage* (Cambridge: Cambridge University Press, 1983) and *Music in the Restoration Theatre* (Ann Arbor: UMI Research Press, 1979).

25. See Burrows, *Handel and the English Chapel Royal* (London: Church Music Society, 1985), Vol. 2, Appendix 4, and Weber, *Rise of Musical Classics*, 111–17.

26. A new edition of *Orpheus Britannicus* appeared in 1721.

27. See the extensive bibliography of such comments in Richard Luckett, " 'Or Rather our Musical Shakspeare': Charles Burney's Purcell," in *Music in Eighteenth-Century England: Essays in Memory of Charles Cudworth*, ed. Christopher Hogwood and Richard Luckett, (Cambridge: Cambridge University Press, 1983), 59–78.

28. Handel had also composed a few anthems, either for the Chapel Royal or for James Brydges at Cannons, which included texts that had previously been set by Purcell (*Let God arise, My song shall be alway*, O *Sing unto the Lord*, and *The Lord is my light*), but the music (by both composers) was unpublished and there were few manuscript copies.

29. On Handel and the relationship of his music to Purcell's, see Burrows, *Handel*, 55, 76, 91–3, 148.

Hearing History

"Dixie," "Battle Hymn of the Republic," and Civil War Music in the History Classroom

JAMES A. DAVIS

In recent decades history teachers from all levels have begun to use primary sources as effective tools in classroom assignments and presentations. These sources vary a great deal depending on the subject and time period under investigation and may include letters, diaries, periodicals, photographs, art works, and more. The benefits of introducing such materials are numerous and often self-evident. At a basic level the use of authentic materials enlivens classroom presentations, offering engaging and entertaining stimuli to what might otherwise be dry or pedantic lectures. Original materials are usually popular with students as working with such objects allows them to feel that they are encountering history firsthand. The use of primary sources also provides a multifaceted platform for integrating disciplines, an issue of growing interest to those involved with educational reform.[1] At a deeper level the use of authentic materials can create pedagogical situations capable of significant and lasting results. Personal involvement with a historical situation encourages students to examine issues more closely than might occur were they to simply read of an event in a textbook. As Alexa Sandmann and John Ahern have noted, "literature gives students the chance to connect with people from other times . . . [it] gives students the chance to learn from others."[2] Likewise the bypassing of the textbook allows students to draw their own conclusions from the material under consideration; they are not merely "learning" history but actually "doing" history.[3]

Scholars know that the intimacy that comes from studying personal documents, to hear the words of the participants themselves, is to touch the past and bring their subject alive. Approaching a subject this way reminds us that history is the story of people: the beliefs, feelings, actions, and all that makes up the human experience. To fully understand historical events one needs to draw on more than just historical "facts" and include the systems of thoughts, values, perceptions, and attitudes that constitute the reality of the participants from both then and now. What better way to approach such topics, especially as teachers, than to use those objects whose primary purpose is directed toward the human experience? Or as some teachers have noted, "It is possible to teach the history of African Americans without referring to their music—but why would you want to?"[4]

Painting, literature, architecture, and dance are all useful in the history classroom, and music in particular can be an effective pedagogical tool. Throughout history music has been used habitually and in a variety of situations; it was and continues to be considered of immense personal importance to those who participate with it and as such has a profound impact on the daily life of people from every social sphere. Within music we can find a portrait of the people involved in history at any given time, thus catching a glimpse of their personal feelings about major events, including their fears, desires, values, and more. By examining music, students can engage with objects that historical figures actually used and simultaneously evaluate for themselves what individuals of the time might have felt and believed.

Other historical artifacts may allow for such an encounter, though music also provides a unique pedagogical opportunity seldom found in other objects. Most artifacts of history are by default treated as museum pieces, removed from their functional environment and placed into an artificial, didactic setting.[5] Certain art works, and music in particular, can still function in some of the ways for which they were originally created. Music allows those from a later time to engage with the artifact as it was intended, that is, as an aesthetic object. Of course it is not possible for students today to experience the work precisely as it was originally intended, as performance practice, aesthetic attitude, educational and social backgrounds, and other factors are impossible to recreate. Yet the possibility still exists for a student to encounter the work as an art object first, to experience the work musically, and from there consider any subsequent issues connected with it. In so doing, students move beyond a cognitive encounter with historical materials and into the realm of emotional experience.[6] Few teachers would deny that an emotional engagement of any kind with the material being studied is an invaluable basis for advanced and effective learning. Participating with a work of music in the history classroom allows students to experience an emotional catalyst from the past while at the same time experiencing their own modern aesthetic response.

Many teachers have found ways to use music in their classrooms with predictably effective results. Music is a popular art with students and is one of the most efficacious ways of enlivening a lecture, though often this involves using music at a fairly superficial level.[7] For too long music has been seen as ornamental in traditional historical studies. Though some history teachers might enjoy drawing on musical references to invigorate their discussions, rarely is music examined in the depth that other artifacts receive, especially letters and other written documents. The unfortunate result is that music in the classroom functions as an amusing sidebar and not an integral part of the educational experience. Other teachers are reticent to include music in their classes, feeling that their own lack of musical expertise would hinder any discussion.[8] Though experience with music theory and history would greatly benefit any teacher, it is not necessary for there to be effective discussion in any level classroom. Care must be taken with what topic is chosen to investigate as well as how the investigation is conducted. Focusing solely on the technical construction of the piece of music requires musical knowledge, yet considering the response to the work does not. In other words, an object-oriented approach is much more likely to require the teacher to possess technical knowledge and skills, whereas a response-oriented approach allows all participants, students and teachers alike, to draw upon their own subjective reactions and function as equals in the discussion.[9]

There are some historical subjects that are particularly well suited for including music as source material. The American Civil War is a subject ripe for investigation from most any perspective, yet ironically this can pose problems for teachers. From the mid-nineteenth century to today the Civil War has captivated this country in a unique way, a defining event for American culture that continues to fascinate and inspire students, scholars, and the public as a whole. In many respects the Civil War has suffered from a glut of historiography, be it from biased accounts in the aftermath of the war to revisionist histories stressing particular social and political agendas at the expense of more general concerns. As a result the events leading up to, involving, and following the Civil War have become dauntingly complex. Current research on the Civil War is refreshingly deep and stimulating as scholars continue to find a wealth of topics to investigate. But what happens when this information is passed down to students? The Civil War will usually occupy only one segment within a larger course or curriculum on American history, forcing teachers to present a condensed version of subjects and events. This is by no means easy, as many of the issues involved in the Civil War contain within themselves contrasting themes that are of substantial complexity. These underlying oppositions form the basis of any civil war and generate the emotional intensity that characterizes internecine conflicts. How then is a teacher to present such complexities without resorting to shallow, predictable and even misleading generalizations? Primary sources are invaluable in this situation, and music in particular can provide a means of revealing latent contradictions in ways suitable for the classroom. The participants in the War Between the States produced and consumed a staggering amount of musical works. Music was present at most every moment of the soldier's day, from the clarion sound of reveille that woke him in the morning and the music of the regimental bands at dress parade, to the consoling tones of a favorite ballad around the campfire. On the home front publishers eagerly produced vast quantities of patriotic tunes and sentimental songs for an eager public, fanning the flames of patriotic fervor while profiting hugely. The result is a vast quantity of music, of various styles and intended usage, consumed by a diverse population; in short, an ideal medium for examining the humanistic background of a major event in American history.

Consider the numerous situations where this music was found and the correlated issues immediately apparent in the music. Much Civil War music was used to bind the people, either through political propaganda or by means of bipartisan songs of hope or sorrow. Music became a primary means of declaring one's loyalties, especially later in the conflict when numerous opposition movements emerged in both the North and South. Singing patriotic songs at rallies and at home was a way for citizens to participate in the war, to be intimately involved in something that was connected to the war movement without being on the front lines. As the war progressed music developed into a primary channel for expressing the tragedy and loss that afflicted so many homes, often in such a way as to minimize geographical differences and anticipate reunification. Singing songs around the piano at home or the campfire in the field was a way of keeping the memory of loved ones fresh and helped to forge an emotional link between soldiers and their families. Some songs dealt solely with emotional subjects, such as the death of a soldier, but other songs often spoke of larger social issues, including slavery, the role of government, conflict of lifestyles, and more.[10]

In all these cases the aesthetic nature of the music allows any topic addressed to be approached from an emotional perspective. It is possible that by studying this music one can begin to examine many of the causes, controversies, conflicts, and contradictions that embody the war; simultaneously it is possible to engage with the artifact at an aesthetic level, thereby tapping into the personal sphere of the participants as well. In this way music provides a medium for forming connections between the historical past and the student's present. Music plays a central role in the life of most students today, and it is not difficult to bring out the many ways in which modern music reflects current events while shaping and reinforcing cultural identities.[11] From there it is a short step to have them engage with a piece from the Civil War to see parallels in how music captures and reflects public attitudes and sentiments. The proper choice of piece will even enable a teacher to elicit a comparison between a contemporary aesthetic reaction and possible historical responses, that is, how a student today may hear and respond to "Home, Sweet Home" versus a soldier in 1865. In this sense they are trying to see into the mind and soul of those actually caught up in the conflict, and personalizing, and even subjectivizing, a major event from our country's past. In these ways music can form a pedagogical link between the abstract concepts that swirled around the participants, the events that resulted from these concepts, and the more intimate interior of the participants themselves. At the same time these pieces still resonate and provide a living bridge between people of today and those who experienced America's greatest tragedy.

An examination of the two musical anthems most commonly associated with the Civil War—the "Battle Hymn of the Republic" and "Dixie"—reveals how much historical depth can be garnered from music and how effective it can be in teaching situations. Much of the music of the Civil War was intrinsically linked with the people and events of the time and set out to capture and celebrate cultural identities.[12] "Battle Hymn of the Republic" and "Dixie" are considered ideal examples of this today. Both are well known and liked, and have achieved a stature few compositions can claim in American culture. In this way they are an ideal starting point for an investigation of the Civil War, as there is already a large degree of familiarity for the students.[13] More intriguingly, there are a great number of anomalies surrounding these songs that are not common knowledge. These irregularities go a long way toward revealing much of the confusion and complexity that existed at the time, as well as highlighting possible misrepresentations by later historians. An investigation of these anomalies can operate at most any teaching level, from public school social studies to the college history course. One of the marvelous consequences of using music is that its inherently abstract nature allows for a broad range of interpretation, allowing conflicting concepts associated with the Civil War to be broached at both basic and advanced levels.[14]

Consider the basic background of both songs. The music for "Battle Hymn of the Republic" was originally a tune titled "Say, Bummers, Will You Meet Us," ascribed to William Steffe of Philadelphia, and eventually adopted as a popular camp meeting song.[15] Men of the Massachusetts Volunteer Militia used this catchy tune for a parody about a member of their battalion, Sergeant John Brown, and the song spread through the ranks and beyond. Those who heard the melody found it captivating, not only as a rousing piece of music for marching, but now as a song honoring the abolitionist John Brown, executed for his raid on the federal armory at Harper's Ferry in October, 1859. In 1861 Julia Ward Howe, a prominent New England socialite and committed abolitionist, was invited to attend a grand review of troops in Washington, D.C. Here she heard many of the tunes popular with soldiers, including "John Brown's Body." A friend encouraged her to write new words for the song and in an early morning burst of inspiration she produced the lyrics now known as the "Battle Hymn of the Republic." The poem was first published in February 1862 in *The Atlantic Monthly*. It was immensely popular, and "Battle Hymn" quickly became one of the most requested and highest selling songs of the Civil War.

Daniel Decatur Emmett was one of the country's most successful composers, particularly of the blackface minstrel shows that were so popular at the time.[16] Born in Mount Vernon, Ohio in 1815, he grew up surrounded by music. He joined the army for a time as a fifer and eventually wrote a manual of instruction for army musicians.[17] Following his military service he became active in minstrel shows, producing a number of future standards, including "Old Dan Tucker" and "Turkey in the Straw." In 1859 he was asked to provide a new tune for the nationally renowned Bryant's Minstrels, and the result was "Dixie's Land." The song rapidly gained popularity and was picked up by numerous other performers throughout the country. As the secessionist movement gathered momentum in southern states, so too did the popularity of "Dixie's Land." Numerous versions appeared, including many with patriotic or martial lyrics supporting the Southern cause.[18] Following the formation of the Confederate States of America, "Dixie" was performed at the inauguration of President Jefferson Davis, thereby helping to establish it as a national anthem for the fledgling country.[19] One of the premier fighting units of the Confederacy, the Washington Artillery, arranged the piece for their band, thereby spreading the tune's popularity amongst soldiers. As one witness noted: " 'Dixie' became to the South what the 'Marsellaise' is to France."[20]

This then is the background of each song as would probably be found in any basic text. Without any further consideration they remain interesting artifacts, musically popular, yet of limited historical value. This basic information fails to reveal a great many anomalies that surround these songs, irregularities that when uncovered reveal numerous tensions and contradictions that lie beneath the Civil War as a whole. It remains to look deeper into the history and nature of these songs, to see what musical, social, economic, and political issues are inextricably bound up with the songs, and therefore what topics are available for teachers to draw upon.[21]

A logical next step is to consider the music to each song to see how they compare.[22] As discussed before, such a comparison can be made with little formal musical knowledge. Each song occupies a somewhat predictable place in terms of the genres they represent; the differences between them may not be extreme, but interesting nonetheless. "Dixie" is very folkish in its construction. In mimics the synthetic Anglo-Irish and slave dance music that was so popular with minstrel shows, including mild syncopations that help to provide rhythmic drive. "Battle Hymn of the Republic" strikes the listener as a march with its walking beat and repeated dotted rhythms. In each case it is not surprising that the songs were popular. The dance-like, singable nature of "Dixie" affords it an immediate appeal, whereas the martial tenor of "Battle Hymn" lends it well to a patriotic setting. The musical structure of "Battle Hymn" is a rigid strophic form, in that there is one musical unit that repeats for both the verses and the chorus, whereas "Dixie" is a verse-chorus structure, with different music separating the verses and the refrain. In terms of the text setting both songs follow a similar approach. They are basically syllabic, with each change of syllable of the text having a corresponding change of note. An interesting difference appears here in that "Dixie" has numerous repeated words in both the verse and chorus. "John Brown's Body" also has repeated words, and in both cases this makes the song easier to remember and sing. "Battle Hymn" has repeated words in the chorus, though in the verses there is no word repetition. Despite being syllabic in its setting, it has a number of forced rhymes and rhythmic settings that make it much more difficult to sing or even remember.

Though the text setting is somewhat similar in each of these songs, the lyrics are vastly different, and a comparison of the texts leads to one of the most notable issues in the reception of Civil War music: who exactly was listening to the music, and where they were listening to it. There is a discernible difference when one compares the most popular songs of the soldiers with those of the civilians, both in the North and South. This disparity widened as the war progressed, seeing an increase in the frustration of the soldiers competing with an almost blind optimism of some civilians (or politicians) or the exhausted despair of those who had lost a loved one.[23] Despite the modern portrayal of "Dixie" and "Battle Hymn of the Republic" as quintessential Civil War songs, the soldiers held a different view from civilians. In fact, the two most popular tunes for both Yankee and Rebel troops were probably "Home Sweet Home" and "Lorena," songs with no reference whatever to the political nature of the conflict around them.[24]

Civilians and soldiers certainly used their music in substantially different ways, and subsequently showed a preference for different types of music. "John Brown's Body" was an extremely effective marching song, especially when compared with Howe's "Battle Hymn." Consider the poetic structure of the opening verse and chorus of each song.

John Brown's Body (anon.)

John Brown's body lies a-mouldering in the grave,
John Brown's body lies a-mouldering in the grave,
John Brown's body lies a-mouldering in the grave,
But his soul goes marching on.

Glory, glory, hallelujah,
Glory, glory, hallelujah,
Glory, glory, hallelujah,
His soul goes marching on.

Battle Hymn of the Republic (J. Howe)

Mine eyes have seen the glory of the coming of the Lord;
He is trampling out the vintage where the grapes of wrath are stored;
He hath loosed the fateful lightning of His terrible swift sword,
His truth is marching on.

Glory, glory, hallelujah,
Glory, glory, hallelujah,
Glory, glory, hallelujah,
His truth is marching on.

The repetitive nature of the lyrics to "John Brown's Body" reflects its suitability for marching. On the other hand, it is difficult to imagine singing the extravagant words of "Battle Hymn" while marching; for that matter, it would seem unlikely that your average Union soldier would sing such words even when sitting around the campfire.[25] The dissemination of these lyrics also shows a significant difference in reception. "Battle Hymn" gained much of its success through publication in major city periodicals, broadsides, and sheet music.[26] Broadsides were popular with and available to the masses, whereas as sheet music was directed toward the upperclasses. In both situations, however, the consumers were primarily urban.

Soldiers in the field had little access to these sources.[27] The two most likely sources for soldiers to learn music, specifically lyrics, were from songsters and through aural dissemination.[28] The lyrics to "Battle Hymn" did not appear in songsters until at least halfway through the war, therefore it is likely that a great many soldiers did not even know the lyrics.[29]

Such concerns lead to a consideration of the intended use of these songs. Many songs during the Civil War functioned as little more than propaganda, and even then served to profit the publishers as much as they promoted popular support for the war.[30] This must be taken into consideration when evaluating the social standing and aesthetic content of these songs. "Dixie's Land" and "John Brown's Body" had little pretension when created, serving as popular entertainment and as a marching song respectively. Only later were they appropriated as propaganda, which undoubtedly impacts their future aesthetic reception. This is equally true of the tunes' modern reception, as this music has achieved patriotic status, directly affecting how people today hear and judge the music. The lyrics to the "Battle Hymn of the Republic" and the revised version of "Dixie" clearly reveal a more political agenda. As the war progressed such songs certainly grew to represent national pride in both a positive and negative way. Upon leaving the city of Atlanta burning in his wake, General William T. Sherman said: "Never before or since have I heard the chorus of 'Glory Glory Hallelujah' done with more spirit or in better harmony of time and place."[31] On the other hand, notable abolitionist William Lloyd Garrison was heard to exclaim "Only listen to that—in Charleston's streets!" on hearing a regimental band play "John Brown's Body" after the war.[32]

There is also the issue of slavery that is so often associated with these songs, and of course with the war as a whole. "John Brown's Body" counts as one of the primary anti-slavery songs due to its appended association with the abolitionist John Brown. This makes it unique as there are remarkably few songs from either side that even address the issue.[33] The subject of slavery is irrelevant in the original adaptation of the song. In fact, there were some at the time who feared the anti-slavery connotations of the song were politically harmful:

The Virginians will think John Brown is worshiped as the Northern hero, in spite of all denials, if even Fletcher Webster's Boston troops sing such a song as this. So on all hands Providence seems to be involving slavery with the war, notwithstanding the most sincere efforts of patriotism and statesmanship to keep the constitutional lines distinct.[34]

"Battle Hymn" approaches slavery obliquely at best. Its religious language can be interpreted in many ways, and there is only one line, "let us die to make men free," which directly addresses slavery, and this line appears only in the fifth and final verse. "Dixie" doesn't address slavery as an issue, though the use of black slang in praise of the South implies satisfaction with the institution of slavery. In fact, the original first stanza was dropped as it was seen to portray slave and master living happily together in "Paradise."[35]

Another provocative way to evaluate the use and popularity of these songs is to examine their performance by regimental bands. These bands were of immense value to the soldiers, and the music performed in camp and at the front had a profound impact on the troops.[36] These bands were also popular with civilians and provided a source of martial music for non-combatants. Northern bands played "John Brown's Body" or "Battle Hymn" but also gave as much attention to other patriotic tunes, most notably "Yankee Doodle," "Hail Columbia," and "The Star-Spangled Banner." Even when reference is made to a band performing "Battle Hymn/John Brown's Body," it is often referred to as "Glory Hallelujah," making it unclear whether the song was considered to be "John Brown's Body" or "Battle Hymn," as both use this phrase in their chorus.

The discussion so far is not intended to refute the popularity of the "Battle Hymn of the Republic." There is no denying that the song, with Howe's lyrics, achieved a great deal of success. The question becomes: to whom was it popular, and where, and when? Evidence would indicate that "Battle Hymn" was popular with civilians, particularly those of the upper classes living in major cities. The soldiers opted for "John Brown's Body." "Battle Hymn" was huge in terms of sheet music sales; yet again, this quite clearly targets a specific segment of society, namely those who can afford sheet music, let alone a piano. This likewise excluded soldiers. It is after the war when "Battle Hymn" gains so much of the prominence it holds today. "Battle Hymn" was popular with civilians during and after the war; "John Brown's Body" was popular with soldiers during the war, yet there was little call for it at the end of hostilities. In subsequent writings following the war, "Battle Hymn" gains almost mythological status. Consider this quote from 1899: "What sublime and splendid words she had written. There is in them a spirit of the old prophets."[37] Though such descriptions are not uncommon in writings after the war, it is rare to find such a description in a soldier's writings from the field. Historiography tends to build upon itself, therefore it is not surprising that "Battle Hymn" grows in prominence in relation to the Civil War, eventually attaining the status of a cultural icon by our time, whereas "John Brown's Body" is relegated to a subordinate position. Today "Battle Hymn" is seen as a quintessential work embodying the beliefs and ideals of the Union during the Civil War. Evidence would seem to indicate that was not the case at the time. Not only do the winners write history, it would seem they sing it as well.[38]

The "Battle Hymn of the Republic" has been elevated to such a degree that it is often viewed as a patriotic or American song reflecting the country as a whole. One need only listen to the marching band when the University of Georgia football team scores to hear the familiar refrain. "Dixie," on the other hand, despite its wide popularity, still retains much of its original geographical reference; it is still a Southern song. There is a striking paradox here, as Emmett's original version was composed for a black-faced minstrel show. From its creation there was no intention for canonical status or any form of patriotic association. It is even more ironic when one remembers that being written for a black-face minstrel show means that the song was presented in a blatantly racist environment, with black makeup and a caricature of black speech, dance, and behavior in general. Certainly this seems an unlikely birthplace for a national anthem; even for a pro-slavery South it seems unlikely that a song which mimics black culture would be seen as capturing white Southern identity. In fact, from the time of the war to today there has been some controversy as to the true origin of the music to "Dixie." Some believe that Emmett first heard the song, or at least a close approximation of it, from black musicians.[39] There were even some at the time of the war who had difficulty with the song:

> It is marvelous with what wild-fire rapidity this tune of 'Dixie' has spread over the whole South. Considered as an intolerable nuisance when first the streets re-echoed it from the repertoire of wandering minstrels, it now bids fair to become the musical symbol of a new nationality, and we

shall be fortunate if it does not impose its very name on our country. . . . What magic potency is there in those rude, incoherent words, which lend themselves to so many parodies, of which the poorest is an improvement on the original? What spell is there in the wild strains that it should be made to betoken the stern determination of a nation resolved to achieve its independence? I cannot tell.[40]

As with "Battle Hymn of the Republic" in the North, it may be argued that the popularity of "Dixie" is more musical than lyrical. Another look at regimental bands supports this. Whereas Union bands opted for various other patriotic tunes aside from that of "Battle Hymn," Confederate bands played "Dixie" at almost any opportunity, but without words. Southern soldiers were no doubt familiar with Emmett's original lyrics, or at least regional or regimental variants; patriotic versions were popularized in Richmond and other urban centers but were not universally known. Just as the emphasis on states' rights prevented the Confederacy from forming a cohesive and effective federal government, so too did regional loyalties lead to a preference for music and lyrics that celebrated individual states and geographical areas. There were some songs written to celebrate national pride, and these achieved significant popularity with civilians and soldiers throughout the South. With the demise of the Confederacy such songs suffered at the hands of Northern-biased historians and failed to gain a place in the post-war canon. "The Bonnie Blue Flag" was the South's first and probably most successful patriotic song, written in honor of one of the Confederacy's first flags. During the war "Dixie" became a "folk" favorite, while "The Bonnie Blue Flag" attained the status of a national anthem. After the war "Dixie" managed to retain its popularity and even gain in significance; not surprisingly, "The Bonnie Blue Flag," an anthem to a short-lived flag for a non-existent country, is consigned to the background.

The evolution of the lyrics to "Dixie" holds a certain similarity to those of the "Battle Hymn of the Republic." At the outbreak of war any number of parodies emerged that are much more reflective of the war movement, the most popular of which was written by Confederate General Albert Pike.

Dixie's Land (D. Emmett)

I wish I was in de land ob cotton,
Old times dar am not forgotten,

Look away! Look away! Look away! Dixie Land.
In Dixie Land whar I was born in,
Early on one frosty mornin',
Look away! Look away! Look away! Dixie Land.

Den I wish I was in Dixie, Hooray! Hooray!
In Dixie Land I'll take my stand, To lib and die in Dixie,
Away, Away, Away down south in Dixie,
Away, Away, Away down south in Dixie.

Dixie (A. Pike)

Southrons, hear your country call you!
Up, lest worse than death befall you!
To arms! To arms! To arms! In Dixie!
Lo! all the beacon fires are lighted—
Let all heart be now united!
To arms! To arms! To arms! In Dixie!

Advance the flag of Dixie!
Hurrah! Hurrah!
For Dixie's Land we take our stand,
And live or die for Dixie!
To arms! To arms!
And conquer peace for Dixie!
To arms! To arms!
And conquer peace for Dixie!

The imitation slang of Emmett's version places it firmly within the minstrel tradition. Despite its blatantly racial presentation, "Dixie" (and its modernized version with "corrected" English) fits well with the music and is easy to sing. Pike's version is much less compatible with Emmett's notes. As was seen with "Battle Hymn" and "John Brown's Body," the original lyrics work much more naturally with the music, whereas the parodies come across as forced and artificial; they seem to function better as poetry than song lyrics. This can be seen in the last line of each verse.

One of the most striking anomalies surrounding "Dixie" involves its composer. It has already been noted that there has been some question as to the origin of the music, whether Emmett derived his music from neighbors or created the music himself. Emmett was an avowed Unionist, and upon hearing the use to which his song was being put exclaimed: "if I had known to what use they were going to put my song, I will be damned if I'd have written it!"[41] Many in the North viewed Emmett as either a traitor or Southern sympathizer, despite the fact that he served for a time in the Federal army. To make matters even more confusing, Abraham Lincoln often stated that "Dixie" was his favorite tune.[42] At the end of the war he requested "Dixie" at a shipboard party; when both the guests and musicians expressed surprise, he responded, "That tune is now Federal property."[43]

Lincoln was not the only Northerner fond of the "Dixie." Consider this account from a Confederate officer at the Battle of Fredericksburg:

> We were attracted by one . . . of the enemy's bands playing . . . their national airs . . . the 'Star Spangled Banner,' 'Hail Columbia,' and others once so dear to us all. It seemed as if they expected some response from us; but none was given until, finally, [they] struck up 'Dixie,' and then both sides cheered, with much laughter.[44]

Such occurrences are far from uncommon and involve many of the most popular tunes from both the North and South. Lieutenant W. J. Kincheloe of the 49th Virginia described one such occurrence: "We are on one side of the Rappahannock, the Enemy on the other. . . . Our boys will sing a Southern song, the Yankees will reply by singing the same tune to Yankee words."[45] Though many song lyrics definitely encouraged the conflict and contributed to negative feeling between the Union and Confederacy, it would seem that the music still managed to transcend the hostilities and provide consolation to soldiers on both sides of the lines.

The impact of the "Battle Hymn of the Republic" and "Dixie" is by no means limited to the period surrounding the Civil War. Both songs have achieved the stature of cultural icons and are used in various ways in contemporary society, from commercial soundtracks and advertising to innumerable recordings and arrangements. Not only have they maintained their musical popularity up to our time, they have retained much of their original social connotations as well. For decades after the war "Dixie" was promoted as a sacred relic for the Confederacy, with heated debates arising in response to proposals for a modification of the lyrics.[46] More recently there has been similar discussion surrounding the lyrics to "Battle Hymn."[47] Both songs have also managed to create controversy as well. At the inauguration of Lyndon B. Johnson in January of 1965 the Mormon Tabernacle Choir sang the "Battle Hymn of the Republic" to the complaints of Southern politicians.[48] "Dixie" likewise has managed to elicit both positive and negative feelings long after the war.[49] In 1999 Chief Justice William H. Renquist led a sing-along of "Dixie" at a judicial conference in Virginia, sparking numerous complaints from those in attendance. Such instances reinforce not only the integral role music plays in both historical and contemporary society, but also provide yet another means for these pieces to function as pedagogical tools.

Teaching a subject like the American Civil War is a challenge to any teacher. There are innumerable complex issues that must be studied if the true nature of the conflict is to be understood. Explaining such complexities or addressing them in a text may be effective, but a personal encounter with such topics is more promising pedagogically. Source materials, particularly music of the time, provide a means for immediate access. Students already know songs such as the "Battle Hymn of the Republic" and "Dixie" and therefore have both aesthetic and historical preconceptions. The lyrics provide a basis for discussion on countless subjects, such as musical function and intended audience; the history of their creation and reception captures much of the tension and contradiction that motivated the Civil War. As works of art each song also generates an aesthetic response that provides a personal foundation from which students can build an understanding of this complex and emotional time.

The added bonus of aesthetic participation propels classroom discussions forward and helps to strengthen the learning experience. Musical taste can be seen as too subjective for historical inquiry, yet this is only the case when the goal is to determine "like" or "dislike." Aesthetic preference and affect can work as the starting point for discussion. How do students' aesthetic choices impact their historical perception? Or in the case of "Dixie" and the "Battle Hymn of the Republic," how might the history of each tune alter their aesthetic choice? And how are the tunes appreciated: musically, lyrically, or historically? If historical association or lyrical content proves to be the deciding factor, then this is fertile ground for discussion. Challenging the received opinion of each song is an ideal way to study how history can bias modern views. To study the Civil War, or any major historical topic, requires not only an examination of principal events and individuals, but also a consideration of those objects that require interpretation and that uncover the subjective reality of those individuals who actually participated in the conflict. What is needed is a dialogue with history; for students to communicate with people from the past, to work not only with the facts of historians, but to listen to the voice of the people, and to experience the emotional, aesthetic, and personal cataclysm that was the American Civil War.

Notes

1. Alexa Sandmann and John Ahern, "Using Literature to Study the Civil War and Reconstruction," *Middle School Journal* 29/2 (November 1997): 25. Using authentic sources such as diaries and letters has been cited as satisfying recent standards set by the National Center for History in the Schools; see Russell B. Olwell, "John Kay's Civil War: A Multimedia Internet Project for Middle School Social Studies," *Social Education* 63/3 (1999): 134.

2. Sandmann and Ahern, "Using Literature," 26. Sean McCollum also notes the personalizing effect primary sources can have for students, and, like Sandmann and Ahern, stresses literary sources; see his "The Road to Gettysburg," *Scholastic Update* 130/1 (September 8, 1997): 18–20.

3. Stephen Kelly, "Reflections of a Music History Teacher," *The College Music Society Newsletter* (March 1992): 1–2, 4.

4. Evelyn Sweerts and Jacqui Grice, "Hitting the Right Note: How Useful is the Music of African-Americans to Historians?" *Teaching History* 108 (2002): 36. See also Alan Simpson, "The Usefulness of 'Aesthetic Education'," in *Aesthetics and Arts Education*, ed. R. Smith and A. Simpson (Urbana: University of Illinois Press, 1991), 171–182.

5. "Even at their best, television and film insist on interpretations that eschew the multiplicity of meaning in behavior, creating instead a bifurcated dialogue in which actors reflect the self-evident truths that inhere to their world. Film productions, unable to explain why individuals act as they do, opt for a reflected rather than refracted sense of reality." Michael Morrison and Robert E. May, "The Limitations of Classroom Media: Ken Burns' Civil War Series as a Test Case," *Journal of American Culture* 19 (Fall 1996): 49.

6. "... [M]usic can provide some genuine empathy for understanding how people in an historical period felt about different things." Steven J. Mastin, " 'Now Listen to Source A': Music and History," *Teaching History*, 108 (2002): 53. Drawing upon emotional connections in teaching the Civil War is also discussed in Olwell, "John Kay's Civil War," 138.

7. See Alex Zukas, "Different Drummers: Using Music to Teach History," *Perspectives: Newsletter of the American Historical Association* 34/6 (September 1996): 27–33.

8. Mastin, "Now Listen to Source A," 49–54. For some very basic angles from which to approach music, see Edith Borroff, "A New Look at Teaching Music History," *Music*

Educators Journal 79/4 (December 1992): 41–43. The general lack of basic musical knowledge remains one of the most embarrassing failures of the American educational system, and one that could be addressed in some measure in collegiate teacher-training programs.

9. A similar discussion can be found in Richard Hickman, "A Student-Centered Approach for Understanding Art," *Art Education* 47/5 (September 1994): 47–51.

10. Dennis E. Fehr effectively shows how rather complex socio-political topics can be approached though art; see his "From Theory to Practice: Applying the Historical Context Model of Art Criticism," *Art Education* 47/5 (September 1994): 52–58. Mastin also provides excellent examples of the interweaving of musical and historical topics in his "Now Listen to Source A." Mugleston discusses a variety of contemporary topics (e.g. impact on the economy, changes in the status of women, civil liberties, African-Americans) that are viable ways of linking the Civil War with today's students; see William F. Mugleston, "Teaching the American Civil War in the Twenty-First Century," *Magazine of History* 12/4 (1998): 71–73.

11. For an entertaining and insightful discussion of "emotional baggage" and contemporary patriotic music, see Arthur Schrader, "Emotional Baggage and Two National Anthems," *The Bulletin of the Society for American Music* 28/2 (Summer 2002): 17–18.

12. Caroline Moseley, "Irrepressible Conflict: Differences Between Northern and Southern Songs of the Civil War," *Journal of Popular Culture* 25/2 (Fall, 1991): 45–56

13. Anna Pendry, et al., "Pupil Preconceptions in History," *Teaching History* 86 (January 1997): 18–20.

14. When used in conjunction with other disciplines it is surprising just how much depth can be achieved; see Rosie Turner-Bisset, "Serving-Maids and Literacy: An Approach to Teaching Literacy through History and Music," *Reading* 35/1 (2001): 27–31. For an example of Civil War music in the public school social studies classroom, see Lynn Waller and William D. Edgington, "Using Songs to Help Teach the Civil War," *Social Studies* 92/4 (July/August 2001): 147–150.

15. The history of the "Battle Hymn of the Republic" can be found in numerous sources, including James Beale, *A Famous War Song* (Philadelphia: James Beale, 1894); Irwin Silber, ed. *Songs of the Civil War* (New York: Dover, 1960), 10–11; Charles Hamm, *Yesterdays: Popular Song in American* (New York: W. W. Norton, 1979), 236; Willard A. Heaps and Porter W. Heaps, *The Singing Sixties: The Spirit of Civil War Days Drawn from the Music of the Times* (Norman: University of Oklahoma Press, 1960); Debbie Williams Ream, "Mine Eyes Have Seen the Glory," *American History Illustrated* 27/6 (January 1993): 60–7.

16. For the history of "Dixie," see E. Lawrence Abel, *Singing the New Nation: How Music Shaped the Confederacy, 1861–1865* (Mechanicsburg, PA: Stackpole Books, 2000), chapter 2; Hans Nathan, *Dan Emmett and the Rise of Early Negro Minstrelsy* (Norman: University of Oklahoma Press, 1977); Richard B. Harwell, *Confederate Music* (Chapel Hill: University of North Carolina Press, 1950), chapter 4; and Silber, *Songs*, 50–51.

17. George B. Bruce and Daniel D. Emmett, *The Drummers' and Fifers' Guide* (New York: Pond & Co., 1861).

18. There were twenty-two lyrical parodies of Dixie, and thirty-nine published arrangements; Heaps, *Singing Sixties,* 48. For some of these parodies, see Harwell,

Confederate Music, 42ff. "Battle Hymn of the Republic" also suffered a number of parodies, though not as many as "Dixie;" see Heaps *Singing Sixties*, 52.

19. James M. McPherson, *Battle Cry of Freedom: The Civil War Era* (New York: Oxford University Press, 1988), 259.

20. Dr. G. A. Kane, "Dixie," *Richmond Dispatch*, 19 March 1893.

21. At more advanced levels the music of the Civil War can raise the issues of slavery, urban/agrarian economies and lifestyles, constitutional government, and more. For the lower grades one can examine "celebrating the cause," "serious soldier life," "Separation," etc.; see Waller and Edgington, "Using Songs to Help Teach the Civil War."

22. There is a fairly in-depth analysis of "Dixie" in Carl B. Holmerg, "Toward the Rhetoric of Music: Dixie," *The Southern Speech Communication Journal* 51 (Fall, 1985): 71–82.

23. For a discussion of recent views on soldiers' motivations, as well as their awareness of larger issues surrounding the Civil War, see Mark Grimsley's review of recent literature in "In Not So Dubious Battle: The Motivations of American Civil War Soldiers," *The Journal of Military History* 62 (January 1998): 175–88.

24. This is evident when one considers the soldiers' letter and diaries, and has been noted by Wiley and others. See also Heaps, *Singing Sixties*, 235.

25. Sandra Lubbers offers an intensive analysis of the lyrics to "Battle Hymn of the Republic," and argues that it captures a "prevailing attitude of the times"; her analysis exhibits a post-war bias, and as has been argued it is unlikely that soldiers or even rural northerners perceived such depth in the words. See her "The Edenic Myth in the Battle Hymn of the Republic," *Student Musicologists at Minnesota* III (1968–69): 110–127. Apparently Julia Ward Howe herself did not believe that her lyrics fit the music all that well.

26. Broadsides were single sheets of paper printed with lyrics to popular songs.

27. Wiley notes that "new" music had little impact on Southern soldiers; see Bell Irvin Wiley, *The Life of Johnny Reb: The Common Soldier of the Confederacy* (Indianapolis: Bobbs-Merrill Co., 1943), 152.

28. Songsters were small, published collections of popular lyrics.

29. An examination of soldiers' writings and songsters reveals that "John Brown's Body" was more popular than "Battle Hymn of the Republic" with Union soldiers; see Bell Irvin Wiley, *The Life of Billy Yank: The Common Soldier of the Union* (Indianapolis: Bobbs-Merrill Co., 1952), 159–160.

30. "Thus, 'popular song' refers to song in actual use by many, and also to pieces prescribed for the populace by aesthetic entrepreneurs." Paul Charosh, "Studying Nineteenth-Century Popular Song," *American Music* 15/4 (Winter 1997): 461. An easy and effective way to evaluate the use of printed music as propaganda is to study the title pages. Many have drawings with blatant patriotic or political themes that have nothing to do with the song.

31. Shelby Foote, *The Civil War, a Narrative, Vol. III: Red River to Appomattox* (New York: Vintage Books, 1986), 640.

32. Foote, *Civil War*, 970.

33. Moseley, "Irrepressible Conflict," 53.

34. *Chicago Tribune*, quoted in Ream, "Mine Eyes have Seen the Glory," 62.

35. John A. Simpson, "Shall We Change the Words of 'Dixie'?" *Southern Folklore Quarterly* 45 (1981): 22.

36. Kenneth E. Olson, *Music and Musket: Bands and Bandsmen of the American Civil War* (Westport, CT: Greenwood Press, 1981); James A. Davis, "Regimental Bands and Morale in the American Civil War," *Journal of Band Research* 38/2 (Spring 2003): 1–21.

37. L. Banks, *Immortal Songs of Camp and Field* (Cleveland: 1899), 165, quoted in Lubbers, *Edenic Myth*, 114. Historians and commentators were and are no doubt attracted to the rhetoric of Howe's lyrics; it is easier to color a text with a phrase like "Mine eyes have seen the glory" as opposed to "lies a-mouldering in the grave."

38. The subsequent popularity of the "Battle Hymn" owes much to proponents such as Bishop McCabe; see William E. Ross, "The Singing Chaplain: Bishop Charles Cardwell McCabe and the Popularization of the 'Battle Hymn of the Republic," *Methodist History* 28/1 (October 1989): 22–32. The possibility for cultural manipulation is addressed in Iain Anderson, "Reworking Images of a Southern Past: The Commemoration of Slave Music After the Civil War," *Studies in Popular Culture* 19/2 (1996): 167–183

39. Howard L. Sacks and Judith R. Sacks, *Way Up North in Dixie: A Black Family's Claim to the Confederate Anthem* (Washington, D.C.: Smithsonian Institution Press, 1993).

40. Henry Hotze, "Three Months in the Confederate Army: The Tune of Dixie," *The Index* I (June 26, 1862): 140; quoted in Harwell *Confederate Music*, 43. Hotze was the Confederate propaganda agent in London. For future portrayals of the South in song, see Earl F. Bargainnier, "Tin Pan Alley and Dixie: The South in Popular Song," *Mississippi Quarterly* 30/4 (1977): 527–564.

41. Nathan, *Dan Emmett*, 275.

42. Kenneth A. Bernard, *Lincoln and the Music of the Civil War* (Caldwell, Id: Caxton Printers, 1966), 13.

43. Foote, *Civil War*, 905–6.

44. Geoffrey C. Ward, *The Civil War: An Illustrated History* (New York: Alfred A. Knopf, 1990), 169.

45. Wiley, *Johnny Reb*, 318.

46. Simpson, "'Dixie," 19–40

47. *North & South*, 2/6 (1999). "Battle Hymn" was for a time put forward as a candidate for our national anthem.

48. Lubbers, "Edenic Myth," 115.

49. Richard D. Starnes, "'The Stirring Strains of Dixie': The Civil War and Southern Identity in Haywood County, North Carolina," *The North Carolina Historical Review* LXXIV/3 (July 1997): 237; see also Sacks, *Way Up North*, 4–5.

The Multitrack Model
Cultural History and the Interdisciplinary Study of Popular Music

Michael J. Kramer

Introduction: The Multitrack Metaphor

. . . the world as experienced by human beings is always multi-tracked and multi-mixed.
>   —*Richard Middleton, "Introduction,"* Reading Pop[1]

A metaphor is at once proposition and resolution. . . .
>   —*Roy Wagner,* Symbols That Stand For Themselves[2]

Among scholars, popular music studies continues to grow as an inter-disciplinary project. A cacophony of approaches now exists, perhaps because, as the critic Greil Marcus has written, "Music is fundamentally ambiguous."[3] The challenge remains to make sense of this ambiguity without narrowing the study of music. How might we organize popular music studies as a field in order to further our collective understanding of pop? Taking the investigation of 1960s rock as a case study while mapping out similarities and differences among academic disciplines, this essay suggests that the metaphor of the multitrack might serve as one way to conceptualize popular music studies.

For the most part, the methodological debates about pop within academia have been three-sided affairs. First, coming to the topic from the formal training of Western art music, musicologists have concentrated on sounds themselves: they emphasize close textual analysis of pop music. Second, embedding their analysis in specific contexts, ethnographers have drawn upon the practices of cultural anthropology to make visible the surroundings of music. Third, by exploring the paradigms and logics through which pop resonates, theoreticians in cultural studies have connected popular music to questions of political ideology and social power. Each of these approaches has provided deep insights into popular music.

Moreover, scholars from each side have increasingly reached across disciplinary divides to generate new strategies for understanding pop. Musicologists draw upon ethnographic interview and connect their focus on sounds to theoretical inquiry. Ethnographers pay close attention to music as sound; so too, they embed interviews and participant-observation in theoretical paradigms. Theoreticians utilize musical texts and contextual evidence to articulate the abstract categories and forces in which they locate pop. However, disagreements across disciplinary boundaries have also limited the development of pop music studies as a field.

As is often the case, interdisciplinarity has been both a blessing and a curse. Musicologists, ethnographers, and theorists have pursued an almost dizzying array of methodological combinations. Yet scholars of popular music still often talk past each other. There is little overarching coherence because the intellectual rewards of the different approaches ultimately drive scholars down divergent paths. The challenge remains to keep popular music studies a wide-open field of inquiry while providing common arenas for debate and discussion. Can we hear the whole song without reducing its many component parts to a monolithic drone?

One place we might start is with a metaphor that comes from the very core of popular music-making: the recording process. As Steve Jones argues, "the technology of sound recording . . . organizes our experience of popular music." Jones's point is that, "Without electronics, and without the accompanying technical supports and technical experimentation, there could not be the mass production of music, and therefore there would not be mass-mediated popular music, or its consumption."[4] From the technology so central to popular music, the multitrack offers a means for conceptualizing interdisciplinary work in popular music studies.

The multitrack allows musicians to record parts of a song separately and then arrange the results into an endless set of mixed and remixed performances. Since this essay is only a preliminary, a rough mix of the multitrack model—a "demo"—what follows is a consideration of but four tracks in relation to my own research on the connections between 1960s rock music and the counterculture movement. This rough mix brings together the three main academic approaches to popular music—musicology, ethnography, and theory—while including a crucial fourth track: cultural history. Of course, there are many other tracks one might add to a fully-conceived multitrack model: non-academic studies by journalists; the thoughts of musicians themselves; the perspectives of engineers, producers, roadies, groupies, collectors, archivists, educators, curators, and others; a focus on the structural, economic dimensions of popular music; and examinations of fiction, poetry, video, and film.

Additionally, one might arrange the tracks differently, isolate or consolidate certain approaches, emphasize a different set of boundaries between tracks, or focus on the common aspects of various methodologies. The multitrack as a metaphor also may not suit all types of music or musical study. Especially as music enters the realm of digital production and consumption, and as musical forms from around the world increasingly intersect and overlap, new metaphors for the study of popular music might be worth exploring. Nonetheless, I hope the multitrack can provide one useful trope for fostering an inclusive interdisciplinary methodology that honors differences among many approaches while insisting on their commonality in the shared pursuit of understanding popular music in all its reverberations.

A word about the fourth track: cultural history. While musicology and ethnography often seek to recapture the meaning of music in the moment, and theory often imposes current concerns onto past sounds, history continually emphasizes the interaction between then and now, past and present. Cultural history serves as a kind of echo track, incorporating the focus of the other tracks into a final layer that completes the overall mix.[5] By itself, this historical track would sound quite odd, a mere whisper of musicology and ethnography's ability to render pop's immediacy in performance and in everyday life. It would also only provide a meek theoretical analysis of music's fully-considered ideological capacities. However, because history considers changes and continuities over time, it provides a perspective on the interaction between immediacy and distance, as well as between practice and theory.

Musicologists, ethnographers, and theorists have always been conscious of history to some extent, but cultural history as a discrete track presents one way to mediate among the three other approaches: musicology's focus on sounds themselves; ethnography's privileging of the voices of participants in order to grasp the surroundings of sounds; and theory's reach to articulate abstract logics, paradigms, and ideologies. By providing a perspective from which to negotiate the other tracks, history helps emphasize the *multi* in the multitrack model. It integrates the other tracks without obliterating their distinctive qualities. More of this in the section on cultural history's echo track; but first to the musicologist's illumination of rock's sounds themselves.

1.   Sounds: Musicology

. . . as if sound were the most absorbent medium of all, soaking up histories and philosophical systems and physical surroundings and encoding them in something so slight as a single vocal quaver or harpsichord interjection.

—*Geoffrey O'Brien, "Burt Bacharach Comes Back"* [6]

For musicologists Sheila Whiteley and Michael Hicks, the sound of rock itself contains a bevy of information. Whiteley's *The Space Between the Notes: Rock and the Counter-Culture* and Hicks's *Sixties Rock: Garage, Psychedelic, and Other Satisfactions* utilize innovative transcription techniques and close textual readings to analyze rock music's sonic relationship to the social codes of the 1960s counterculture.[7] By staying close to the music while incorporating limited aspects of ethnographic, theoretical, and historical approaches, they produce rich sonic accounts of rock that begin to reveal the music's larger significance. Their books demonstrate the ways that pop musicologists have moved beyond the traditional question of their field, which was what makes this particular piece of music great, to issues of social meaning-making. But Whiteley and Hicks continue the best practices of musicology, repeatedly grounding their observations in close listening to the sounds of rock themselves.[8]

In *The Space Between the Notes*, Sheila Whiteley focuses on "progressive rock" and the British counterculture. The concept of homology, in which specific sounds map directly onto particular meanings, serves as Whiteley's crucial analytic device. Taken from the theories of British subcultural studies, homology allows Whiteley to interrogate sounds as if each expressed a precise idea.[9] This allows her to utilize a theoretical notion from the third track of the multitrack model while honing in on close textual analysis of the sounds themselves, the first track. Whiteley hears "a homology between musical and cultural characteristics" in "the association of acid and universal love with sounds in the music."[10] Asking how "a musical language" can "express an alternative 'progressive' viewpoint," Whiteley decides that there was a "psychedelic coding" in the music.[11] This coding correlated to the countercultural search for a "progressive" mind-expanding consciousness. According to Whiteley, six aspects of the music connoted the "trip," as participants called their search for new modes of imagination, self-expression, and behavior. The musical aspects were: 1. manipulation of timbres (blurred/bright/overlapping); 2. upward movement (connoting "psychedelic flight); 3. harmonies (oscillating/lurching); 4. rhythms (regular/irregular); 5. relationships (foreground/background); and 6. collages (compared to "normal" treatments).[12]

Whiteley focuses on songs by Cream, Jimi Hendrix, Pink Floyd, and other groups to demonstrate various incarnations of the six aspects of "psychedelic coding" and how they directly represented countercultural yearnings for expanded consciousness and freedom. For instance, she closely analyzes the harmonic and rhythmic progressions of the song "I Feel Free" by Cream. The title and central lyric of the song, of course, suggest its meaning. But Whiteley goes much further, demonstrating how the music evoked, even produced, the countercultural ethos. "The song is based on two contrasting styles," Whiteley explains, "the first a gentle and floating around the beat, the second more didactic with a strong emphasis on the vocal and the walking bass line. A sense both of freedom and of continuity is achieved by the subtle interplay of the basic motifs established in the introduction."[13] By closely analyzing the music of "I Feel Free" as sound, Whiteley is able to show how the sounds embodied meaning for the 1960s "progressive" counterculture.

Continuing in this vein, Whiteley transcribes and describes "Astromony Dominé" by Pink Floyd, tracing how, "the dip shapes in the guitar solo create a strong feeling of floating around the beat, and this is reinforced by the lazy meandering around the notes, again suggestive of a state of tripping where the fixed point takes on a new reality."[14] To Whiteley, the sonic and the cultural come together in music. She documents a similar "trip" in Jimi Hendrix's guitar improvisations. Utilizing the standard staff notation of Western musicological transcription, Whiteley innovatively adds boxes of text that mark the ascent "into trip," the "start of trip," and finally the "climax." In the box about the climax, she offers textual description as well as musical notation: "climax: electronic manipulation and bending of notes: bending of notes: tripping around notes: high excitement bars 6–7."[15] With this transcription, we can literally see the sounds of countercultural rock mapped out in an updated form of traditional Western notation. We can follow with our eyes as well as our ears the visual representation of psychedelic music, annotated with descriptive text.

Overall, Whiteley's study is rich in this sort of sound-based analysis. But she never delves particularly deeply into the social milieu through which rock music loudly reverberated in the 1960s. Her musical analysis describes a number of the ways that rock communicated "psychedelic" notions through aural signals, but it only begins to explore the actual spaces in which rock seemed to open up psychedelic alternatives. We can follow the notes on paper, but we have little sense of the environments in which they were first produced: London's UFO Club or countless individual hi-fi systems, headphones, and bedrooms around the United Kingdom and beyond. We can hear the correlation of sounds to "psychedelic codings," and this helps to deepen our appreciation of the sounds, but the larger context remains at a remove. Whiteley's attention to rock music as homological text lets us hear the society as it was represented in the sounds, but it does not reveal with any depth the sounds as they moved through the society.

Like Whiteley, Michael Hicks explores the sonic incarnations of psychedelia. Adopting an emphasis on the circulation of certain key songs, he focuses on the musical journeys of widely covered tunes such as "Hey Joe" and "Light My Fire," which he tracks through close sonic analysis. To this focus on the sounds, Hicks adds an attention to genre. By addressing the names, origins, and histories of two ambiguous genres in rock, "garage" and "psychedelic," Hicks begins to uncover the ways that music helped to define, even create, a kind of vernacular, youth-led avant-garde movement in the United States. The history of music genres, rooted in Hicks' focus on the sounds of rock themselves, is then able to feed into a larger history of social transitions and connections during the 1960s.

Hicks' chapter on "Avant-Garage" is especially insightful. Drawing upon the art-historical theories of Renato Poggioli, Hicks explores how during the mid-1960s, "activism and antagonism, hallmarks of avant-garde movements, permeated garage rock and the mentality of those

who played it." Hicks continues: "it was the music that bound the participants together in a cohesive, symbol-laden community.[16] Though he
focuses on the sounds, Hicks utilizes the notion of genre and Poggioli's
theories of the avant-garde to begin to move toward a fuller multitrack
version of 1960s rock. The idea of genre contextualizes the sounds of
garage and psychedelia, while Pogglioli's theory locates the social use of
the sounds in a larger ideological paradigm.

First, Hicks examines garage rock. The genre's "musical traits express
activism and antagonism yet serve to build a community," Hicks notes of
garage's seeming contradictions. "In garage rock," he explains, "riffs, fuzz,
and other musical details serve as musical signs, conversational details
passed from recording to recording in a way that tied the whole garage
movement together."[17] Sensitive to the circulation of "musical signs," Hicks
primarily concentrates on the sounds themselves, but links the sounds to
other aspects of the multitrack: the surroundings fostered by shared sonic
traits and theories guiding the making of these common sounds.

Tracing garage's links to psychedelic-rock, Hicks is then able to tell us
something new about the genealogy of the counterculture movement in
America. He conveys how garage and psychedelia, though distinct genres, were marked by similar sounds of "activism and antagonism" that
were able to foster "community." The fuzz-toned, overdriven sounds in
common heralded a politics of egalitarian participation and noisy dissent emanating out of cheap guitar amps. Though psychedelia has often
been conceptualized as a highbrow reaction to the more gritty, working-
class form of garage-rock, which is interpreted as more authentic, Hicks
traces the sonic links between psychedelic-rock and garage to argue
that, in many ways, pyschedelia was an extension and elaboration on
garage. As Hicks puts it, the counterculture as expressed in rock was the
"flip side," the b-side, to garage's a-side.[18]

Letting the musical sounds of rock guide him, Hicks navigates countercultural connections such as these, which involve contextual and
theoretical issues of class, race, gender, and generational identity. Yet
his art-historical-based analysis of genre only begins to move from the
sounds themselves to their larger social situatedness. We might ask many
questions that Hicks does not address. What was the relationship of
garage rock and psychedelia to the marketplace? Were the communities
these genres enabled "consumption communities," to borrow a phrase

from Daniel Boorstin, or were they political communities, or both?[19] The relationship of the marketplace to genre is not explored in detail.

Other questions emerge: what racial issues did garage and psychedelic rock musicians and fans negotiate (or fail to negotiate) in borrowing ideas from the free jazz of John Coltrane and others?[20] How did questions of gender and identity affect avant-garage and psychedelic rock?[21] What do we make of the class issues involved in the fact that, according to Hicks, "garage rock showed contempt for the trappings of middle and upper-class society," while "psychedelic rock was more subversive, using new forms, unusual chord progressions, sophisticated technology, and novel gadgets to undermine the conventions of popular music and, implicitly, of the whole cultural environment"?[22] A close analysis of the sounds and the genre configurations of 1960s rock is crucial, but questions about context and theory remain even after we scan our eyes over Hicks's transcriptions of the lengths of various performances of "Light My Fire" by The Doors.[23]

Whiteley and Hicks insist that the sounds of rock in the 1960s mattered *as sounds*. Even as they begin to bring context and theory to bear on rock, they go far beyond simply treating the music as if its sole purpose was to be the background for socially conscious lyrics.[24] And in their close textual readings of particular songs, Whiteley and Hicks flash strobe lights on the larger cultural context of rock music in the 1960s. But because their musicological methodology focuses so intently on sounds themselves, a deeper, richer accounting of the counterculture remains at a distance. How do we get more inside this experience?

2. Surroundings: Ethnography

All music is what awakes from you when you are reminded by the Instruments. . . .
—*Walt Whitman, "A Song for Occupations," Leaves of Grass*[25]

Just as musicology helps us hear the sounds of popular music in richer ways, ethnography assists in hearing the wider context within which those sounds exist. Ethnographic methods point to the value of carefully studying the surroundings in which humans create, receive, reject, share, celebrate, and use music. Of course, ethnographers have little interest in sacrificing the musicological understanding that the direct study of sounds conveys, nor are they interested in separating the contextualized experiences of sound from larger theoretical notions of popular music or severing those experiences from history. But most of all, ethnographers seek to deepen our perspectives on the social worlds in which sounds resonate. They can turn us more fully from the musicological focus on sound to a sense of music as social experience. As the second track of this multitrack model, ethnography emphasizes the reception of sounds and the ways in which popular music is embedded in the lives of its makers and listeners.

Recent ethnographies present methods and approaches that might apply to 1960s rock. Barry Shank's emphasis on the constitution of a local "scene" in Austin, Texas, in the 1970s and 1980s helps us think more about the creation of scenes in 1960s rock locales. Based on his intensive participant-observation, Shank argues that, "The rock 'n' roll scene in Austin, Texas, is characterized by the productive contestation between these two forces: the fierce desire to remake oneself through musical practice, and the equally powerful struggle to affirm the value of that practice in the complexly structured late-capitalist marketplace."[26] This collision between, on the one hand, the ground-level energies of scene creation centered around remaking the self and, on the other, participation in national and international flows of capital through the mass media and the mass distribution of consumer goods reminds one of earlier musical settings such as San Francisco in the 1960s. While one obviously cannot draw upon direct ethnographic evidence as Shank did in his study of Austin in the 1970s and 1980s, the careful use of source materials and participant interviews can begin to contextualize the music of the "San Francisco Sound" along ethnographic lines.

Shank himself does not rely only on ethnographic interviews. To develop his suggestive findings, he incorporates the history of Austin music-making, issues of Texan identity, and Lacanian psychoanalytic theory into a multitrack-like approach he calls "critical cultural studies ethnography."[27] But above all, he honors his ethnographic evidence, even when it is in tension with other aspects of his interdisciplinary method. For instance, when the musician John Croslin tells Shank that Croslin's group, The Reivers, "are a band that thrives on personality . . . the most important part of the band is our personalities going back and forth," Shank takes care to note that, "The local language of 'personalities' . . . conflicts with my language of subject positions and enunciative possibilities."[28] For Shank, the challenge in *Dissonant Identities* always becomes how to find a way to connect the theoretical and historical dimensions of his study to the viewpoints of his interviewees. No matter how far away he reaches for analytic tools to help him grasp his topic, everything must return to the ethnographic track: the concrete, lived experiences of participants in the Austin scene.

While Shank keeps his focus on social life in one specific place, other ethnographers have explored the manner in which social surroundings connect to more spiritual, ethereal realms. Without losing site of the insider's perspective on the direct contexts in which sound is experienced, these studies examine the ways in which sound transcends immediate settings. The social meanings of sound in these ethnographies become not merely their place in an economic system or a network of music makers and consumers or a particular "scene" (important as those are), but the deeply affective religious qualities of sound that contributes to music's power. At once social and transcendent, these religious qualities are significant because they embody how, through music, insiders reach outward, away from surroundings to forces that feel as if they exist beyond the social.

Daniel Cavicchi's study of contemporary Bruce Springsteen fans presents the ability of ethnography to deepen our understanding of how insiders experience their fandom along religious lines.[29] While Cavicchi insists that fandom is not the same as religion, he argues that the parallels "point to the fact that both fandom and religion are addressing similar concerns and engaging people in similar ways." Among these, Cavicchi notes, are an intense experience of "turning" or conversion; the interest in applying the signs and symbols discovered in a body of materials (whether it be liturgy or Springsteen's songs) to their own lives; the urge to belong; and the creation of shared rituals of devotion.[30]

Cavicchi's parsing of the religiosity of Springsteen fandom suggests the kind of careful analysis that historians might develop about past music such as 1960s rock. Many participants in 1960s rock music described their experiences in religious terms. For instance, the critic Albert Goldman characterized the New York rock club the Electric Circus as, "a votive temple to the electronic muse, crammed with offerings from all her devotees."

Goldman provided a striking description of listening to rock at the Electric Circus, offering details about its qualities that might serve as ethnographic evidence. "Magnetized by the crowd," Goldman wrote, "impelled by the relentless pounding beat of the music, you are drawn out on the floor. Here there is a feeling of total immersion: you are inside the mob, inside the skull, inside the music."[31]

Linking a religious framework to hunches about underlying, deeply felt erotic impulses and desires, Goldman continued, "Strangest of all, in the midst of this frantic activity, you soon feel supremely alone; and this aloneness produces a giddy sense of freedom, even of exultation. At last you are free to move and act and mime the secret motions of your mind. Everywhere about you are people focused deep within themselves, working to bring to the surfaces of their bodies deep-seated erotic fantasies."[32] If we treat Goldman's writing as ethnography, it articulates musical experience not only as socially constituted, but as a medium between the concrete social world and subconscious desires and yearnings. The music also pointed toward religious transcendence, the "giddy sense of freedom, even of exultation" that Goldman mentions. Barry Shank's use of psychoanalytic theory offers one way of interpreting the unspoken, even unconscious, dimensions of musical experience to which Goldman alludes. Add to this Cavicchi's approach to Springsteen fandom and Goldman's observations suggest that there is much interpretation to be drawn from careful readings of the religion-tinged language used to describe the experience of 1960s rock in its day.

"At issue here," Glenn Hinson writes in his ethnography of African-American gospel music, "is transcendent encounter, the experience of the holy, a feeling that so transcends the everyday that it grants certain knowledge and rounds ardent faith. Without addressing such encounter, and without according it the essential centrality granted it by the saints, ethnographic inquiry—like religion without feeling—would be a hollow exercise."[33] Ethnography has tended to emphasize everyday life and has produced many insights into daily practices. But, as Hinson suggests, grasping the transcendent nature of music is also essential. Ethnography can be effective in the ways it locates sounds in their immediate social contexts; but these microscopic studies of participants also illuminate the ways music moves between specific surroundings and the transcendent realms toward which sound can leap.[34]

3. Schemes: Theory

Music, like cartography, records the simultaneity of conflicting orders, from which a
fluid structure arises, never resolved, never pure.

— *Jacques Attali,* Noise[35]

While theorists borrow from the methods of musicology and ethnography, they interpret pop music's sounds and surroundings as particular manifestations of larger forces at work in society. More than any other segment of the multitrack model, theory concentrates on revealing these larger forces, often drawing upon Marxist or other visions of the hidden ideological powers that lurk beneath the surface of everyday life. The theories of popular music might be thought of as schemes in both senses of the word: first, as *schemata*, or the mapping out of the deeper cultural forces that theorists perceive as driving musical expression and experience, and, second, as blueprints or proscriptive efforts to shift society in new directions.

Theoreticians of rock have been especially interested in articulating the ideologies and politics within which sounds and their surroundings have existed. In doing so, they have not only wanted to understand the history of the music, but also to present normative valuations for future experiences of the music. This interest in grasping rock within its larger ideological forces in order to attend to current political and ideological concerns has led certain theorists to declare rock "dead" as a genre, while others have reaffirmed its continued relevance. It has all depended upon which theoretical paradigm the theorist has located rock.

The groundbreaking theoretical scheme for rock put forth by Simon Frith set the stage for arguments both for and against rock's future. Rejecting both the belief that rock was a revolutionary folk music of the young that emerged outside the mechanisms of consumer society and the counter-position that it was merely commercial manipulation foisted on listeners by corporate powers, Frith argued that rock revealed the dialectical struggles at the heart of late twentieth-century consumerism. Rock was a musical form generated from the contradictions of capitalism.[36] "We have to try to make sense of rock's production and consumption on the basis of what is at stake in these processes—the meanings that are produced and consumed," Frith writes. "Rock is a mass-produced music that carries a critique of its own means of production; it is mass-consumed music that constructs its own 'authentic' audience." Caught between its exchange value as a commodity within capitalism and its use value as a form of expression linked in fundamental ways to identity, community formation, and aesthetic power, rock could help constitute certain types of politics, but only within the ideologies of the economic system that produced it. For Frith, "the needs expressed in rock—for freedom, control, power, a sense of life—are needs defined by capitalism."[37] If authentic community and the politics that might spring from it were to be found in rock, to Frith the music had to be understood as a commercial medium with powers that could, at times, seem to momentarily propel itself beyond the marketplace alone.

Expanding upon Frith's positioning of rock within the ideologies of capitalism, both Lawrence Grossberg and Theodore Gracyk explore 1960s and post-1960s rock music within other political frameworks. Grossberg explores rock as a popular music that could have possibly produced a democratic socialist consciousness within the fragmenting, postmodern context of late twentieth-century capitalism—a moment when stable individual identities and communal affiliations were being ruptured by new economic processes. He is most interested in how 1960s rock failed to foster socialist beliefs in the postmodern moment, and how advocates of progressive, socialist values might learn from rock's shortcomings. In particular, Grossberg examines how rock ironically wound up asserting and consolidating a cultural hegemony of passivity and conservatism by reshaping what constituted "the popular."

Gracyk, by contrast, examines rock as a form of mass culture rather than of "the popular." He is interested in rock's relationship as a commodity form to the ideologies of modern liberalism, particularly its conceptions of individual freedom, and puts forth normative models of understanding rock in the spirit of liberal pluralism. Grossberg focuses on how rock's collective possibilities were contained and limited while Gracyk explores rock's capacities for individual flexibility in the making of hybrid identities. That the same music could lead to such different interpretations tells us something about the slipperiness of theory. As a track by itself, theory can become abstract to the point of pure speculation; but in connection with the tracks of sound, context, and history, theory can become a significant mode of grasping music at its most expansive.

Lawrence Grossberg is explicit about his theoretical project. He is most concerned with the overarching cultural paradigm that guides rock. "I have never been interested in the concrete as a local, empirical phenomenon," he explains, distinguishing his work from musicologists and ethnographers, "but in the formation of rock culture at the broadest level."[38] Grossberg argues that at this overarching position, we might grasp the logic of what he terms the "rock formation," a mode of thinking and being that shaped particular instances of musical experience in relation to feelings of political empowerment and impotency. Grossberg's goal in discussing the abstract idea of the "rock formation" is to "propose a strategy that will allow us to map out the positive differences between major forms" of rock.[39] Offering explanations and charts that schematize how various "apparatuses, scenes, and alliances" within rock music relate to the larger "rock formation," Grossberg provides a model of how rock music, in all its guises, has operated through a linked paradigm. Particular rock performers, songs, albums, and receptions of the music are marked by "articulations" of authenticity, rebellion, affirmation, negation, fun, pleasure, and boredom within the vectors of the larger "rock formation."

Turning toward the normative analysis of how rock has failed to communicate or enact progressive, socialist political beliefs and values, Grossberg develops an argument about what he sees as the end result of the "rock formation": instead of a receptivity to more progressive socialist attitudes and policies, its cultural logic led to a mood of "popular conservatism." In Grossberg's account, rock music provided its makers and fans with powerful shared emotions of rebellion and authenticity, which Grossberg calls "affective alliances."[40] The music especially allowed its participants to mark themselves as different from parents, and from other music fans. But, limited by the "rock formation," the music offered no truly sustainable alternative outside of the dominant structures of society: it only could articulate difference from family to school to mass consumerism and leisure; it proffered mobility, but with no place to resettle but within the existing lifeworld; it gave pleasure and respite from boredom, but only in temporary doses. The music, for all its furious energy, ultimately expressed the feeling of having nowhere to go. This fostered a "postmodern" sense of futility in which all authenticity felt beyond attainment, and hence a passive, conservative posture seemed to be the most sensible stance for fans to adopt. Grossberg's somewhat pessimistic sense of rock music culture's political efficacy stems from his probing for the music's socialist possibilities, especially rock's potential capacities for collective transformation in the face of postmodern fragmentation and futility. Grossberg concludes that rock represents an expression of the turn toward passitivity and conservatism.

Coming at rock not as a herald of progressive politics but as an aesthetic form deeply linked to the liberal tradition, Theodore Gracyk reaches quite different conclusions: he hears rock as a startling expression of liberal pluralism, with its emphasis on individual autonomy and freedom. As a philosopher, Gracyk creates a different scheme in which to understand rock, and from this scheme, he offers an alternative vision of the normative ways in which rock should be heard and interpreted.

The different schemes of Grossberg and Gracyk have their origins in different conceptualizations of the music's form. Grossberg thinks of rock as an ideological and affective "formation" that is part of the larger political struggle to shape what feels popular.[41] Gracyk, by contrast, interprets rock as a form of *mass* rather than popular culture. To Gracyk, rock is a commodity form that expresses a continually renewed commitment to liberalism's articulation of the autonomous, free individual in the face of postmodernism's claims that this individual no longer exists: "When rock songs proclaim that rock will never die, this now looks less like a claim about the enduring attraction of the music and more like an expression of commitment to a liberal ideology at odds with the main themes of postmodernism," Gracyk writes.[42] To Gracyk, the guiding paradigm of liberal individualism motors rock music; it is the source from which rock music springs and to which it returns. In this way, according to Gracyk, "rock's continued vitality depends on the continuing power of an ideological abstraction. In its turn, liberalism is refreshed with new modes of expression."[43] Rock depends on liberalism's abstract ideal of the independent individual; simultaneously, this abstract ideal is reenlivened by rock's ability to give it material and aesthetic expression.

While Lawrence Grossberg believes that larger forces of the "rock formation" shape individual being, Gracyk argues that rock continues to promulgate the opportunity for individuals to control the making of their own identities. As recorded sound created through innovative uses of the mass-production technologies in studios rather than as a work of music meant to be performed from written notation, rock points the way toward a range of personal expression far richer than traditional Western classical music. Not just musical notes, but sonic qualities of echo, reverb, distortion, and electronic manipulation become essential to the defining qualities of rock. From what Gracyk emphasizes as the ontological diversity of rock as a recording medium, "musical pleasure positions listeners to share community with persons performing otherwise threatening or previously unimagined identities."[44] According to Gracyk, even the most powerful stereotypes, such as gender identities, can go by the wayside. "The very breadth of subject positions," Gracyk concludes about a Bonnie Raitt vocal performance, "has the effect of challenging the stability of any identity that we might assign to her."[45]

In Gracyk's schemata of rock, the music becomes a resource for destabilizing identity without fracturing it into postmodern despair. "The real contribution of popular music may be its power to expose listeners to a vast arsenal of possible identities," Gracyk argues. "In allowing a listener to 'inhabit' new positions without bearing any of their real-life consequences, mass art can suggest life options that were previously unthinkable."[46] For Gracyk, rock conveys the liberal ideology of a pluralistic society in which independent subjects are able to alter and change their identities through profound aesthetic experiences. Offering a normative, prescriptive political position of "disinterested listening," Gracyk puts forth a scheme for rock in which, "those who bother to listen and look will find that rock exhibits a staggering variety of identities that can serve as models in the performance of personal identity."[47]

Whereas Grossberg hears the politics of rock as a formation of cultural artillery fired across the war-torn landscape of battles fought over popular culture, Gracyk hears the politics as a costume party in which mass culture makes available a proliferation of identities to autonomous individuals, and the masquerade can perhaps lead to new modes of equality and freedom of choice. For both these theorists, popular music takes place within larger cultural logics and paradigms, schemes that provide the framework for the making and experience of music, and schemes that also provide blueprints for the ways in which popular music might function in the future.[48] There is a history to rock, of course, and a wider context that both Grossberg and Gracyk are concerned in tracing, but the complexity and contingency of this history and historical consciousness are subordinated to schemes of the music's abstract ideological underpinnings.

4.   Echoes: Cultural History

The cultural historian does not seek to know past experience, that is, to reexperience it in any sense. Rather he seeks to discover the forms in which people have experienced the world—the patterns of life, the symbols by which they cope with the world. . . . But the problem is a complicated one for the historian, for in order to do his job he must, as a matter of fact, also create forms so that he can best understand the forms that make up the culture he is studying.

—Warren Susman, *Culture as History:* The Transformations of American Society in the Twentieth Century[49]

If theorists such as Grossberg and Gracyk scheme with ears cocked toward the future, historians listen more intently back in time. What they hear there is less an orderly scheme than a cacophonous echo of sounds, contexts, actions, interactions, accidents, ideas, beliefs, values, attitudes, emotions, fantasies, dreams, and doubts. As Warren Susman points out, obtaining knowledge about the past is always difficult. It is informed by the historians' starting position in the present. Moreover, points in the past are themselves affected by earlier cultural forms and layers: the past has its own pasts. Cultural historians of popular music can harness this ongoing negotiation between past moments and present reference points to evoke a rich description of the relationship between music and history. This dialectical movement back and forth, between perspectives of then and now, creates an echo track that serves as an effective final layer in the multitrack model.

Because it continually moves between positions, cultural history never rests comfortably in any one mode of analysis. In the spirit of musicology, cultural history pays close attention to sounds themselves; it also concentrates on ethnography's pursuit of immediate cultural surroundings; and history always explicitly or implicitly involves theory's wide-angle lens on the conceptual paradigms in which popular music has existed and continues to reverberate. Scholars in musicology, ethnography, and theory have, of course, already been integrating these different approaches. So too, they have been aware of history. But thinking of a special echo track of cultural history offers a particularly effective way to incorporate approaches without obliterating their differences.

Two examples of cultural history's echo track can be found in Dominick Cavallo's A *Fiction of the Past: The Sixties in American History* and Nick Bromell's *Tomorrow Never Knows: Rock and Pyschedelics in the 1960s*.[50] Cavallo seeks to place the efforts of 1960s rock musicians along with other radical youth culture participants of the era "in the American grain"; Bromell attempts to elucidate the kind of historical consciousness that rock music and psychedelic drug use helped spark in the 1960s. Cavallo's book is a good example of well-researched historical inquiry into social practices, cultural forms, and their effects; Bromell's is a striking meditation somewhere between memoir and historical analysis. Both books suggest the value of listening carefully to the echo track.

Dominick Cavallo seeks to integrate the radicalism of the 1960s youth movement into larger strands in United States history. He explains that "the goal . . . is to weave the radical youth culture into the American experience." Exploring the influence of everything from the romanticization of the Wild West in film to child-rearing practices, Cavallo argues that, "The sixties of youthful rebellion has not been sutured to the country's past. Rather than being explained and made a crucial part of that history, this crucial aspect of the decade dangles in time. It is generally unhinged from what went before, and painfully alien to what followed. It remains, therefore, inevitably misunderstood and misinterpreted."[51]

Most histories of the 1960s position rock music as a sphere of leisure, pleasure, and consumption, but Cavallo looks to the productive sensibilities informing musicians. He detects deep-rooted, pre-corporate American values of artisinal control over labor resurfacing among 1960s rock musicians. Of the Grateful Dead, Frank Zappa, and Neil Young, he writes, "Most of them wanted money and fame. But these artists were equally intent upon achieving personal autonomy through their labor."[52] Exploring the language and practices of 1960s rock music-making, as an ethnographer might, Cavallo is able to illuminate the lingering ideologies of autonomous labor on which a theorist might concentrate. Moreover, moving between his own perspective and the 1960s moment, and more significantly, between the 1960s and perceptions of history available during that era, Cavallo is able to demonstrate how what seemed new and futuristic in the 1960s—rock music's electronic sounds—also possessed deep historical roots.

Perhaps even more than Cavallo, Nick Bromell's study of the experience of rock music and psychedelic drug use in the 1960s is marked by sensitivity to time. Bromell's title, *Tomorrow Never Knows*, taken from the Beatles, speaks to the historical consciousness that permeates his study. Developing readings of rock songs themselves, as musicologists would, while paying close attention to the words of rock critics and his own memories of the era, as a memoirist might, Bromell outlines a theory of how "the fusion of rock and psychedelics either inaugurated a way of being in the world, or simply coincided with it, and in either case helped articulate and objectify it."[53] This way of being in the world was most of all a sensibility about history. "It was the widely shared sensation that history was ending in the '60s," Bromell decides.[54] And yet, alongside this apocalyptic mood, rock music and drugs inspired a feeling of joining an immense flow of time.

Bromell believes that this combination of millennial fervor and an expanded awareness of being embedded in time's ceaseless waves profoundly radicalized its listeners by heightening their historical consciousness. Rock and psychedelics seemed to accentuate the utopian potential of the moment, but also provided, "a way of seeing and being in the world that underwrites the possibility, indeed declares the inevitability, of rapid and ceaseless social change." To Bromell, "it is here—where the vision of existence as a profound instability looks liberating at one moment, then suddenly malevolent the next—that 60s rock and 60s politics flowed into each other."[55]

To Bromell, popular music and drug use help reveal the criss-crossing of cultural and political energies in a manner typical political histories cannot. "Because these complex feelings are seldom named by conventional politics and political language," Bromell writes, "they have been omitted from the picture of the 60s given to us by historians concerned with the New Left and other political movements." Understanding rock and drugs more clearly, however, helps emphasize the uncertainty, the contingency of past moments in history—a feeling of instability that Bromell argues was especially key for grasping the meaning of the 1960s. "Historians of the 60s who have caught hold of the terms 'breakthrough' and 'breakdown' have tended to arrange them in a neat linear sequence,"

Bromell explains, "from Woodstock to Altamont, or from the Summer of Love to the Chicago Convention. But at the time, as . . . many . . . songs of the 60s show, these two states were inseparable, concurrent, inter-penetrating each other and forming one feeling-state."[56]

The notion of a "feeling-state" in which breakthrough and breakdown were part of the same process reflects not a linear historical progression, but an awareness of the ironies and strangeness of history. One irony that Bromell argues is essential to understanding 1960s rock is the manner in which rock's predominantly young, white, middle-class rock fans were so moved by a music that was, largely, an extension of the African-American blues form. The blues, according to Bromell, presented a past mode of musical expression that resonated for rock listeners because it gave expression to the alienation, loneliness, and longing for authenticity that rock's listeners themselves felt. There were troubling problems with this appropriation of culture across the boundaries of race and time. But there was also communion.[57] As a blues-descended music, rock became a resource for countercultural rockers to grapple with their own experiences. "The blues (like all forms of music)," Bromell argues, "are a force, not a mirror. They do much more than merely 'reflect' certain historical conditions." Instead, the blues provided, "a way to work through . . . responses to those conditions." For the adolescent counterculturalists seized by rock, the "force" of the blues form was its ability to resonate with their own historical moment while also feeling like it linked them to a deep tradition.[58] To Bromell, rock became a music both of immediacy and roots; in the process, it enlivened its listeners sense of being embed-ded in time. Rock, as a blues-descended form, produced a "feeling-state" of historical consciousness.

In Bromell's study, the sounds, surroundings, and theories of 1960s rock lap backward and propel forward in time. As with Dominick Cavallo's study, Bromell is sensitive to the reverberations of earlier cultural forms on 1960s rock. So too, he is quite aware that he is considering the music of his own youth as it recedes into the past. As he considers the tricky ways in which 1960s rock drew upon its own constructions of the past, and the fact that he himself only can hear the music through the passage of time, Bromell mingles musicological, ethnographic, autobio-graphical, and theoretical approaches effectively. He listens carefully to songs by the Beatles, Bob Dylan, the Rolling Stones, and Jimi Hendrix, contextualizes them within materials from the 1960s such as criticism, film, literature, and significant political events, and develops theoretical schemes about the music as it related to the expressive form of the blues and the widespread usage of drugs among rock's participants. As Bromell claims of his methodology, "this book isn't conventional history or cultural studies or popular culture analysis or musicology or memoir, but a hybrid of all these."[59] In the historical echoes that this hybrid approach addresses, we can hear popular music more fully.

Conclusion: Playing Back the Multitrack

"There must be some way out of here," said the joker to the thief,
"There's too much confusion, I can't get no relief."
                    —Bob Dylan, *"All Along the Watchtower"*[60]

The many ways of approaching popular music can begin to create too much confusion and demand some relief. Methods overlap. Sounds quickly lead to surroundings. Surroundings wind up rooted in theoretical paradigms. Theories must rely on historicization. History returns to the sounds themselves for evidence. To cope with the intersections that occur in the study of popular music, academics across disciplines have increasingly borrowed methodologies from one another. The multitrack can help to sort out this interdisciplinary project.

So too, the multitrack might be an effective tool for guiding future research. We might utilize the multitrack to analyze the biographies of particular artists, the study of specific scenes, the mutations of genre definitions, the changing global networks and structures of the music industry, the relationship of music to political forces, the meanings of popular music to various audiences, and the shifts in pop music's power and significance over time. Even one song's many levels can be revealed through the multitrack. If we examine "All Along the Watchtower," we might think of the sounds, surroundings, theory, and history of this song in 1960s rock in order to identify its many dimensions.

First, we might consider the *sounds* of "All Along the Watchtower" more closely. Written by Bob Dylan and released on the album *John Wesley Harding* in 1967, the most famous version of the song was recorded by Jimi Hendrix and released on his album *Electric Ladyland* the following year.[61] Comparing the sound of the two versions illuminates the relationship between the genre of folk music and the "psychedelic coding" of rock that Sheila Whiteley examines. The song itself is built from three chords (C-sharp minor, B major, A major in Dylan's original) that descend and ascend repeatedly, like a man climbing up and down a stepladder. Dylan's version is performed on acoustic guitar, bass, and drums, with Dylan's voice a tense, throaty mutter. The song has a thudding, restrained, wooden quality. The lyrics, an inscrutable parable about a joker, a thief, a prince, and a confrontation that beckons but never arrives, conveys a sense of rubble-strewn trails and stormy forests. As a whole, Dylan's "All Along the Watchtower" evokes a sense of the American primitive: folksy but taut with anxiety.

By contrast, Hendrix's version of the song booms into sonic overdrive from its first chord. His version of "All Along the Watchtower" embodies a "psychedelic coding" rather than a folk music ethos. Emphasizing the song's chord pattern in a rhythm that hints at flamenco, with its castanet-style rattle, Hendrix and his band immediately push harder at the song, with a fuller reverb and echo that signals a much larger sense of scale. The drumming is much more aggressive and active. Hendrix's singing is more open and direct than Dylan's elliptical, grunted style. Additionally, adopting a practice from his rhythm and blues days, Hendrix has tuned his guitar strings down a half-step (meaning he is playing the same frets on the guitar as Dylan but the resulting tones are a half-step lower in pitch). This incremental change perhaps helps accentuate the warbling quality of the guitar since the strings are looser. And it gives the notes an extra bite when Hendrix bends his guitar strings.[62]

The resulting mood of the song is one of disorientation: are we in the ancient land of medieval Spanish castles or in outer space? *Is this tomorrow or just the end of time?* Taking us through this time warp, Hendrix's electric guitar soars, swoops, buzzes, crackles, and twists around the song's insistent up-and-down chord repetitions. In his guitar solo midway through, Hendrix takes a solo using a wah-wah pedal, a foot device that manipulates the electronic signal generated by the guitar. The notes open and close in tones at once robotic and yet emulating a crying human voice. Compared to the original version of "All Along the Watchtower," in which Dylan's harmonica evokes the smallness of the human voice as Dylan puffs out single plaintive notes, Hendrix's guitar dizzies the mind with its epic might. Dylan evokes intimacy, almost whispering to us from close by; Hendrix conveys a voice blasting through the power grid, an electronic roar screaming across the circuitry, panning from stereophonic speaker to speaker, announcing its dislocating movement across our consciousness. As the "power trio" of Hendrix, Noel Redding on bass, and Mitch Mitchell on drums crash and thunder toward the song's conclusion, the guitar lines crescendo and peak, taking us up to the stratosphere in one last sudden rush higher.

We have briefly considered the sounds of "All Along the Watchtower" in order to think about the ways in which Dylan's version clings to certain folksy tropes, while Hendrix's interpretation pushes toward the disorientation of "psychedelic coding." Investigating the song's surroundings, however, offers a means of placing "All Along the Watchtower" more fully into context. The reception of Dylan's album and Hendrix's cover version provides one way of accessing this ethnographic information. We turn to the second track of the multitrack model.

Critics heard *John Wesley Harding* as a return to Dylan's early career as a folk balladeer in the tradition of Woody Guthrie after his mid-1960s leap into electric rock: Dylan was harkening to the more traditional world that folk music sought to symbolize, with its connotations of small towns, farms, itinerant hoboes, and outlaws in the hills. But they also sensed in this the album's commentary on the state of the United States and the world in 1967. Ellen Willis heard in the album, "folk lyrics. Or more precisely, affectionate comments on folk lyrics—the album is not a reversion to early work but a kind of hymn to it."[63] Yet in this awareness of memory and the past, Willis and others heard *John Wesley Harding* as very much about its contemporary moment, especially the Vietnam War. Jon Landau states, "Dylan manifests a profound awareness of the war and how it is affecting all of us. This doesn't mean that I think any of the particular songs are about the war or that any of the songs are protests over it. All I mean to say is that Dylan has felt the war, that there is an awareness of it contained within the mood of the albums as a whole."[64] By trying to "not speak falsely," Landau claims, alluding to a lyric from "All Along the Watchtower," the album explored the complexities of morality in folk-like songs that, despite their rootsy sounds, served as allegories for 1960s American and the Vietnam War.

If Dylan's version of "All Along the Watchtower" merely alludes to the Vietnam conflict, Hendrix's interpretation seems to place us in Vietnam itself. With its soaring, jet fighter guitar lines and mood of impending doom mixed with grizzled self-confidence, Hendrix's take on "All Along the Watchtower" intersects with his other songs about the United States and Vietnam: his startling version of the "Star-Spangled Banner" and his song "Machine Gun," which Hendrix explicitly dedicated to Vietnam soldiers when he performed the song in concert. The static crackle, Doppler-effect sounds, and lyrics about fighters approaching and look-out posts seem sonically to transport a listener to the Vietnam frontlines.

Indeed we know from memoirs and journalistic accounts that the song—and Hendrix's music in general—was quite popular among American fighters in Vietnam itself. In *Dispatches*, the journalist Michael Herr describes a black soldier in the 101st Airborne Division (which Hendrix himself had been discharged from in the early 1960s), listening to Hendrix on a portable cassette player while on a mission in Vinh Long.[65] Veterans recall hearing Hendrix on portable record players and underground radio stations.[66] A "Top 30 Countdown" from October of 1968, broadcast on the Armed Forces Radio Network in Vietnam, finds disc jockey Scott Manning introducing "All Along the Watchtower" by speaking of "the electric Jimi Hendrix," who is "watching for you."[67]

This contextual evidence points to the ways in which 1960s rock was not just part of a counterculture movement *against* the war in Vietnam, at least not in any simple way. A careful consideration of the surroundings of rock suggests that songs such as "All Along the Watchtower" expressed a more complex mood for listeners on the home front and in the war effort. The song did not stop the war but rather helped give musical expression to contradictory feelings about Vietnam. Perhaps "All Along the Watchtower" mingled anxieties about war with a sublime feeling of the drama of battle; it launched a listener into an expansive, reverberating soundscape. It reproduced the excitement of being enmeshed in something grandly historical where life was on the line; the song even signaled that one might gain access to the tools of war, to the power of automatic rifles and bomb navigation systems whose sounds seemed embodied in Hendrix's explosive electric guitar solos. As the rock critic Albert Goldman wrote of listening to Hendrix in general (he does not specify what song he was listening to), "In the tight little world of the earphones, I heard thunderous sounds like salvos of howitzers. . . . I began to cringe as the roar of a jet engine mounted in my ears—but something magical happened. The intimidating sounds became an esthetic object; impulsively I thought, How beautiful are our noises!"[68] True, just one listener's experience, but it provides one piece of ethnographic evidence of the complex manner in which Hendrix's music was received. A song such as "All Along the Watchtower" could communicate the terror *and* the attractive beauty of warlike sounds and feelings all at once.

Backing away from direct experiences of "All Along the Watchtower," from an ethnographic approach to the song, in what kinds of paradigms can we interpret "All Along the Watchtower"? We arrive at the multi-track's third band: theory. One area of consideration scholars have considered is the racial logic in which Jimi Hendrix functioned, and against which he struggled. Viewing Hendrix as abandoning the pop orientation of early 1960s black rhythm and blues for the sonic experimentation of psychedelia and the large mass audiences of rock, the historian Brian Ward hears Hendrix as "succumbing to, but playing with, white expectations." This, to Ward, "was ultimately a pyrrhic victory; a temporary mental survival ploy wrapped in a sound commercial strategy which left pervasive white assumptions unchallenged and tacitly endorsed." Ward dismisses as "mostly just hippie doggerel" Hendrix's attempt toward the end of his short life to develop and advocate a kind of proto-multicultural philosophy that Hendrix called the "electric sky church."[69]

But other scholars, such as Lauren Onkey, take Hendrix's later musical and philosophical ideas seriously. Onkey theorizes that with the electric sky church, "Hendrix suggests here that if the revolution were to succeed, it would need to take hold in the imagination apart from the commercial and political realms." Beginning with his own multi-ethnic heritage as Native American, African American, and Caucasian American, Hendrix took seriously music's ability to open the heart and mind to new ideas and perspectives, according to Onkey. Sensing in the psychedelia of the counterculture a strand of empathetic pluralism, "Hendrix held out the possibility of a psychedelic, imaginative reordering of the world." To Onkey, Hendrix was able to model a spiritually bold vision of cosmopolitan, hybrid identity that was liberating for individuals and groups alike. Hendrix, in her analysis, sought for us all to be "Stone Free," as the title of one of his songs put it.[70]

Ethnicity as well as race certainly figures in a song such as "All Along the Watchtower." A song written by a Jewish Midwesterner (who adopted a Welsh surname) and made most famous by an African American/ Native American/Caucasian Northwesterner (whose first success came in England), it resonated with long-running exchanges of culture across racial and ethnic lines.[71] Charles Shaar Murray alludes to this in *Crosstown Traffic: Jimi Hendrix and Post-War Pop* by emphasizing how deeply influenced Hendrix was by Dylan's new mode of surrealist, symbolist songwriting in the mid-1960s when Dylan went electric.[72] In a presentation at the 2003 Pop Music Conference at the Experience Music Project, Hendrix biographer Charles R. Cross made even more of the connection between Dylan and Hendrix, arguing that rather than being the "black Elvis," as a number of critics called him, Hendrix longed to be the "black Dylan."[73] Though Cross does not place his biographical work on Hendrix in a larger theoretical analysis, one might think of a song such as "All Along the Watchtower" as a crucial point of transit between black and white participants in the counterculture movement: the song is informed not only by the ambiguous relationship between folk music and psychedelic rock, but also the kinds of exchanges rock opened up across the color line, and the kinds of blockages it either maintained or created. Whether one adopts Ward's critical position or Onkey's more celebratory argument on the topic (or pursues still another interpretation), one can certainly spot ethnicity and race as theoretical constructs operating in "All Along the Watchtower."[74]

The song also heralds another cultural paradigm that the theoretical track can reveal. "All Along the Watchtower" seems to manifest a larger cultural logic of conspiracy that arose in the late 1960s and into the 1970s. The song's lyrics hint at nefarious collusions and sinister forces operating in mysterious ways, but we aren't quite sure how the pieces of the narrative puzzle fit together. We are able to hear bits of an elliptical conversation between a joker and a thief, two figures who seem to be a team, but who may not entirely trust each other. "Businessmen, they drink my wine, plowmen dig my earth," the joker complains. "There are many here among us who feel that life is but a joke," the thief responds. But, there is "no reason to get excited," since "you and I, we've been through that, and this is not our fate." The thief insists to the joker that they should, "not talk falsely now" because "the hour is getting late." Meanwhile, as this strange conversation occurs, suspicions arise on the parapets of the watchtower, where "the princes kept a view" and "all the women came and went, barefoot servants too."

The song seems to emanate from an overarching mood of distrust. Knowledge fragments and perspectives shift in a manner linked to the sense of fissure, rupture, and crisis that Frederic Jameson identifies in his work on postmodernism. We are being watched from the watchtower, or we are doing the watching ourselves, a conspiratorial regime that Stephen Paul Miller has explored in his book on the decade following the late 1960s, *The Seventies Now: Culture as Surveillance.*[75] "All Along the Watchtower" can be heard as embedded in a framework of conspiracy, or perhaps adrift in a swirl of conspiratorial chaos might be a better way of phrasing it. As the song concludes, we are left with ominous lines that seem to circle us back to the beginning of the story. Having started out by listening in on an inscrutable conversation between a joker and a thief, we leave learning that "two riders were approaching and the wind began to howl." Trapping us in its endless loop, "All Along the Watchtower" conveys a world in which devious forces plot from on high, looking down upon us as from a panoptic tower. There are stirrings of rebellion among the "women" and "foot soldiers," but all we can hear are a few incongruous quips and comments as the wind begins to kick up and we wonder when the apocalypse will rain down upon us.[76]

Theoretical paradigms such as race, ethnicity, and conspiracy already suggest a historicization of the 1960s era. But how might we further historicize the song? We can better hear its echoes on the fourth track of the multitrack model if examine the many cover versions recorded since the 1960s. Of course, Dylan's original itself already sounds like a cover of a lost nineteenth-century badman tune from frontier days in the United States, with stories of outlaws and bandits reverberating in its lyrical and musical tensions. The song's allegorical nature and Dylan's instrumentation flood the original version with its own sense of the past.

Once he heard Hendrix's cover version, however, Dylan intriguingly chose to perform his own song along the lines of Hendrix's interpretation. Captured live with the Band on the album *Before the Flood* (1974), on *Live at Budokan* (1979), on *Dylan and the Dead* with the Grateful Dead (1988), sung by Neil Young on *The 30th Anniversary Concert Celebration* (1993), and on Dylan's *MTV Unplugged* appearance (1995), one hears "All Along the Watchtower" interpreted and reinterpreted again as an echo of

Hendrix's cover version. From Jerry Garcia's lilting homage to Hendrix's guitar playing on the version with the Grateful Dead to Neil Young's sneering version at the 1992 celebration of Dylan's thirty years in the music business to Dylan's terrified vocal performance at the *Unplugged* session, one hears a song that seems to reexamine the lessons learned in the 1960s in light of newer aesthetic and historical situations. The Dead sound festive, nostalgically remembering their survival, celebrating and perhaps even recreating the communal joys of the 1960s counterculture. Young's angry, gut-wrenching performance perhaps expresses a feeling of failure about the utopian dreams of the 1960s. Dylan's own reinterpretation of the song, in which his bleary voice rushes toward the end of each vocal line, ominously lowering the notes, sounds as if he has turned headlong toward the future and finds himself staring directly at the final conspiracy: old age, mortality, and death itself.

Add to these versions the many other cover versions of "All Along the Watchtower" and one can hear the song as a meditation on the 1960s as a whole. As both Simon Frith and George Lipsitz have argued, rock music in particular (and popular music in general) are particularly powerful conveyors of memory.[77] Bobby Womack, a friend of Hendrix's the early 1960s rhythm and blues circuit, performs a straight-up soul version, as if the song could help recover the memory of Hendrix's pre-psychedelic persona.[78] Meanwhile, younger musicians, such as U2, the Indigo Girls, and the Dave Matthews Band, among others, especially seem to play "All Along the Watchtower" as a way of signaling their allegiance with the anti-establishment politics of the 1960s counterculture. Ironically, they also use the song to brand themselves as part of "classic rock," that is as part of the very heart of the music business establishment.[79] "All Along the Watchtower" continues to serve as contested terrain for understandings of 1960s rock as both an oppositional music and an expression of success in the dominant mainstream of commercial society.

In these multiple ways, "All Along the Watchtower" has become a key text in the historical consciousness of the 1960s and the counterculture as a whole. As Nick Bromell writes in his afterword to *Tomorrow Never Knows: Rock and Pyschedelics in the 1960s*—tellingly titled, " 'Our Incompleteness and Our Choices': Forgetting the '60s and Remembering Them"—he listens now to "All Along the Watchtower" and believes that "Hendrix playing Dylan represents the consummate fusion of the blues tradition with the psychedelicized hunger of white youth enmired in loneliness and looking for a new self, trapped in history and looking desperately *for some way out of here.*" The song's persistence down to this day speaks to the fact that, "teenagers still stand there on the watchtower and wait and wonder."[80] Trapped in history, yet empowered by the consciousness it can invoke, we continue to reflect on the 1960s, rock music, the counterculture, and popular music as a whole through songs such as "All Along the Watchtower."

Putting together the four tracks—musicology, ethnography, theory, and history—allows us to hear even this one song with a richness and depth that interdisciplinary study can offer. The multitrack presents one metaphor for managing this interdisciplinarity. Of course, I have left out many other positions that one might incorporate into the model.[81] So too, by focusing on 1960s rock as a case study, I leave to others the development, revision, or rejection of the multitrack metaphor with regard to different musical forms. That said, I have especially attempted to show how cultural history offers a special track—an echo track—that enriches the multitrack as an interdisciplinary endeavor without obliterating the other modes of analysis.

Music and history have a special connection. As Gene Santoro writes, "Music not only captures time; it mimics time. The ebb and flow that shapes the emotional tension between sound and space, spiked by dynamics and tonal colors, creates a rhythm analogous to the way we pass through history."[82] My hope is that as a mode of interdisciplinary analysis, the multitrack model can make the "ebb and flow" of both music and history more palpable and powerful to our ears.

Notes

1. Richard Middleton, "Introduction," in *Reading Pop: Approaches to Textual Analysis in Popular Music*, ed. Richard Middleton (New York: Oxford University Press, 2000), 14.

2. Roy Wagner, *Symbols That Stand For Themselves* (Chicago: University of Chicago Press, 1986), 11. Quoted in Steven Feld, "Aesthetics As Iconicity of Style (Uptown Title); Or, (Downtown Title) 'Lift-Up-Over Sounding': Getting Into the Kaluli Groove," in *Music Grooves: Essays and Dialogues*, ed. Steven Feld and Charles Keil (Chicago, IL: University of Chicago Press, 1994), 115.

3. Greil Marcus, *Ranters & Crowd Pleases: Punk in Pop Music, 1977–1992* (New York: Doubleday, 1993), republished as *In the Fascist Bathroom: Punk in Pop Music, 1977–1992* (Cambridge, MA: Harvard University Press, 1999), 213.

4. Steve Jones, *Rock Formation: Music, Technology, and Mass Communication* (Newbury, CA: Sage, 1992), 1.

5. For useful descriptions of cultural history as a methodology, see Lynn Hunt, ed., *The New Cultural History: Essays* (Berkeley: University of California Press, 1989); Peter Burke, *Varieties of Cultural History* (Ithaca, New York: Cornell University Press, 1997); and Victoria Bonnell and Lynn Hunt, eds., *Beyond the Cultural Turn: New Directions in the Study of Society and Culture* (Berkeley: University of California Press, 1999).

6. Geoffrey O'Brien, "Burt Bacharach Comes Back," *New York Review of Books* (6 May 1999): 48.

7. Sheila Whiteley, *The Space Between the Notes: Rock and the Counter-Culture* (New York: Routledge, 1992); Michael Hicks, *Sixties Rock: Garage, Psychedelic, and Other Satisfactions* (Urbana: University of Illinois, 1999).

8. John Covach writes eloquently about the study of rock music in terms of the more traditional musicological question, what makes this sound great, arguing that musicological "theorists should pay more attention to rock music *because it is interesting*" [italics in the original]. See John Covach, "Won't Get Fooled Again," in *Keeping Score: Music, Disciplinarity, Culture*, ed. Anahid Kassabian, David Schwarz, and Lawrence Siegel (Charlottesville: University Press of Virginia, 1997): 85. For additional examples of this sort of methodological argument, see John Covach, "Popular Music, Unpopular Musicology," in *Rethinking Music*, ed. Nicholas Cook and Mark Everist (Oxford: Oxford University Press, 1999), 452–70; John Covach, Graeme M. Boone, eds., *Understanding Rock: Essays In Musical Analysis* (New York: Oxford University Press, 1997); Kevin Holm-Hudson, ed., *Progressive Rock Reconsidered* (New York: Routledge, 2001); and Wilfrid Mellers, *Twilight of the Gods: The Music of the Beatles* (1973; reprint, New York: Viking, 1974). Also see essays in Richard Middleton, ed., *Reading Pop*. For a critique of the traditional musicological approach from within musicology as a field, see Susan McClary and Robert Walser, "Start Making Sense!: Musicology Starts Making Sense," in *On Record: Rock, Pop, and the Written Word*, ed. Simon Frith and Andrew Goodwin (1995; reprint, NY: Routledge, 2000), 277–292.

9. Paul Willis traced a homological relationship of expressions of style to class identity in his groundbreaking study, *Profane Culture* (New York: Routledge, 1978). See also, Stuart Hall, Tony Jefferson, John Clarke, eds., *Resistance Through Rituals: Youth Subcultures in Postwar Britain* (1975; reprint, New York: Routledge, 1995). For a complication of the homological approach using the notion of *bricolage*, see Dick Hebdige, *Subculture: The Meaning of Style* (1979; reprint, New York: Routledge, 2002). For a critique of homology, see Keith Negus, *Popular Music in Theory: An Introduction* (Hanover, NH: University Press of New England/Wesleyan University Press, 1996), 23–24.

10. Whiteley, *The Space Between the Notes*, 2.
11. Whiteley, *The Space Between the Notes*, 2.
12. Whiteley, *The Space Between the Notes*, 4.
13. Whiteley, *The Space Between the Notes*, 7.
14. Whiteley, *The Space Between the Notes*, 32–33.

15. Whiteley, *The Space Between the Notes*, 21.

16. Hicks, *Sixties Rock*, 27.

17. Hicks, *Sixties Rock*, 38.

18. Hicks, *Sixties Rock*, 59.

19. Daniel J. Boorstin, *The Americans: The Democratic Experience* (New York: Random House, 1973), 89–164.

20. An intriguing book from the 1960s on the connection between rock and free jazz is Jon Sinclair and Robert Levin, *Music and Politics* (New York: The World Publishing Company, 1971).

21. Among others, Sheila Whiteley has addressed the issue of rock and gender in *Women and Popular Music: Sexuality, Identity, and Subjectivity* (New York: Routledge, 2000) and in her edited volume, *Sexing the Groove: Popular Music and Gender* (New York: Routledge, 1997). See also, Simon Reynolds and Joy Press, *The Sex Revolts: Gender, Rebellion, and Rock 'n' Roll* (Cambridge, MA: Harvard University Press, 1995).

22. Hicks, *Sixties Rock*, 73–4.

23. Hicks notates various recorded and live performances to trace the different ways the Doors presented their hit song, reading into the performances their perspectives on their mainstream success. *Sixties Rock*, 82.

24. The lyric-driven approach dominated much of the early work on rock music. See, for example, James T. Carey, "The Ideology of Autonomy in Popular Lyrics: A Content Analysis," *Psychiatry* 32, 2 (May 1969): 150–164.

25. Walt Whitman, "A Song For Occupations," *Leaves of Grass* (New York: Houghton Mifflin Riverside Editions, 1959), 158.

26. Barry Shank, *Dissonant Identities: The Rock 'n' Roll Scene in Austin, Texas* (Hanover, NH: University Press of New England/Wesleyan University Press, 1994), x.

27. Shank, *Dissonant Identities*, xi.

28. Shank, *Dissonant Identities*, 138–139.

29. Dan Cavicchi, *Tramps Like Us: Music and Meaning Among Springsteen Fans* (New York: Oxford University Press, 1998). Cavicchi participated in an earlier project along similar lines. See Charles Keil, Susan Crafts, Dan Cavicchi, *My Music* (1993; 2nd edition, Hanover, NH: University Press of New England/Wesleyan University Press, 2002). For other inquiries into pop music fandom, see Lisa Lewis, ed., *The Adoring Audience: Fan Culture and Popular Media* (New York: Routledge, 1992).

30. Cavicchi, *Tramps Like Us*, 186–187.

31. Albert Goldman, "The Emergence of Rock," in *Freakshow: Misadventures in the Counterculture, 1959–1971* (1971; reprint, Cooper Square Press, 2001), 14.

32. Goldman, "The Emergence of Rock," 14.

33. Glenn Hinson, *Fire In My Bones: Transcendence and the Holy Spirit in African American Gospel* (Philadelphia: University of Pennsylvania Press, 2000), 8.

34. For additional examples of the range of pop music ethnography, see Sara Cohen, *Rock Culture in Liverpool: Popular Music in the Making* (New York: Oxford University Press, 1991); Jeffrey Arnett, *Metalheads: Heavy Metal Music and Adolescent Alienation* (Boulder, CO: Westview Press, 1996); Harris M. Berger, *Metal, Rock, and Jazz: Perception and*

the Phenomenology of Musical Experience (Hanover, NH: University Press of New England/Wesleyan University Press, 1999); Lauraine Leblanc, *Pretty in Punk: Girls' Gender Resistance in a Boys' Subculture* (New Brunswick, NJ: Rutgers University Press, 1999); and David Muggleton, *Inside Subculture: The Postmodern Meaning of Style* (Oxford: Berg, 2000). Ethnomusicology offers another vast literature of ethnographically-grounded research. Among many worthy studies, see Feld and Keil, *Music Grooves*; Charles Keil, *Urban Blues* (1966; reprint, Chicago: University of Chicago Press, 1991); Paul F. Berliner, *The Soul of Mbira: Music and Traditions of the Shona People of Zimbabwe* (1978; reprint, Chicago: University of Chicago Press, 1993); Charles Keil, *Tiv Song: The Sociology of Art in a Classless Society* (Chicago: University of Chicago Press, 1979); John Chernoff, *African Rhythm and African Sensibility* (Chicago: University of Chicago Press, 1981); Steven Feld, *Sound and Sentiment: Birds, Weeping, Poetics, and Song in Kaluli Expression* (1982; reprint, Philadelphia: University of Pennsylvania Press, 1990); Peter Manuel, *Cassette Culture: Popular Music And Technology In North India* (Chicago: University of Chicago Press, 1993); Ingrid Monson, *Saying Something: Jazz Improvisation and Interaction* (Chicago: University of Chicago Press, 1996); Timothy Taylor, *Global Pop: World Music, World Markets* (New York: Routledge, 1997); and Kay Kaufman Shelemay, *Let Jasmine Rain Down: Song and Remembrance Among Syrian Jews* (Chicago: University of Chicago Press, 1998).

35. Jacques Attali, *Noise: The Political Economy of Music*, trans. Brian Massumi (1977; trans., Minneapolis, MN: University of Minnesota, 1996), 45.

36. For more on the contradictions of capitalism as, on the one hand, demanding a productive code of restraint and discipline and, on the other, promoting a consumer drive toward gratification and excess, see Daniel Bell, *The Cultural Contradictions of Capitalism* (New York: Basic Books, 1978).

37. Simon Frith, *Sound Effects: Youth, Leisure, and the Politics of Rock 'n' Roll* (New York: Pantheon, 1981), 11, 272. For an overview of the popular music studies debates between "cultural Marxists" and "material Marxists," see David Sanjek, "Funkentelechy vs. the Stockholm Syndrome: The Place of Industrial Analysis in Popular Music Studies," *Popular Music and Society* 21, 1 (1997): 77–98.

38. Lawrence Grossberg, *Dancing in Spite of Myself: Essays on Popular Culture* (Durham, NC: Duke University Press, 1997), 16–17.

39. Grossberg, *Dancing*, 49.

40. For Grossberg's explanation of "affective alliances," see especially Lawrence Grossberg, "Another Boring Day in Paradise: Rock and Roll and the Empowerment of Everyday Life," *Popular Music* 4 (1984): 225–258.

41. Grossberg draws on theories of cultural hegemony articulated by Antonio Gramsci and expanded by Louis Althusser and Stuart Hall. See Antonio Gramsci, *The Antonio Gramsci Reader: Selected Writings 1916–1935*, ed. David Forgacs (1988; reprint, New York: New York University Press, 1999). Louis Althusser, *Lenin and Philosophy, and Other Essays* (1971; reprint, New York: Monthly Review Press, 2001). Stuart Hall, *Critical Dialogues in Cultural Studies*, eds. David Morley and Kuan-Hsing Chen (New York: Routledge, 1996). He also utilizes theories of power developed by Michel Foucault and Gilles Deleuze and Felix Guattari. See Michel Foucault, *The Foucault Reader*, ed. Paul Rabinow

(New York: Random House, 1984). Gilles Deleuze and Felix Guattari, *A Thousand Plateaus: Capitalism and Schizophrenia* (Minneapolis: University of Minnesota Press, 1987).

42. Theodore Gracyk, *Rhythm and Noise: An Aesthetics of Rock* (Durham, NC: Duke University Press, 1996), 226.

43. Gracyk, *Rhythm and Noise*, 226.

44. Theodore Gracyk, *I Wanna Be Me: Rock Music and the Politics of Identity* (Philadelphia, PA: Temple University Press, 2001), 236.

45. Gracyk, *I Wanna Be Me*, 209.

46. Gracyk, *I Wanna Be Me*, 215.

47. Gracyk, *I Wanna Be Me*, 227, 217.

48. Of course, there are many other schemes. One of the most intriguing places rock within the framework of romanticism. See literary scholar Robert Pattison's *The Triumph of Vulgarity: Rock in the Mirror of Romanticism* (New York: Oxford University Press, 1987) for a negative interpretation, and Perry Meisel, *The Cowboy and the Dandy: Crossing Over From Romanticism to Rock and Roll* (New York: Oxford University Press, 1999) for a more positive interpretation. Peter Wicke's *Rock Music: Culture, Aesthetics, and Sociology* (New York: Cambridge University Press, 1990) emphasizes the effects of mass-media and technology on the ideologies of rock: he claims they created a new cultural paradigm in which collective and individual liberation merged through a romantic ideology of creativity. Jason Toynbee's *Making Popular Music: Musicians, Creativity and Institutions* (New York: Edward Arnold, 2000) expands upon Wicke's ideas by examining the rhetorics and practices of creativity in popular music in more detail. A different scheme is put forth by the political theorist Carson Holloway, who argues that popular music can be heard through theories of classical republicanism. See Carson Holloway, *Music, Passion, Politics* (Dallas, TX: Spence Publishing Company, 2001).

49. Warren Susman, *Culture as History: The Transformations of American Society in the Twentieth Century* (New York: Pantheon, 1984), 185.

50. Dominick Cavallo, *A Fiction of the Past: The Sixties in American History* (New York: St. Martin's Press, 1999); Nick Bromell, *Tomorrow Never Knows: Rock and Psychedelics in the 1960s* (Chicago: University of Chicago Press, 2000).

51. Cavallo, *A Fiction of the Past*, 9.

52. Cavallo, *A Fiction of the Past*, 146.

53. Bromell, *Tomorrow Never Knows*, 10.

54. Bromell, *Tomorrow Never Knows*, 19.

55. Bromell, *Tomorrow Never Knows*, 128.

56. Bromell, *Tomorrow Never Knows*, 87.

57. Bromell notes the outlining of these problems by Eric Lott, Steve Waksman, and others but argues that rock should not be interpreted as a kind of false consciousness; Bromell, *Tomorrow Never Knows*, 194. See Eric Lott, *Love and Theft: Blackface Minstrelsy and the American Working Class* (New York: Oxford University Press, 1995); Steve Waksman, *Instruments of Desire: The Electric Guitar and the Shaping of Musical Experience* (Cambridge, MA: Harvard University Press, 1999). For more on the issue of race and music, see Ron Radano, ed., *Racial Imagination and Music* (Chicago: University

of Chicago Press, 2000) and Greg Tate, ed., *Everything But the Burden: What White People Are Taking From Black Culture* (New York: Harlem Moon, 2003).

58. Bromell, *Tomorrow Never Knows*, 51–52.

59. Bromell, *Tomorrow Never Knows*, 6.

60. The song originally appeared on Bob Dylan, *John Wesley Harding* (Columbia Records, 1967).

61. The Jimi Hendrix Experience, *Electric Ladyland* (Reprise, 1968).

62. I owe a debt of gratitude to Andy Flory, graduate student in the Music Department at UNC-Chapel Hill, for these observations on Hendrix's guitar-tuning; email with author, 25 May 2004.

63. Ellen Willis, *Beginning to See the Light: Sex, Hope, and Rock-and-Roll* (1981; 2nd edition, Hanover, NH: University Press of New England/Wesleyan University Press, 1992), 24; from an essay originally published in *Cheetah* 1, 6 (March 1968): 34–37, 66–71.

64. Jon Landau, "John Wesley Harding," *Crawdaddy!* 15 (May 1968): 16.

65. Michael Herr, *Dispatches* (New York: Knopf, 1977), 181–182.

66. Among other sources, see Lee Andreson, *Battle Notes: Music of the Vietnam War* (Superior, WI: Savage Press, 2000), and Stephen Roby, *Black Gold: The Lost Archives of Jimi Hendrix* (New York: Billboard Books, 2002), 96.

67. From "Top 30 Countdown with Scott Manning," *Armed Forces Radio Network Vietnam (AFVN)* (October 1968). At one point, this archival recording was available in real audio format at the website, www.geocities.com/afvn.

68. Albert Goldman, "Superspade Raises Atlantis" (1968), in *The Jimi Hendrix Companion: Three Decades of Commentary*, ed. Chris Potash (New York: Schirmer Books, 1996), 60.

69. Brian Ward, *Just My Soul Responding: Rhythm and Blues, Black* Consciousness, *and Race Relations* (Berkeley: University of California Press, 1998), 246–247. For a critique of Ward's book, see Robin D. G. Kelley, "A Sole Response," *American Quarterly* 52, 3 (September 2000): 533–545.

70. Lauren Onkey, "Jimi Hendrix and the Politics of Race in the Sixties," in *Imagine Nation: The American Counterculture of the 1960s and 70s*, ed. Peter Braunstein and Michael William Doyle (New York: Routledge, 2000), 209. For another interpretation of Hendrix and race, see Steve Waksman, "Black Sound, Black Body: Jimi Hendrix, the Electric Guitar, and the Meanings of Blackness," in *Instruments of Desire*, 167–206.

71. The literature on this topic is vast, but among other books, see David R. Roediger, *The Wages of Whiteness: Race and the Making of the American Working Class* (1991; revised, New York: Verso, 1999); Paul Gilroy, *The Black Atlantic: Modernity and Double Consciousness* (Cambridge, MA: Harvard University Press, 1993); Eric Lott, *Love and Theft: Blackface Minstrelsy and the American Working Class* (New York: Oxford University Press, 1995); Michael Rogin, *Blackface, White Noise: Jewish Immigrants in the Hollywood Melting Pot* (Berkeley: University of California Press, 1996); W.T. Lhamon, Jr., *Raising Cain: Blackface Performance from Jim Crow to Hip Hop* (Cambridge, MA: Harvard University Press, 1998); Matthew Frye Jacobson, *Whiteness of a Different Color: European Immigrants and the Alchemy of Race* (Cambridge, MA: Harvard

University Press, 1998); and Jeffrey Melnick, *A Right to Sing the Blues: African Americans, Jews, and American Popular Song* (Cambridge: Harvard University Press, 1999).

72. Charles Shaar Murray, *Crosstown Traffic: Jimi Hendrix and Post-War Pop* (1989; revised ed., London: Faber and Faber, 2001), 14.

73. Charles R. Cross, "Meet the Dylan: How a Chance Encounter Between Bob Dylan and Jimi Hendrix Forever Changed American Popular Music," Paper delivered at *Skip a Beat: Challenging Popular Music Orthodoxy, EMP Pop Conference*, April 2003.

74. Among other inquires into Hendrix and race, see David James, "Rock and Roll in Representations of the Invasion of Vietnam," *Representations* 29 (Winter, 1990): 78–98; David James, "The Vietnam War and American Music," in *The Vietnam War and American Culture*, ed. John Carlos Rowe and Rick Berg (New York: Columbia University Press, 1991), 226–294; Mary Ellison, "Black Music and the Vietnam War," in *Vietnam Images: War and Representation*, ed. Jeffrey Walsh and James Aulich (New York: St. Martin's Press, 1989); and Katherine Kinney, *Friendly Fire: American Images of the Vietnam War* (New York: Oxford University Press, 2000).

75. Frederic Jameson, *Postmodernism, Or, the Cultural Logic of Late Capitalism* (Durham, NC: Duke University Press, 1992). Stephen Paul Miller, *The Seventies Now: Culture as Surveillance* (Durham, NC: Duke University Press, 1999).

76. One might develop a whole theoretical interpretation of "All Along the Watchtower" utilizing Foucault's theory of the panopticon. See Michel Foucault, *Discipline & Punish: The Birth of the Prison* (1977; reprint, New York: Vintage, 1995), 195–228.

77. Simon Frith, "Rock and the Politics of Memory," in *The 60s Without Apology*, ed. Sohnya Sayres, *et. al.* (Minneapolis: University of Minnesota Press, 1984), 49–69. George Lipsitz, "Who'll Stop the Rain: Youth Culture, Rock 'n' Roll, and Social Crises," in *The Sixties: From Memory to History*, ed. David Farber (Chapel Hill: University of North Carolina Press, 1994), 206–234.

78. Bobby Womack's version appears on *The Facts of Life* (originally released on United Artists, 1973; re-released by The Right Stuff, 1994).

79. U2's version appears on *Rattle and Hum* (Island Records, 1988); the Indigo Girls' version appears on *Back on the Bus Y'all* (Epic Records, 1991); Dave Matthews Band performs the song on a number of live albums, among them *The Central Park Concert* (RCA, 1993), *Live at Folsom Field, Boulder Colorado, 7/11/01* (RCA, 1992), and *Live in Chicago, 12/19/98* (RCA, 1991). For more on this process of countercultural affiliation in relation to the music industry, see Fred Goodman, *The Mansion on the Hill: Dylan, Young, Geffen, Springsteen, and the Head-On Collision of Rock and Commerce* (New York: Times Books, 1997).

80. Bromell, *Tomorrow Never Knows*, 149.

81. To name but a few: Christopher Small's notion of musical reception as an active social process that he calls *musicking* (a theory that Nick Bromell utilizes); John Shepherd's similar work on the social dimensions embedded in musical performance; Shepherd and Peter Wicke's careful inquiries into how music communicates not as spoken language but through its own non-semantic logics of discourse; Jacques Attali's theories of music, noise, and social control; George Lipsitz's utilization of the Bakhtinian idea of the dialogic; Harris Berger's deployment of phenomenology; and perspectives on African-American

music and expressive culture put forth by Ralph Ellison, Albert Murray, Amiri Baraka, Tricia Rose, and others. See Christopher Small, *Musicking: The Meanings Of Performing And Listening* (Hanover, NH: University Press of New England/Wesleyan University Press, 1998); John Shepherd, *Music As Social Text* (Cambridge: Polity, 1991) and *Music Of The Common Tongue: Survival And Celebration In Afro-American Music* (1987; New York: Riverrun Press, 1994); John Shepherd and Peter Wicke, *Music and Cultural Theory* (Malden, MA: Blackwell, 1997); Jacques Attali, *Noise*; George Lipsitz, *Time Passages: Collective Memory and American Popular Culture* (Minneapolis: University of Minnesota Press, 1990), "Listening to Learn and Learning to Listen: Popular Culture, Cultural Theory, and American Studies," *American Quarterly* 42, 4 (December 1990): 615–636; and *Dangerous Crossroads: Popular Music, Postmodernism and the Poetics of Place* (New York: Verso, 1997); Harris M. Berger, *Metal, Rock, and Jazz: Perception and the Phenomenology of Musical Experience* (Hanover, NH: University Press of New England/Wesleyan University Press, 1999); and Harris M. Berger and Giovanna P. Del Negro, *Identity and Everyday Life: Essays in the Study of Folklore, Music, and Popular Culture* (Hanover, NH: University Press of New England/Wesleyan University Press, 2004); Ralph Ellison, *Shadow and Act: Essays* (1964; reprint: Vintage, 1995); Albert Murray, *The Omni-Americans: Some Alternatives to the Folklore of White Supremacy* (1970; reprint, New York: Da Capo Press, 1990), *Stomping the Blues* (1976; reprint, New York: Da Capo Press, 1989), *The Blue Devils of Nada: A Contemporary American Approach to Aesthetic Statement* (New York: Vintage, 1996); Leroi Jones (Amiri Baraka), *Blues People: Negro Music in White America* (1963; reprint, New York: William and Morrow, 1983); Tricia Rose, *Black Noise: Rap Music and Black Culture in Contemporary America* (Hanover, NH: University Press of New England/Wesleyan University Press, 1994).

82. Gene Santoro, *Stir It Up: Musical Mixes from Roots to Jazz* (New York: Oxford University Press, 1997), iv.

Response

JEFFREY H. JACKSON AND STANLEY C. PELKEY

As practitioners of two different academic disciplines, whenever we have come together and shared stories and conversations about our teaching or our research, each of us has come away having gained something. Talking about what we do has often pointed us to ways in which we can cooperate because we have seen that although we ask different questions and seek different answers, much of what we do as scholars is ultimately quite similar. But talking about our own fields of study in light of the other has sometimes been uncomfortable, even painful. Doing so can make us wonder about why we have chosen to look at the world in a particular way, and it forces us to ask whether the other person might really have more insight. Are the tools that we each use truly the best ones just because they were handed to us by our mentors or because they have been time-honored ways of investigation? Working together can be rewarding, but it can also produce a certain amount of intellectual anxiety.

For historians, changes in the discipline over the last decades such as those discussed in the introduction have proven useful in opening up new doors, including the investigation of music. The new worlds discovered by those who do "interdisciplinary history" have helped to change how the past is examined. But do we have further to go? We have learned much from disciplines like anthropology, literary studies, and sociology. Now, does musicology have anything to tell us when we confront that basic question: What is the appropriate topic for the historian to study, and are there questions that we have yet to ask? Likewise, musicologists have been asking similar basic questions, especially: What is music? Just as historians have wondered about where their boundaries are, so too musicologists are rethinking how to define the very subject of their study.

This collection of essays also begs the question "What is music?" The answer is not so easily given, and how one thinks about music and its "metaphysical status" has profound implications for one's place in each discipline and in the interdisciplinary space between the two. It also implies much about the kinds of music that one sees as worthy of serious study, the kinds of methods of discussion and exploration that will ultimately inform one's research, and the kinds of evidence that one will bring to bear on a topic.

First, we have tried to answer the implied question, "What music is worthy of our serious and sustained attention?" Having included essays on jazz, rock, blues, and nineteenth-century popular music, among others, this collection as a whole moves beyond the more traditional repertoire boundaries of historical musicology. Although musicologists and historians have been scrutinizing those traditions for several decades now, our authors here offer further proof that many kinds of music can be worthy subjects for serious study. These choices have implications both for musicologists and for historians. Hearing the multitude of voices contained within these very different styles complicates our picture of the musical past because it asks whether, in fact, "music is music" everywhere it is performed or whether different meanings accompany it in different contexts. Music is not so simple after all.

Second, our choice of essays and the kinds of music that they treat also suggest an answer to the related question about what methods can be employed: the music that the historian and the culturally or historically minded musicologist often prefer to study may not be understood most effectively by the techniques developed for studying the styles and works of the mainstream of Western classical repertories. For the historian, that often means delving more deeply into the issues of culture that have informed much scholarship recently. We have studied the work of anthropologists and ethnologists, but now we may learn much more from the culturally oriented ethnomusicologists than we ever have before. Some historians have certainly looked at music in terms of sociology or political relations, but the cultural approach takes us inside the minds of music makers and music consumers to understand how they make sense of music in their worlds.

Ethnomusicologists, like cultural historians, delve deeply into the social, cultural, and political contexts of music and music making, but

for most of its history as a field, historical musicology has been dominated by the study of masterpieces that can be examined, analyzed,
edited, and perhaps most importantly performed again and again with
continued aesthetic appreciation. In this view, musical works are comparable to great books and even with important visual art works. The
metaphor of the museum has been used to describe the classical concert
and the canon as they have evolved during the past two centuries.[1] In her
essay, Laura Mason reminds us of this fact, and rejects such a narrow
focus, when she speaks of more traditional definitions of music being
too closely tied to compositions and institutions.

Given the traditional emphasis in musicology on institutions and
"great works," the "bridging" that is going on may have to be between
history and a particular kind of musical study, one in which we either do
not focus on the great canonical masterpieces or examine repertoires,
styles, or pieces not so much on aesthetic grounds but because they have
been ways in which people have expressed (potentially competing)
social, cultural, and aesthetic practices and values within a community
that is now separated from us across time. Again, Mason speaks of the
often "untouched . . . dimensions of musical experience that become
apparent in performance." As Michael Kramer notes in his essay, some
genres, such as rock, reject the written notation of classical repertories
and aim not at reproduction but rather at an expressively rich music
that is intended for performance in the moment.

Still, the canon of classical music has a history, as Donald Burrows and
William Weber help to show us. Furthermore, Dorothy Potter notes that
in the past, audiences and performers were less conscious of a separation
between popular and classical repertories of music than they are today.
Because it has a history, classical music can be contextualized, and thus
we can ultimately include it in our efforts at bridging the disciplines.

Third, all music creates a type of evidentiary problem. Musical pieces
are distinguished from other kinds of documents by their sound. They
represent the masterful use of (and sometimes even the masterful rejection of) a collection of stylistic tools available to the composer or
performer. If scholars do not engage with the sound, we may lose something important about the musical piece or experience.

Thus to be treated fully, music must be "translated" into its historical
context, and the sounds of the music must also "translated" or given

sense. This is where the bridge between music and history is the shakiest. "Translation" is a skill unique to musicologists unless historians have a background in musical performance or analysis; even then, they may not have the tools or the experience to ask the right questions. What does music-as-sound mean? How will we decide which words to use to describe both the meaning of the technical features of the music and our aesthetic response to the music so that we can crack the musical (and social) codes of meaning? This may seem to take us far from history, but not necessarily. Cultural history draws directly on the notion of cracking codes, but the same codes are often understood differently by different scholars. And that's where the collaboration may be particularly fruitful in creating a broader, fuller meaning.

We should pause for a moment, however, because the attempt to crack the code of a piece of music brings us full circle back to questions about the definition of "music." Pieces of music can be appropriated differently through time and in such ways as to suggest that those pieces do not remain the same. Different listeners will recognize different, even competing, social and political meanings for the same pieces of music. Mason reminds us of this through her discussion of "Marseillaise," as does James Davis in his account of the origins of "The Battle Hymn of the Republic" and "Dixie" and in his discussion of how these two songs were used in both the nineteenth and twentieth centuries. Likewise, Stanley Pelkey argues that musical styles and traditions that arise in one nation can be appropriated by listeners of a second nation and become part of the latter's national cultural heritage. If pieces of music and musical styles are this unstable in their meaning, from a cultural point of view, then pieces, styles, and even texts may be far less important for our bridging of history and music than are the histories of performance, reception, and appropriation.

Furthermore, we should acknowledge the possibility that concern with style, sound, or the "music itself" may blind us to the systems of belief and practice that hide behind or within the music and of which Sandra Lyne reminds us in her essay. Furthermore, Michael Antonucci demonstrates in his discussion of the meaning of the "frank" in blues pieces that it may not be the sonic that is the most important element of a piece of music or a repertoire in regards to that music's social effect. And Charles Freeman shows us that understanding a particular historical moment can enliven musical interpretation and may even reshape how musical styles are understood.

But what if we do not want to "interpret" a piece, simply contextualize it, or a repertoire, a style, or set of musical practices? For historians, "interpretation" and "contextualization" are often the same thing. For musicologists, though, many of whom have embraced aspects of literary theory, the very nature of such "texts" and the relationship of texts to the world and to "the past" may be up for grabs in a way that they still are not for those working within the limits of history as a discipline. This point is still in dispute for many historians, especially those who have also been influenced by literary theory. But historians are ultimately bounded by evidence. The musicologist's version of "context" or "interpretation" may sometimes be a bridge that historians cannot cross. Indeed we can see differences in evidence and argument across disciplines contained within the essays in this volume. Some musicologists argue by analogy or by textual/contextual similarity between music and other cultural phenomena rather than by the historian's preferred goal of drawing strong links between text and context at a particular moment in time. It is precisely that quest for strong links that governs the essay by Burton Peretti, who seems to hope that we can do better than simply "leap" between musical trends and intellectual and ideological culture.

One might avoid the entire problem of "interpretation" by engaging more often with musical practices or musical institutions, such as Helen Marsh Jeffries does in her essay. Or one might address musical pieces from outside the classical repertoire that were created with less concern about the evolution of style history, such as popular songs or folk music from across several centuries or from a different culture. The further virtue here is that an analysis of text can replace an analysis of sound. But even songs, operas, chants, and other such texted music are surely more than mere words. The fact that these texts were set to music demonstrates that the communities where they emerged greatly valued the act of singing itself. So should the scholar—musicologist or historian—not engage with sound here too? The words are, of course, still important. Indeed, throughout the past one thousand years of Western history, some religious texts, for example, have been set, generation after generation, to profoundly different melodies from very different styles for use within changing social contexts. There must be some way in which scholars can meaningfully engage contexts, texts, and sounds if, in fact, music in total means something distinctive to each society and culture at a particular moment in time.

These comments regarding definitions of music, methods for study, and types of evidence are food for thought as we begin a larger dialogue. Hopefully, we can engage the best of each of our disciplinary traditions to shed light on our common interests. But we also know that the best of our traditions will inevitably pull us apart. At the end of the day, our questions are, in fact, different, and our answers will be too. As Michael Kramer notes in his essay, "the intellectual rewards of the different approaches ultimately drive scholars down divergent paths." Nevertheless, by revisiting those sites of common interest, we can continue to exchange ideas, learn from each other, enrich our own disciplines, and produce work that is intellectually more stimulating because we took the risk of crossing over into each other's disciplines.

Note

1. See Lydia Goehr, *The Imaginary Museum of Musical Works: An Essay in the Philosophy of Music* (Oxford: Clarendon Press, 1992).

Contributors

Michael A. Antonucci teaches African American literature and culture at the University of Illinois-Chicago. His scholarship and creative work has appeared in *African American Review, Brilliant Corners, Near South, Obsidian III* and *Poetry Motel*.

Donald Burrows is professor of music at The Open University, Milton Keynes, Great Britain. His publications include a biography of Handel, a catalogue of Handel's musical autographs and an edition of documents about music and theatre from the Earl of Malmesbury's archive. He is vice-president of the Händelgesellschaft and chairman of the Handel Institute; in 2000 he was awarded the Händel-Preis of the City of Halle.

James A. Davis is associate professor of musicology and chair of music history at the State University of New York at Fredonia. His interests include American music, pedagogy, and philosophy, and his work has appeared in publications such as the *Journal of Aesthetic Education, Journal of the History of Ideas, Music Review,* and the *Journal of American Culture*. He is currently completing a book featuring the letters of a Civil War musician.

Charles Freeman is a musicologist in Tallahassee, Florida, and has served as a visiting assistant professor of music at Florida State University and at Texas Tech University. His publications and presentations have been included in such forums as the International Conference on Nineteenth-Century Music, the International Conference on Romanticism, the Society for American Music, *Opera Journal,* the National Opera Association, and chapters of the American Musicological Society.

Jeffrey H. Jackson is the author of *Making Jazz French: Music and Modern Life in Interwar Paris* (Duke University Press, 2003). He received the 2002 Charles R. Bailey Prize for best article from the New York State

Association of European Historians for his article "Making Jazz French: The Reception of Jazz Music in Paris, 1927–1934" which appeared in *French Historical Studies*. He teaches history at Rhodes College in Memphis, Tennessee.

Helen Marsh Jeffries is currently completing a PhD on music at the court of Edward IV at Royal Holloway, University of London. She has articles forthcoming this year on the minstrels of the court of Edward IV (*Plainsong and Medieval Music*) and John Plummer at St George's Chapel, Windsor (Proceedings of the 2002 conference on St George's Chapel, Windsor). She is patron of MUSEA (Music School of Eastern Africa), which is based in Kisumu, West Kenya (www.members.aol.com/museakenya).

Michael J. Kramer is a doctoral candidate in United States history at UNC-Chapel Hill. He is currently working on a dissertation whose working title is "Exile on Main Street: The Civics of Rock Music and the Formation of the Sixties Counterculture."

Lawrence W. Levine is professor of history and cultural studies at George Mason University and Margaret Byrne Professor of History Emeritus at the University of California, Berkeley. His books include: *Black Culture and Black Consciousness*, *Highbrow/Lowbrow*, *The Unpredictable Past*, *The Opening of the American Mind*, and *The People and the President*. He is currently writing a cultural history of the Great Depression.

Sandra Lyne is a language and literature PhD candidate at the University of Adelaide, South Australia. Her publications, conference papers, and general research have concentrated on race and femininity in literary production and associated media, and on the performance of race in theatre and opera. Her many years of experience as a performer with the State Opera of South Australia have enriched her research into the history of nineteenth- and twentieth-century European and Asian relations.

Laura Mason is an associate professor of history at University of Georgia. She is the author of *Singing the French Revolution: Popular*

Culture and Revolutionary Politics, 1787–1799 (Cornell, 1996) and *The French Revolution: A Document Collection* (Houghton-Mifflin, 1999).

Stanley C. Pelkey is an assistant professor of music at Gordon College where he teaches courses on music history, world music, and the fine arts. He has published articles in the *New Grove Dictionary of Music and Musicians* (2001), the London Handel Institute Newsletter, and the *Early Keyboard Journal*.

Burton W. Peretti is an associate professor of history at Western Connecticut State University. He is the author of *The Creation of Jazz: Music, Race, and Culture in Urban America* (1992) and *Jazz in American Culture* (1997).

Dorothy Potter is an assistant professor of history at Lynchburg College, Lynchburg, Virginia. She has frequently published articles and read papers dealing with various aspects of Mozart and Anglo-American culture. In 2002 she edited the journal of Mary Freman Caesar, the wife of an eighteenth-century British member of Parliament; Mrs. Caesar was keenly interested in politics and was a friend of Alexander Pope and Jonathan Swift.

William Weber, professor of history at California State University, Long Beach, has written *Music & the Middle Class* and *The Rise of Musical Classics in Eighteenth-Century England,* and he has co-edited *Wagnerism in European Culture and Politics.* He is presently working on a history of concert programs across Europe in the eighteenth and nineteenth centuries, a project begun when he was Leverhulme Visiting Professor at the Royal College of Music in London in 2002.

Index